OOPS!

We Forgot the Kids

OOPS!

We Forgot the Kids

A STORY ABOUT RELATIONSHIPS AS
PARENTING AND SELF-CENTEREDNESS COLLIDE

Doyle Roth

PO Box 469, Littleton, CO 80160

Oops! We Forgot the Kids
ISBN: 0-93608-326-3

Cover Design: Resolution Design (www.resolutiondesign.com)
Cover & Interior Illustrations: Dan Pegoda (dannigin@aol.com)
Editorial Team: Steve Wamberg
Typography: Marty Shull

Printed in the United States of America
First Printing / 2007

To receive a **free catalog** of books published by Lewis & Roth Publishers,
call toll free: 800-477-3239. If you are calling from outside the United States,
please call 719-494-1800.

Lewis & Roth Publishers
P.O. Box 469
Littleton, CO 80160
www.lewisandroth.com

CONTENTS

ACKNOWLEDGEMENTS

Books just don't pop out of nowhere, nor do authors just start writing about anything. It takes time for authors to develop and ideas to incubate. Long before I was aware of it, the *OOPS!* books were in the hopper as God orchestrated a beautiful symphony of events and people that made them a reality.

I married **Nancy** in 1963. For over 40 years we've been collecting life experiences on how to stay married, raise children and live godly lives. I can't say enough about Nancy's contributions to the *OOPS!* projects. Throughout our marriage she's faithfully been the helper of her husband. She's been stretched, frustrated and truly sacrificial with my insane schedule, all the while devoting herself to being a Titus 2:4,5 woman who "loves her husband...loves her children...is sensible, pure, a worker at home, kind, subject to her own husband, so the word of God will not be dishonored." Without Nancy there would be nothing to write about. No Nancy, no book!! Thanks, my dear! You're truly a miracle.

And there were others:

- **Our four terrific children** who became the test cases for our parenting ideas. They validate this *OOPS!* book, not because of our parenting but in spite of our parenting because God is large and in charge. He's given each of them a wonderful spouse, and they parent our twelve delightful grandchildren. Believe me, it's wonderful to watch. Rowdy, Raney, Shane, Kacy and families, I love you all.
- **My men's Bible study group in the 1970s**. You guys helped me take the Bible to a whole new level. I salute you brothers: Jim, Bob R., Rick, Bob C., and Ron.
- **Jim and Louise Wright**, our marital mentors. In 1969 they helped Nancy and me answer the question, "How did our marriage get into such a mess?" Thanks again.

- **Our godly friends and camping buddies** who've managed to keep us focused on the delicate balance between family and ministry: Alex and Marilyn, Dave and Marilee, Ken and Jo, Mike and Chris. You're all terrific!
- **The hundreds of families that have entered my counseling office.** I've learned so much about myself, my failings and my stubbornness through your tears and frustrations. You made me dig deep for Biblical solutions to family troubles. Thanks for being so transparent.
- **The many lost people we've encountered through the years**. You kept the Great Commission alive in our home, and so kept our home from becoming a sterile Christian commune. You gave my family purpose and mission.
- **Dr. Craig VanSchooneveld** who never ceased encouraging me to keep writing. My editor **Steve Wamberg** who made sense of my ramblings, my artist **Dan Pagoda** who put my life on display through cartoons, **Marty Shull** who magically put the text into book form and **Eric Anderson**, the graphics guy who tied it all up in a nice knot. I appreciate each of you.

In closing, 1 Thessalonians 5:18 says it best: "In everything give thanks, for this is God's will for you in Christ Jesus." To God be the glory.

Doyle

OOPS! We Forgot the Kids is a collection of parenting principles, not just a book of survival tips and tricks.

Don't get me wrong. All parents need some tricks up their sleeves, but tricks alone don't constitute purposeful parenting. That's right: technique alone comes up short in our lives as parents.

Long-term solutions are principle-based, not just a "to do" list of formulas. Parents must answer the question, "**Why** do I parent the way that I do?" before they can resolve trivial issues like "**What** do I do when Little Albert pitches his hot dog?"

That's why *OOPS! We Forgot the Kids* is a must for every parent. Through the media of email, the characters in the book talk through real life parenting principles and how to apply them. The emails you're about to encounter expose family struggles. They ask questions and address issues similar to yours. They also teach meaningful parenting strategies and down-to-earth parenting skills one email at a time. You'll find that most parents are just like you, so expect to see yourself as you peek into the lives of others.

Over the years, I've seen my own life in the lives of others. While sitting across the counseling table from a struggling couple, I could see through the fog of their frustrations to my own blindness. Someone else's hurt feelings and heartbreak would ring a bell in my own head and I could see the hurt I was causing my wife and family. (Strange how that works, isn't it?) While trying to sort through someone else's parenting struggles, I was often reminded of my own. When I gave counsel to others, I was in a strange way counseling myself. You see, I was learning by default as I observed the failures of others.

Now it's time for you to become a true observer... a fellow learner by default. Allow yourself to sink deep into the lives of my friends who are in desperate need for direction. Remember, they're people just like you and me. They get frustrated and angry so they scream and yell. They want to love and be loved but feel taken advantage of and ignored. They want to be effective as parents but at times live with regret and despair. But like all of us they want to learn... to grow... to improve.

After all, who doesn't want to start over again with renewed hope and better relationships at home? My friends did. So did I and so can you.

Now it's time to dig in. Grab a soda, a few chips and a comfy recliner. Then... enjoy!

Doyle Roth
Sedalia, Colorado
January 2007

Carter and Minnie
live in Colorado and have been mentoring couples and teaching marriage and family classes for many years. They were invited to join the email Parenting Co-op and share their insights on parenting. **Their four children are all married and on their own.**

AJ and Jenny
are in the midst of a horrible family crisis. Their children are rebellious and their marriage is in desperate need of help. **Their children (Troy, Carrie, Tyler) are teenagers.**

Gerry and Sue
are friends of Carter and Minnie and live in Wyoming. Sue is also Jenny's sister. **Their children (Clayton, Jessica) are pre-teen.**

Stu and Stacy
live in Texas close to AJ and Jenny and by coincidence are friends of Gerry and Sue. **Their children (Tanya, Rusty) are pre-school age.**

Do you ever wonder why families can't get along? Why do they bicker, argue and fight with one another?

It seems like husbands constantly disagree with their wives. Wives incessantly complain their husbands are uninvolved or controlling. Parents scream at their children, and children scowl at their parents. It's as if there's no end to this domestic turbulence in sight. Every once in a while you get a solemn reminder of how serious family problems can get when someone you know picks up the phone and calls you for help. No, you're not a professional counselor, but they want someone to talk to or maybe even a shoulder to cry on. What do you say? What do you do?

For sure, they want you to help them sort through their latest disagreements. They want some assurance and hope that things will calm down. But where do you go from there?

Well, I can tell you that if it wasn't for some of *our* good friends who weren't afraid to get involved, God only knows the predicament AJ, Jenny and their three children would be in. Frankly, if it weren't for the loving intervention of these Christian friends, their family would have been torn to shreds. It's an amazing story of determined Christian love, honesty, confrontation, commitment and discovery. So, here we go!

It all started December 29th, a couple of days before New Year's Eve. Like any other holiday, AJ spent it fighting with my sister Jenny and their kids Troy, Carrie and Tyler. They couldn't agree on anything, let alone on how to raise the kids. So the New Year's Eve school dance gave them something to disagree about like fresh meat to a hungry lion.

"I don't care how old Carrie is! She's not going to any dance," AJ argued. (Incidentally, Carrie's 16½-going-on-19.) "You know what happens when you get a bunch of adolescent, testosterone-driven boys dancing with scantily dressed, hormone-saturated girls. Aren't you smart enough to figure that out, Jenny?"

Jenny's caustic and often critical responses only frustrated AJ even more. "Carrie is asking to go with friends to a chaperoned school event at the high school gymnasium, not to a night club or an all night event at a friend's house. So what's so wrong with that, AJ?" she taunted him.

Carrie jumped into the heated fracas like a frog onto a lily pad. "Yeah, what's so wrong with that?" she insisted.

As if the stress wasn't piling up fast enough, their oldest son Troy, who's almost 18, piped up and said "Yeah, Carrie, maybe you could meet your big hulk at the dance and do some playing around on one of the library sofas."

Of course, this comment made Carrie's hair stand on end. Blushing, Carrie told Troy to take a hike. She then abruptly reminded him of his latest escapades after the so-called Christmas party Friday night at Ugly Dave's house. Dave always made fun of Carrie's braces, so she gave him the nickname "Ugly Dave."

"Remember the beer incident, Troy?" she fired back. Of course, this not only shocked AJ and Jenny, but also fueled AJ's concern that his children were getting totally out of control. AJ's personal boiler was steaming away, and he was getting madder and madder by the moment. "Sometimes you must take control," he said through clenched teeth to Jenny.

That was nothing new for AJ. He had a habit of forcing his way through almost every disagreement using his temper as a launching pad. Brute force was his way of getting control. Time and again AJ justified his habit by saying, "Sometimes you need to make a point by stomping your feet, hitting your fist against the wall and throwing a few things. A little screaming and yelling doesn't hurt either. It lets everyone know who's really in charge."

That evening, before you could say "Jack be nimble," AJ tore into Carrie like a beaver on a green aspen log. "Carrie, you're not going to the dance and I don't care what your mother says. If you think you can mouth off to me about it, you've got another thought coming. End of the discussion. Go to your room." With that he left the room, but the excitement wasn't over.

I mean, who rips the phone cord out of the wall just to make a point? Slapping Carrie in the face because she talked back to him was downright abusive, and damaging Troy's car was just mean. Apparently Tyler, their 12-year-old son, was frightened by all the horrible screaming, dish breaking and malicious threats that were part of AJ's tantrum. So he slipped out of the house like a scared rabbit and ran to some neighbor's house for refuge. They called 911 and alerted the police of the situation.

When the police arrived at the house and witnessed the damage, it was apparent to them that AJ and Jenny needed some help with their parenting techniques. By the time the courts, legal eagles and Social Services were done with AJ and Jenny, they had a renewed interest in becoming better parents. It took about 11 months for the situation to quiet down. However, the legal process was only a very small part of their education.

It's important for you to understand that, as Jenny's younger sister, it's been real hard for me to help because we live so far away. My husband Gerry and I are both very concerned, but we're in Wyoming and Jenny's in Texas. So what could we really do about their situation? Pray? Hope? What really could we do?

But I remember so well the night Jenny called and talked with us about the meltdown at their house. We were horrified. "How could this happen?" Gerry asked.

"Well, it's been coming for some time," I replied, remembering numerous phone conversations with Jenny about their marriage problems. She'd confided in me that AJ would often blow a fuse, lose control of his emotions and push them around while throwing things. It all seemed to be part of his scare tactics. I think he thought it was just normal behavior for a husband and father.

Jenny told us that she would provoke AJ while trying to defend or protect the children simply by making sarcastic comments. It was her way of redirecting his anger toward her rather than the children. You understand, don't you? Jenny and the children were scared to death by AJ's emotional outbursts, but didn't know what to do. Her meltdown call was different. Jenny was not only afraid, but also despondent and searching for some help as a drowning person would hope for a life jacket.

Anyway, after an hour-long phone conversation, Gerry told Jenny, "It's time to take the bull by the horns and get you and AJ some help. Jenny, what do you say? Is it okay with you if we contact some of our friends who do marriage and family counseling and get some direction? We know you need some help, and we know just the right people. I think they'd be a great place to start. What do you think?"

When I hung up the phone, I stopped momentarily to reminisce about my own family problems a few years back and how our friends helped us work through them. They helped Gerry deal with his anger, and helped me be more constructively assertive instead of destructively critical.

Gerry and I were filled with self-centeredness. We'd disregarded God in our family and were failing as parents. But that's when crazy Carter and his lovely wife Minnie showed up. Just like so many other couples, Gerry had called Carter and asked him for some help with our marriage. As I think about Carter, even now he makes me laugh. That old rancher, whose skin is as tough as shoe leather, didn't mince any words in confronting our despicable behavior. Yet at the same time, we could feel his warmth and sincerity even when he compared us to farm machinery, ranch tools or truck parts. Carter always had something funny to say even when talking about something pretty serious. I remembered Gerry kept a list of all the names Carter called him. Names like "slacker," "slug," "sissy," "turkey," "dimples," and "peaches" all became a part of their friendship.

Frankly, Carter and Minnie were unusual people. Their Christianity actually made it into shoe leather. The teachings of the Bible are very important to them (most of the time) except when Carter was fishing, hunting or driving too fast. (At least that's what Minnie told us. I just bent over laughing again!)

I actually wondered if AJ and Jenny would react negatively to Christian teaching on family life. After all, they weren't very interested in spiritual stuff. But you know something, neither was Gerry at first. When the going got tough between Carter and Gerry over the spiritual stuff, Carter simply said, "Well my friend, you're a stubborn one but God can 'break you to lead,'" and with that he'd head to the cooler for a couple cans of Pepsi. Because of that understanding, Gerry didn't feel any pressure and was very open to listen to Carter.

Carter would send us emails in addition to his many phone calls and counseling sessions at his office. We both knew he was genuinely concerned about us, and before you knew it we had worked through our marriage troubles and were well on the road to spiritual and family recovery. Thanks to our real true friends who confronted our behavior and told us what we needed to hear when we needed to hear it, Gerry and I have been growing and maturing in our relationship with Jesus Christ, with each other and with the children ever since.

Isn't that a wonderful story? As I sat there reflecting on those troubled days, I got goose bumps all over just thinking about it and tears of joy filled my eyes. Now I wondered if those same friends might be helpful to AJ and my sister. Would Carter and Minnie be willing to counsel AJ and Jenny via email?

When we finished the phone call from Jenny, I was struck with a sense of urgency and felt sadness for my sister and her family. You know the feeling, don't you? You want to help, but the future looks pretty bleak. At that very moment Gerry returned to the kitchen. He knew I'd been crying.

"Sue, are you all right?" Gerry asked. It was at that moment I returned to my senses, and Gerry and I realized that it was time to contact Carter and Minnie.

Well, it's been almost a year of emails back and forth with wonderful results. AJ and Jenny wanted you to know the whole story. They've agreed to let you in on all the details. So sit down, gather up some low calorie ice cream, some chips, dip and a soda and we're off to the races again. Enjoy!

Sue and Gerry

TO: CARTER and MINNIE
FROM: GERRY
SUBJECT: Parenting problems in El Paso, Texas

Hey, you two! We both enjoyed going with you to the Stock Show last month. Carter, you looked so cute with your big cowboy hat and those red elephant skin boots. Why did you choose red? Minnie, can't you dress the old guy better than that?

But the looks on your faces far outweighed Carter's fashion sense that day. You both looked so proud as your grandson took his turn in the Mutton Bustin' Competition. He actually rode that woolly critter a pretty long time, considering his rear end spent most of the time dragging in the dirt. When he fell off, I don't know who hurt the most—the little cowboy down in the arena or the old cowboy up in the stands with a little tear running down his sunburned cheek. Carter, was that a tear from a proud grandpa or were you tearing up because your grandson didn't place in the money? Or was it because your grandson got a kiss from the Rodeo Queen and you didn't? Come on Carter, 'fess up! (By the way, why didn't you let your grandson hold his own trophy? You rascal!)

On a more serious note, there are problems brewing down in Texas and I'm not talking about moonshine. It's Sue's older sister Jenny and her husband AJ. Things have been pretty turbulent lately for their family, but now the turbulence has turned into all out war. Their marriage is falling apart. Their three children are a mess.

Troy, their oldest, is 17. Carrie is their 16-going-on-19-year-old daughter. Tyler, their 12-year-old, is a mama's boy filled with lots of anger. That's no wonder, considering all that's been going on.

You see, this past week AJ lost his cool. It all started over a simple disagreement about Carrie going to the New Year's Eve school dance. What started out being a simple difference of opinion soon escalated into emotional meltdown. Before it was over, AJ broke some dishes, damaged the dining room table, pushed Jenny head first into the couch, smashed out the windshield of Troy's car, took his car keys and grounded him for the rest of the school year (or for the rest of his life, whichever lasts longer). AJ was even physically abusive to his daughter. He slapped Carrie in the face and gave her a bloody nose.

Thankfully, their youngest son Tyler ran to the neighbors up the street and they called the police. Seems to me this was probably the only responsible act the entire night. It got very ugly. I can understand why the police felt Jenny and the children were in danger, and why they left that night for a safer location.

Now Social Services wants a complete investigation before the children return home. Jenny is devastated. AJ's angry at Social Services for sticking their noses into something that isn't their business.

Isn't that the way it often goes? Generally, destructive parents try to avoid personal responsibility by shifting the blame to someone else. It's either the neighbor kids who are at fault or the school, the computer, the church, the television, or the pastor. Seldom is the issue ever the parents' fault.

Self-centered behavior sure wrecks a family, doesn't it? When you mix self-centeredness, anger, lack of good communication skills and no self-control all together, you get this kind of a mess. In fact, you can see how self-centered living has practically destroyed their family relationships. The Bible reminds us of the folly of being hot-tempered. This family proves it!

Carter, you've told us that being a happy family is all about *knowing*. *Knowing* God, *knowing* your spouse, *knowing* your child, *knowing* the biblical principles of selfless living, *knowing* what to do, *knowing* what not to do, *knowing* how to be self-controlled and *knowing* how to get help when it's needed. Frankly, AJ and Jenny really don't *know* how to be a family and don't *know* where to begin. Would you be willing to help them learn?

I can't promise you that AJ will listen, or that Jenny will follow your advice. At times it looks pretty hopeless to us but I know what you're thinking! You've quoted Hebrews 11:6 to me plenty of times: "Without faith it is impossible to please God." Do you think we can move forward in faith, believing God will reach out to AJ and Jenny through us?

Carter and Minnie, please let us know if you'd be willing to help. By the way, AJ's quite a fisherman. Does that help you decide? I'm tempting you a bit, but for a good reason.

That's enough for now. Sue and I will be anxious to hear from you. Our love to you both!

Gerry

P.S. Since email worked before, why not try the same kind of thing with AJ and Jenny? What about an email Parenting Co-op? We could send emails back and forth with the purpose of learning how to improve our family situations. Frankly, we could use your counsel on parenting as well. Sometimes our kids just drive us to the nutty farm—so nuts that occasionally we don't even act like Christians. You could send copies of your teaching emails to both families. I hope we'll be back in the email business soon. Join us, will you?

TO: AJ and JENNY
FROM: SUE
SUBJECT: Let's make a deal!

Jenny, we're so thankful you felt free to call us. Be assured of our prayers. We've been very concerned about your family—but honestly, we didn't know what to do or say. Since your phone call, we're even more concerned.

It's shocking to us about the children. Please try to stay positive. Hopefully, something good will come out of this ordeal and the children will be home in no time. Gerry and I are very sorry, but try to realize that God can make something beautiful out of ashes. He specializes in difficult situations. In the meantime, it's probably necessary for everyone to collect their thoughts, get control of their emotions and start learning how to properly live together.

I can just imagine how difficult it is to raise teenagers. They have minds of their own and the size to back it up. Our children are much younger and yet are a pretty big handful. We also get pretty frustrated, lose control and fight amongst ourselves. We certainly understand your frustration!

AJ and Jenny, even though several hundred miles separate us, please remember that we love you and are praying for you. Both of us are trying to figure out what we can do to help, but as inexperienced parents ourselves we don't know what to recommend. We have our hands full with our own parenting problems. Jenny, can you remember when your children were nine, seven and four years old like ours? You can relate to our parenting issues as well.

Anyway, a thought came to us. What if we got some people together to discuss parenting techniques via email? In other words, wouldn't it be helpful for all of us to learn from each other's experiences? We need the help, the tools and the creative ideas to improve our own relationships. Fact of the matter is, we often parent by the seat of our pants. Honestly, who wouldn't want to learn about better parenting via email?

To top it all off, we know a couple in Colorado who've already raised their children. Gerry and I have asked Carter and Minnie to join our little email co-op of needy parents. They have a boatload of experience and lots of practical tips to back it up. They have four adult children and a truckload of grandchildren. I'll bet they're bursting with creative ideas for needy moms and dads. What do you say?

By the way, don't you have to go through some form of counseling required by the courts? Maybe the courts would allow you to counsel with Carter. He does family counseling and serves as an elder in his church. Doesn't hurt to ask!

We don't want to stick our noses into your personal business but maybe we can all get some help at the same time. The email idea might be just the ticket. Would you be willing to share your parenting experience with other interested parents using email? What about learning from Carter and Minnie? Does any of this sound interesting to you?

Just let us know. Gerry and I love you both.

Sue

P.S. Incidentally, tell AJ that if he likes hunting, fishing, racquetball, football, soccer, baseball, swimming, skiing, gymnastics, bowling, eating or channel surfing, he'll love Carter.

TO: STU and STACY
FROM: SUE
SUBJECT: Matthew 25:35-36, 40: "… unto the least of these…"

I can't believe what happened! God is constantly surprising us with miraculous realities. We knew you were moving but little did we know you'd move that close to AJ and Jenny! It's a small world, isn't it? Who would have guessed their neighbors are in your Bible Study group?

In our devotions this morning we read from Philippians 1:6, "He who began a good work in you will perfect it until the day of Christ Jesus." The same chapter, verse 12 says, "Now I want you to know, brethren, that my circumstances have turned out for the greater progress in the gospel." These verses reminded us that with God, there are no coincidences! God has a plan for everyone and He will perfect it and our circumstances will turn out for greater progress in our spiritual lives (Romans 8:28). We thank God that He has a plan for AJ and Jenny. He's even using their bad circumstances and great neighbors like you folks for His divine purposes.

Thanks, Stu and Stacy, for putting your Christianity into shoe leather. I'm sure your unexpected visit and cherry pie said quietly, "God loves you." Your kindness reminded us of another passage in the Bible where Christ encourages us to reach out to the "hungry, the thirsty, the strangers" because in doing so, we do it unto Christ Himself. It would have been so easy for you to just go about your business and occasionally wave at them while driving by but you actually went out of your way to meet them. We just want to say thanks. I'll be sending you a coupon to Dairy Queen. Have a malted milk on us!

I'm writing to personallly invite you to join our email group. Jenny thought you might be interested. Actually, Gerry and I have been interested in developing a group of three to four families that would be willing to trade parenting experiences and insights via email. We're struggling with various aspects of our own parenting and are often frustrated by our lack of experience and knowledge. Just this afternoon, my two youngest got in a spat over the Legos and both ended up crying. I didn't know what to do, so I just sent them to their rooms. Oh well! We really don't have anyone to bounce ideas off of. Plus, I think we could use someone looking over our shoulders and holding us accountable for our behavior. I must confess that sometimes it isn't a pretty sight.

As you know, I've presented this idea to Jenny. I think she's OK with it, but I don't know about AJ. Wouldn't they be a great addition to the group? Here's what I have in mind. Let's get you two, AJ and Jenny, Gerry and me and crazy Carter and Minnie into an email Parenting Co-op. I've already asked Carter and Minnie to help with AJ and Jenny and join us in the email co-op. I'm hoping they'll jump at the chance. They're lots of fun and they'll have good advice for us. I imagine Old Carter will probably have all kinds of ranch illustrations about raising cattle, horses, dogs, kittens, mice, rabbits, chickens, gerbils and parakeets that apply to parenting children. He's often said, "I've broken horses to ride, cows to lead and dogs to growl so kids aren't that difficult."

Let us know.

Sue

P.S. We'd sure like AJ and Jenny to get involved in a good church. Could you help in that direction?

TO: GERRY and SUE
FROM: JENNY
SUBJECT: I need to be in your group

Count me in! If anyone needs help with her kids, it's me. My children are living with another family, eating with strangers and are afraid to come back home. I need all the help I can get. So does AJ, but he refuses to admit it.

AJ's just like his father. His dad lived most of his life with his head in the sand. He totally denied the lousy condition of his marriage and family. Like father, like son!

AJ's so stubborn it's sickening. It's been over a week since everything went to pieces and we've yet to discuss the problem. Can you believe that? It's like if we ignore the problem, it'll vanish. And here I am, caught right in the middle of dealing with AJ's indifference and encouraging the children. I can't win for losing! I scream, demand and cry but it's no use. I've been walking this tightrope for 17 years and I've had it!

I just wish there was someone who could gain AJ's trust so he'd open up and face his past as well as deal with our present problem. I'm willing to join your group because my family is fighting for survival. I don't know about AJ. I showed him your last email but his only response was, "Let the courts provide the 'quack.'" See what I'm dealing with?

I'm anxious to meet Carter and Minnie, especially since they've been down this teenage road before. Who couldn't use a parental mentor? I'll show AJ all the emails, but I can't do anything beyond that right now. He's being too bullheaded. I'm sorry.

Actually, I did breach the subject of counseling with the social worker last week. It'll be mandatory that AJ gets anger management counseling. We'll also need some local parental supervision and guidance. Our caseworker encouraged me to learn from whatever sources were available. It'll look good on our record when our case goes to court, which is scheduled to happen in two weeks. We'll just have to wait and see about the counseling, but let's move forward with the email idea. The sooner the better!

Isn't it unusual how we met Stu and Stacy? Out of the clear blue sky here's these people standing at our door with a cherry pie, introducing themselves as friends of my sister. How amazing is all this? I'm glad Stu and Stacy will be a part of our email group. Stacy was pretty excited about it and wants to get started right away.

Yesterday, Stacy and I went out for ice cream. You know, I haven't had any real friends down here until now. Now I have someone to talk with and a friend to confide in. I really enjoy her phone calls.

Later, Sis.
Jenny

TO: GERRY and SUE
FROM: STU and STACY
SUBJECT: We're in -
it's either medication for the kids, or for us

We still attend Community Bible Church here in town. No, they haven't thrown us out—yet! It's actually only three miles away. We'll try to get AJ and Jenny to go with us, but I think that's down the road a piece. Right now we need to work on our relationship so they can trust us.

When I read the heading on your last email (". . . unto the least of these. . ."), Stu and I were very touched. It's exciting to be a part of God's work in the lives of others! When we took the cherry pie over to AJ and Jenny, we never thought all this would happen. But that's what makes it a "God thing."

We're going to have fun with the Parenting Co-op idea. Stu's overwhelmed with the whole deal of parenting. Having never had children of his own and ending up with two of them almost overnight has him backpedaling as fast as he can. I can't believe how a six-year-old and a four-year-old can take a 200-pound muscle man and turn him into a marshmallow in seconds. While he wants to be a good father, he's like a fish out of water. He doesn't know how to go about it. He was pretty self-centered in his pre-Christian days, and it takes time for all that to go away. But what's new?

Hey, hold on a minute! I let Stacy write up to this point, but now it's my turn. Stacy's the most disorganized parent ever. It's a wonder that I haven't broken my neck on a roller skate or a rubber ball.

Stacy thinks that "turning up the volume" is the only way to make the children obey. I guess I've learned that the more the volume goes up, the more the children tune out and the bigger my headache gets. We discipline differently. Stacy thinks "time out" means putting the child in the corner for five minutes. I think time out means Stacy and I leave the house for five days with no children. See how different we are?

Of course we want to be a part of your email group. I know the email idea really works because it was so helpful when Stacy was going through all her marital problems. It's so much more personal than sitting down and reading a book of "how-to's." I'm anxious to hear from crazy Carter and Minnie. I hope they join us or the group might simply turn into a pooling of ignorance. When does it all start?

Actually, I think it's already underway!

Later!
Stu and Stacy

P.S. Just one other footnote. I got a call from Jenny yesterday. We must have talked for 30 minutes. That girl has plenty of problems in her life, and is she ever depressed over them. I took the liberty of sharing my personal faith in Christ and how He has made such a huge difference in my life. Getting me through my marriage problems and the death of Mitch was no easy assignment, even for God. She didn't seem to be offended. We're going to get together again next week and discuss our families. And Stu had coffee with AJ the other day to get a little more acquainted and plan a fishing trip. Keep praying!!

TO: GERRY and SUE; STU and STACY
FROM: CARTER
SUBJECT: Wise as serpents, harmless as doves

God is wonderful! The Bible teaches that before the foundation of the world, God ordained that Stu and Stacy would move right under AJ and Jenny's noses. If a person doesn't believe in God, it's understandable they might attribute such things to coincidence. But as a believer I understand this to be God's providential care of those He loves. Don't you?

Would you mind if Old Carter gave you a pat on the back for a minute? Thank you! I am so impressed by the way each of you are ministering to AJ and Jenny. Your example to them is very wise, and very Christ-like. They must be embarrassed about their circumstances, but you neutralized their problems in such a loving way. Nobody likes being an example of bad parenting. When others are willing to be transparent about their own marital or parenting failures, it builds bridges that everyone feels comfortable crossing. I like your email group idea. It offers AJ and Jenny lots of protection, and it's a great vehicle for sharing ideas. Maybe over time they'll both want to get involved. Minnie and I would sure be honored to be a part of it. We're both real anxious to meet AJ and Jenny.

When I move cattle from one pasture to the other, the most important thing is to get all the cattle gathered and headed in the same direction. Oftentimes my horse needs to work pretty hard collecting the stragglers who are hesitant to join the rest of the herd. One thing's for sure: it doesn't help to go screaming and yelling after the strays, but rather patiently and persistently encourage them to join their cow friends. Otherwise I might have cattle everywhere. Sometimes the strays are afraid, and other times they're just plain stubborn. In either event, getting them onto the trail with all the other cows is very important but takes patience. Did you get that? **It takes real patience!**

It seems like we have a nice group of folks who want to go in the same direction—all except one, and that's AJ. Everyone will need to work hard and be very careful not to spook him or he'll end up running in the wrong direction. He might be a little stubborn, even fearful, but deep down in his heart I know he loves his family. Persistence will pay dividends if we're patient, and trust God to touch his life.

Sue, I read your last email to us very carefully. I focused on the sentence where you mentioned that self-centeredness ruins or drains the life out of family relationships. I like the word "drain" because it speaks of a gradual process. That's exactly how it happens with families. It's like a slow leak in a stock tank. Over time the water leaks out, leaving a huge mud hole in the process. To make matters worse, the cows who come to drink are out of luck.

Family relationships are a lot like that. If we're not careful, our family relationships gradually drain out over time through the hole of self-centered living and leave our families thirsty for life-giving relationships. AJ and Jenny have lost their relationships, haven't they? It's our opportunity as their Christian friends to guide them to the "water of life." They need supernatural help to fill up their family with selfless relationships **that only GOD can provide**. They need God to plug up the hole of self-centered living and quench their thirsty souls. Notice what Isaiah 55:1-3 says: "Ho! Every one who thirsts, come to the waters; and you who have no money come, buy and eat. Come, buy wine and milk without money and without cost. Why do you spend money for what is not bread, and your wages for what does not satisfy? Listen carefully to ME [God Himself], and eat what is good, and delight yourself in abundance. Incline your ear and come to ME. Listen, that you may live." God is the answer for families who've lost their direction and are drying up on the inside. Let's make sure everyone gets that message! Right?

Initially, maybe Jenny can have AJ just read our emails. Then with a little "planting and watering" God can work in their hearts and cause that seed to grow. Always remember that unless the Lord builds the house, when we build, we labor in vain. Let's be praying now for God to give us direction in building a bridge over to AJ. Stu taking AJ out for coffee was the first step in that bridge. Good work!

Thank you for inviting Minnie and me to be a part of your parenting work. We're saddled up and ready to chase cows! Check your cinch!

Carter

Life at the Lazy-U reminds me of AJ and some other parents.

TO: STU and STACY
FROM: CARTER
SUBJECT: Start your parenting journey with
a healthy marriage

Stu and Stacy, you old rascals. How in the heck are you? It sounds like we'll have a hoot in this Parenting Co-op provided nobody gets offended by my poor English.

Doesn't God have a delightful sense of humor? He gives children to young people who know very little about parenting, yet have unbelievable energy. But He doesn't give them to older people who have more life experience, and generally more wisdom. Go figure!

What that tells me is this: *it takes more energy than brains to raise kids.* That's a very good principle to keep in mind. If you're a young parent and you're spending a lot of time in the recliner, you must have your parenting on backwards.

Stu and Stacy, parenting is one of life's most important and challenging tasks. All parents struggle in the process. That's why our hair turns gray if we don't pull it out first. We develop chest pains, occasional ulcers and diarrhea. To say nothing about all the emotional effects including anxiety, guilt, frustration, feelings of incompetence and the temptation to murder. Just kidding!

Parenting's tough. What are parents to do? Everything is so goofed up! Our country is collapsing into the abyss of no absolutes and no convictions about anything, from the absence of prayer in schools to immorality on television. Is it any wonder parents are running for cover—taking refuge in churches and private educational systems? Yet as pathetic as the condition of our country is, we parents have the great opportunity and privilege to raise our children under these challenging conditions. Even though it seems like the wheels are coming off faster than we can put them back on, God is still in heaven and sits on the throne. That, in and of itself, should empower us to be courageous and confident as parents knowing the truth of 1 John 4:4: "Greater is He that is in you than he who is in the world." (KJV)

Stu, this parenting business must be pretty challenging for you. You're the most recent spouse and parent in our email co-op. Stacy's been parenting for a few years and has some on-the-job training but not you. You might be hesitant to step into the role of father knowing that there's a protective mother just around the corner. Tanya and Rusty are Stacy's children and you lack experience in parenting. Stacy might be a little nervous about that. You might even be a little fearful of her disapproval. All this makes for a confusing situation.

That's why communication and strategy are so important. Blended families, families with physically or mentally challenged children, families with only one parent, families with an inexperienced parent and even traditional family models all will benefit from good communication and strategy. If you don't communicate and have some strategy to your parenting, then look out!

Because Minnie and I are Christians, we use the Bible in our counseling. Unless those reading this email are willing to learn from biblical principles and the experience of others, raising children can be a very painful proposition. I know what you're thinking, Stacy. Yes, even with biblical counsel and a good strategy, parenting can still be very painful. But more times than not, the pain will be reduced by learning how to parent from the written Word of God, and from the wisdom and knowledge of other Christian parents.

Before we get to this matter of parenting, I'm going to take the liberty of picking on you. (Just remember I'm sending this email to everyone in the group as well.) Stu and Stacy, did you memorize your wedding vows? Do you recall what they said? Think, Stu! As you spoke your vows to each other you must have been so proud. You entered into your new relationship with conviction and determination to make God the center of your relationship, didn't you? Good going! You're on the "first base" of parenting.

Stu, one of the most important components of good parenting is how you treat your children's mother. We often overlook this important ingredient. So, I recommend that you make arrangements for a babysitter and take Stacy out for a nice meal at the corner steakhouse. As you're enjoying a big T-bone steak, tell her how much you love her and how thankful you are for her. Tell her how you appreciate all her efforts to keep the house clean and organized, to clothe the children and to see to it that all of you are gaining weight through her wholesome meals.

Stacy, you need to appreciate the work Stu puts in to keep food on the table. Thank him for his leadership. Let him know that you haven't forgotten about his dedication to his work.

Make sure you do these special dates with each other on a regular basis. Your children will watch the way you act toward one another, and they'll take careful mental notes. When a father is disrespectful or distant it not only hurts the children, but also gives them license to treat Mom in a similar way. When a mother is demeaning or critical, it also gives the kids permission to treat Dad like that. You should never let the children be disrespectful of your spouse. That's especially hard for children to understand if *you're* being disrespectful of each other.

You should support each other so the children learn that Dad and Mom are a loving team. Show kindness and affection to each other. That way, the children will learn to be respectful and caring toward their parents.

Here's a question for the group: what should happen if one spouse becomes verbally or emotionally abusive to the other? What then? It's very simple. Someone needs to be taken out back to the woodshed by some loving friends and thumped a bit. Don't you agree? There's no excuse for this kind of negative behavior.

Let's do a little recap exercise:

Point #1: Parents, if you want your children to grow up and be successful young people, start by loving each other. Kids notice how you talk and act toward each other.

LIFE at the LAZY-U

I GUESS ONLY ADULTS CAN FIGHT WITHOUT GETTING GROUNDED.

Point #2: During dessert on your date nights, take some time to discuss some mutual **expectations and goals** of your parenting. Take a napkin and jot down some goals that you can work toward together. For example:
1. Being more consistent in discipline
2. Objectively evaluating your parenting
3. Structured family times (no phone or TV distractions)
4. Lowering your voice and controlling anger

My point is simply this: you must be headed in the same direction or you'll have nothing but confusion in your parenting. Always keep in mind that parenting is something a father and mother do together, not independently of each other.

I'll send another email in the next couple of days.

One other thing. Minnie and I are planning a trip down south and would love to drop in and see you folks. We plan on being in El Paso for an insurance meeting from March 2nd to the 5th. Minnie says she found some money under the mattress and wants to buy you all dinner. What do you say? We'll bring a housewarming present if we can find some more money under the couch.

Til then, crank out some romance,
Carter

P.S. Does it surprise you that marriage is one of the most significant issues with parenting? If parents can't discuss their parenting together, then parenting is a free-for-all. The kids work the parents against each other and the parents work the kids against their spouse. Let me ask you again, does your marriage create a safe place for your children to live? Does your marriage have the strength it takes to raise your children effectively? If not, then first things first! Get busy working on your marriage. Pronto!

TO: AJ
FROM: CARTER
SUBJECT: Fishing and pig hunting

Good Morning, AJ! My name is Carter. I've known Gerry and your sister-in-law Sue for many years (against my better judgment, I might add) and in fact, just got an email from them. They told me you're quite the fisherman. Is that true? I don't know if I'm a fisherman, but I *do* know I like to go fishing. I always hesitate asking someone for fishing directions. Generally, though, one fisherman is always willing to help out another fisherman—provided that when they go fishing together, he promises to not catch more fish.

Here's the deal. I'm coming down to Texas the first part of March and I'd like to go fishing down on the coast. I've never fished "deep sea" style. I'd like to try it. I know that you're very busy with your own work, but wondered if you might know somebody who would be willing to make a few bucks ($300) and take me fishing. I'll pay for the boat rental and whatever else I might need, including a huge freezer for my trophy whale.

What do you think? Could you lead me to someone? I'd certainly be willing to go with you, as well, if you could work it into your schedule. The $300 would probably fit just as good in your pocket as it would in somebody else's.

I'll bring my Ruger 6mm Magnum if you can arrange a pig hunt as well. That's another one of my 17 weaknesses. I love to hunt anything from blondes (elk) to brunettes (bear) to say nothing about squirrels, badgers, white tail deer, black tail deer, mule deer and rattlesnakes. I even like hunting for friends like you.

In any event, I sure am looking forward to meeting you and Jenny in March.

Check your "fly,"
Carter

TO: CARTER
FROM: AJ
SUBJECT: How about some of each – fishing
and pig hunting?

I know who you are. Your bad reputation goes before you. You have other friends down here in Texas. Stu and Stacy were talking to us the other day and they told us all about you. I understand that you're a lousy fisherman on top of it all. Well, that's OK. I specialize in lousy fisherman.

Carter, I already have a boat, all the gear, and plenty of time. I don't need your $300, so you can stick it where the sun doesn't shine. I'll be going fishing whether you go or not, so having another person go along is no big thing. Bring your own raincoat in case the boat sinks!

If the fishing is good, we'll bag the pig hunting. If the fishing stinks, we'll go chase hogs. How's that? If neither of those is productive, we'll chase antelope with my jeep.

Now, *that's* one heck of a lot of fun. You get in the jeep with the top off and head out across the beautiful Texas landscape. When you see some antelope, off you go with rope in hand. The idea is to get close enough to them critters so you can rope one out the side of the jeep. I understand you're quite the cowboy.

Incidentally, the last guy I took antelope roping got so excited he fell out the side of the jeep and broke two fingers on his right hand. When he hit the dirt, all I could see was his hardhat bounce straight up in the air. Don't ask me why he was wearing a hardhat. I can't remember. Through the rear view mirror I could see my ex-friend crawling around on the ground like a disoriented squirrel looking for his stash of acorns in a cactus. He was actually looking for his glasses.

You want to rope some antelope, or are you as big a sissy as Stu says?

See ya' in March!
AJ

TO: THE PARENTING CO-OP
FROM: CARTER and MINNIE
SUBJECT: Sperm donor dads vs. real dads

It looks like the Parenting Co-op is well underway, so here's another teaching email. You can respond, if you wish, by sending back your specific comments and any questions that might apply to your individual family needs. I'll also try to answer your questions broadly enough with general applications so that each family can easily apply them.

For your information, I've found one solid friend down in Texas. At least there's one real man who fishes and hunts. Thanks to AJ, I hope to bag the biggest fish and the meanest pig ever. The only problem I see is that he probably won't get out of bed. The guy is a slacker. AJ my man, you know I'm kidding. I'm really looking forward to hanging out with you.

This email is principally to the men. It concerns their responsibilities connected to parenting. Now ladies, this doesn't exclude you from your responsibilities so read on.

Dads play a very critical part in the parenting process, don't they? I've learned that unless men are willing to face their tremendous parental responsibilities head on, much of our time and energy coaching families will be wasted.

I get emails from wives and mothers who are concerned about how their husbands are treating (or not treating) the children. Many dads treat their children too rough. Others are distant and uninvolved. Some scream and yell constantly. Others are so passive they're virtually inconspicuous. Some dads spend huge blocks of time at work and play. Others are spending an exorbitant amount of time in front of the blasted TV or the computer screen.

I can't believe how many dads disconnect from their responsibilities, and just leave the parenting to the mother. Oh, they might play with the children while Mom cooks the evening meal. But after dinner, it's back into the recliner. They might yell at the children from the recliner now and then, but to creatively parent or deal with discipline effectively is out of the question. More times than not, it's off with their buddies to do something away from the children. You can often find them in a foursome playing a round of golf with higher-handicapped shooters or shooting skeet at the local gun club. Absentee fathers call this "male bonding." I call it a bunch of bull.

Incidentally, I just got an email from one woman who said that last week her husband was home with the children a total of two hours. He's apparently a golfing fanatic. A lousy one at that, I understand. She is one ticked woman! I can tell you this much, if she ever does with his five iron what she threatened to do with his five iron, he's going to be in one heck of a lot of pain just below his belt. (I can't criticize him too much, because I've needed to dig the five iron, a pitching wedge and a putter out of my hide several times before. Minnie's great at hiding my golf clubs.)

I guess all of us guys struggle with the same problem. Being involved with our kids is a tough assignment. It takes focus, discipline and strategy.

Let me illustrate this with a personal illustration from my parental arsenal. I have four kids, one of each kind. Our two sons and two daughters are each as different as day and night. My youngest son was always an interesting challenge for his parents, as well as his teachers at school. He might be a lot like one of your kids.

From the very beginning of his first year in school, he was not a happy camper. He felt that his schooling was radically interfering with his education at the ranch. Frankly, he wanted to stay at home and punch cattle all day. The school would have no part of that, so off to school he went. Getting him to school was easy because he was locked up in the bus and couldn't escape. However, *keeping* him at school was a much more daunting exercise. You're getting the picture, aren't you? He basically made it miserable for everyone.

His teachers were obviously running out of gas when Minnie and I got a special invitation to a parent-teacher conference with the entire school hierarchy. "This is cool!" I thought. "Maybe they legalized handcuffs!" Anyway, it was a meeting with several high-powered educators to discuss how to "fix my son." You see, they saw my son as the problem, not my son's parents.

His teacher was present. So were the principal, special education teacher, two social workers and one child psychologist who wasn't married and didn't have any children of his own. However, he did have a bunch of empty theories. It was a pretty impressive lineup for a little country school! The only person who wasn't there was the brand inspector.

We all crowded into a little room. They proceeded to answer the question, "What are we going to do with this little trouble-maker?" Around the circle of higher learning, the question went ricocheting off the walls like a stray bullet. They were going to do everything from drug the lad to incarcerate him in the corner of his room until he had underarm hair that was long enough to braid. All of their actions seemed so right. Punish the boy! Medicate the lad! Reject the disobedient little rascal! It all sounded so right.

But not once in the entire meeting were his problem *parents* ever addressed or questioned. Never once did the brain gang confront me, my absence in the family or my indifference to my son's problems. Never once did this think tank consider how my son's father played into his disobedience and behavioral problems. Did they even consider how distant I was from the parenting process? Couldn't they figure out that my anger was being reproduced in the life of a frustrated little guy?

Didn't they know that the marriage problems Minnie and I were having caused stress and insecurity in this little feller's life as well? Didn't they care about that? Apparently not! They never once asked me about my personal life, or a single thing about our home life. I just figured they knew how to fix my son. Mistake Numero Uno!

Over the next couple of days, Minnie and I became very uneasy about our meeting. Then it hit me. Like a bolt out of the blue, I was struck square in the heart: *Why does my son need to suffer the consequences of me being such a lousy dad?* Why should the brain gang discipline, reject and medicate my son for problems resulting from my personal failure as a dad? His school problems were an extension of my lack of involvement in his life. There was nobody to blame but me, especially not the little guy in overalls who had a tear running down his cheek because "nobody liked him."

Within the week, there was another meeting of the "think tank of higher learning." This time, I called the meeting and Minnie and I led the discussion. By the time the meeting was over, everyone had learned two very valuable lessons:

Lesson #1: Don't mess with a problem child until you talk with his problem parents.
Lesson #2: Commitment and involvement are essential to good parenting.

With the cooperation of the school and direct involvement on our part, we began a written daily evaluation of my son's performance at school. Every evening at home, his performance review was discussed. We encouraged him if it was positive, and encouraged him accordingly if it was negative. We had an incentive program whereby he could earn points for his good performance at school, then be cut loose to do something else he really enjoyed—like riding his horse.

By the end of the school year, a different boy emerged. His teachers, the principal, both social workers and the brand inspector were all very impressed with his progress. More importantly, by the end of the school year, I was a very different parent.

During that year I learned a very important lesson about raising kids: **you must first raise their parents!**

Sometimes we parents need to be made aware of our parental responsibility. Yes, children do stupid things. That's why our job as parents is to guide and counsel them. It is our job to properly teach and train our children. It takes hours and hours of training, patience and creativity. Frankly, I spent more time training my cattle dog to drive cows than I did training my own flesh and blood to deal with school. What a sorry dad I was!

Now let me ask you fathers a question. Do you spend more time exercising, surfing the net, watching TV or doing a hobby than training your own flesh and blood? Learn from my mistakes, men, and get down to business with your children. After all, it's your responsibility.

Later alligator! In the meantime, check your cinch....
Carter

TO: GERRY and THE MEN
of THE PARENTING CO-OP
FROM: CARTER
SUBJECT: Silent and not-so-silent child abuse

Gerry, thanks for your phone call. I was glad to hear my last email upset you. I know you aren't physically abusive to your children, but you raised a couple of interesting questions:

1. What's the difference between the physical injuries sustained by a child at the hands of an angry or frustrated father and the emotional injuries sustained by a child at the hands of an absent, disconnected or indifferent father?

2. What's the difference between the emotional damage done to a child by a father who screams, yells, hits or has temper tantrums and the emotional injuries resulting from a passive, uncommunicative, controlling, manipulative or distant father?

Well, Gerry, I see children who've been physically crippled by abusive fathers who take out their frustrations on them. Yesterday, I read a story about "Shaken Baby Syndrome." Seems an irresponsible father shook his little baby so hard that the little guy suffered several critical injuries which included a severely cracked skull, swelling of his little brain and contusions in both eyes. My heart rate shot up to an all time high! To make matters worse, his little twin sister was placed in foster care after the doctors found that she had also sustained serious injuries including a broken arm and leg. The mother of the two injured children explained to the investigators that she had seen the father, Mr. Bonehead, shake the children. However, she didn't think he'd rattled them to the point of injury.

The article reported that this sorry, out-of-control dad shook his children because he was angry and frustrated. All I could do was wish that somebody would grab him and shake him around a while to see how he likes it. What kind of person takes a seven-week-old baby and just shakes the tar out of him? Picture this 180-pound man holding his little fifteen-pound baby in his hands. He screams, yells and shakes the poor baby mercilessly. It just breaks my heart and makes me madder than a disgruntled old bull. How about you?

This kind of incident happens all the time. What's wrong with fathers? They don't stop long enough to think about anybody but themselves. Even little helpless babies are at the mercy of their self-centered, self-absorbed, self-serving and self-willed fathers. The Bible tells us in 2 Timothy 3:1-4 what men will act like in the latter days. It says, "Men will be lovers of self… arrogant… ungrateful… unloving… without self-control… brutal, haters of good, treacherous, reckless… lovers of pleasure rather than lovers of God."

I guess we've arrived at the latter days, haven't we? These terms often describe fathers and husbands who have lost their moral compass and revert to sinful behavior that is repelling and inexcusable. So it is with the father I just described. Do any of these terms apply to your parenting?

Dads, here's a word of warning: if you can't control your anger, keep your hands in your pockets where they won't hurt anybody. Never take out your frustrations on little people or your wives.

The answer to the problem of parental child abuse, as well as every other parenting problem, is to *fix the parents*. Educate the parents that crying babies aren't the problem. Neither are rebellious teens. We need to train parents to learn self-control and manage their emotions more effectively. It's the parent's anger, frustration, impatience and lack of self-control that's the issue. These self-centered behaviors make parenting less effective and more destructive.

I've said all this to suggest that as parents, we need someone to teach us how to be selfless, controlled and wise in our parenting. We need to be taught how to be responsible and effective parents who have learned to control their emotions and frustrations when the going gets tough.

Just look around and observe the number of parents that are at their wits' end when it comes to dealing successfully with their children. Through my counseling work, I'm constantly brushing shoulders with parents that have run out of energy, ideas, time and patience. Parents shouldn't focus all of their time and energy on the problems of their children, but rather allocate some time and energy to solving their own problems as parents. How about we focus on the parental problem of self-centeredness? That covers parental laziness, impatience, inappropriate discipline, lack of creativity and unwillingness to teach and train.

I know these physically abused children have been emotionally hurt as well. But there's another distinct group of emotionally crippled children we don't like to discuss. Especially in Christian circles. They're the sons and daughters of preachers, elders, deacons, Sunday school teachers and hard workers—moms and dads alike—who never affirm, validate or approve of their kids. These parents do a lot of damage to their children as well. It's just not as noticeable as physical abuse.

Let me impress this on you! There are many emotional side effects to children from fathers who are disconnected, uninvolved, and non-affirming. Often these children end up with their brains scrambled in a different way. Far too often they turn to drugs, alcohol, and sex in their quest for parental love and approval.

The horrible tentacles of irresponsible and self-centered parenting, whether physical or emotional, eventually reach into every aspect of a kid's life. Take King David as a good biblical example of this. For all the good David did in his life, he was pretty uninvolved with his children and the results were horrific. Let me give you some food for thought from 2 Samuel, chapter 13. What would you do as a dad if one of your daughters was raped by one of your sons? Do you know what King David did? Not a thing, except get a little angry. So his son Absalom took matters into his own hands and ordered his servants to kill the rapist, his younger brother Amnon.

Now if your son, like Absalom, wanted to patch things up with you, how long would it take for you to set up the meeting? Read on in 2 Samuel 14. King David wasn't in any hurry. It took him *over two years* to see Absalom. From that point on, Absalom's anger got the best of him. He continued on an evil, angry path. Consequently, Absalom set out to steal the hearts of all the men in his father's kingdom. He eventually sought to kill his own father.

As the saga continues, a battle ensued between the army of David and the army of Absalom. As an act of belated "fatherly kindness," David told his generals to win the battle but preserve Absalom's life. That was thoughtful! Late, but thoughtful.

Sometimes later in a father's life, he begins to see more clearly the broken relationships between him and his children. I believe this was the case with David. I think he finally realized all the damage and distance between him and his son Absalom. Sparing Absalom's life seemed to be the only answer to his heartfelt grief and regret. However, during the battle Absalom's donkey went under a large oak tree and Absalom's beautiful hair got tangled in the tree. There he hung until Joab, one of David's trusted generals, arrived.

Joab was so angry with Absalom that he ignored David's orders. Joab thrust three darts into Absalom's heart. Then Joab's armor bearers surrounded Absalom and killed him. When King David finally heard the news about his son's death he cried, "Oh my son Absalom, my son, my son Absalom! Would God I had died for thee, O Absalom, my son, my son!" (2 Samuel 18:33, KJV)

Absalom reached out for his father's approval, but David was too busy running his kingdom. Absalom wanted a relationship with his dad, but David was preoccupied with so many other things that he just didn't have the time or interest to love Absalom. Absalom suffered the emotional abuse of an uninvolved father. Do you get my point? There were no physical scars to tell of David's abuse, but his neglect of Absalom left emotional scars that tormented the boy his entire life.

I've said all that to say this: fathers are responsible to properly, and I emphasize *properly,* teach, train and discipline their children. Your children don't need visible bruises on their bodies to indicate child abuse. All they need are broken spirits from an angry, indifferent, controlling and distant father who is verbally or emotionally abusive. They want you to love them, but maybe you're too busy with other things and other people. They long for your approval but maybe you're too far removed from their lives, and too self-consumed to plug in. Oh, how they want you to pat them on the back, give them a hug of approval and love them. Will you do that? Could it be you're too busy patting yourself on the back?

Is it this way with you? I sure hope not. Let's face it. Fathers are often disconnected from the parenting process. Mom's circuits are fried and the kids are absolutely driving her to the funny farm. Dad goes to work, or out with the guys after work, oblivious to the underlying needs of his family. And we wonder why kids are screwed up! Well, folks, it's time for a wake up call! **Maybe it's time for Dads and Moms to get a little shaking**! How about calling this the "Shaken Parents Syndrome"?

The Shaken Parents Syndrome, when done properly, **unscrambles** your brain and gets your parenting back to "sunny side up." Are you still with me?

Meditate on these things, and I'll wrap up my remarks in another email tomorrow. Till then give your kids a hug, OK?

Carter

P.S. I need to have you answer a question before my email tomorrow. Some dads and moms are involved to a fault. They're controlling, legalistic and virtually "smother" their children. They don't allow their children one ounce of independence and demand the children do everything just like they want. These kids grow up always looking over their shoulders for a critical, judgmental and smothering parent who doesn't allow them to be individuals. Do you see a problem with this kind of **negative involvement? What does that do to a child?**

TO: THE MEN of THE PARENTING CO-OP
(continued)
FROM: CARTER
SUBJECT: Bible illustrations about uninvolved dads

Sorry I couldn't finish my email yesterday. Minnie and I went on a hospital visit and were late getting back to the ranch. Of course, I needed a piece of pie after our visit. By the time we returned home I had other things on my mind, like getting some shuteye.

So here we go again. Since the Bible has so much to say about parenting, let's use another illustration right from its pages. We all know the Bible reminds Christians and non-Christians alike to stay involved with their children, to teach, train and discipline. They should avoid an angry spirit, be patient and self-controlled. So let's learn together in spite of our spiritual differences. Who knows? Maybe we'll not only be better informed about parenting, but also learn a lot more about God Himself and His wonderful plan of salvation. So why not try a little Bible reading?

The most important parenting principle we learn from the Bible is that we should follow the model of our heavenly Father. He loves us as His children. God disciplines His children with loving care as a gracious parent. He is involved in every aspect of His kids' lives. What a great example God sets for parents to follow! However, unlike God, many parents choose to raise their children using the latest fad in parenting instead of the time-tested biblical principles. Can you say "disastrous"? Or they rely upon the model of their earthly fathers instead of their heavenly Father. Say "disastrous" one more time! Here's the problem of relying on your earthly father.

A few years ago, a man came to my office for counseling. Another pastor in town had referred him to me. This guy was probably 40 years old and had a very obvious physical disability. He told me about how, while he was growing up, his father punished him by hitting him on the side of the head. The damage to this man's body was the result of an abusive father who hit him in anger. Do you know why this man was in my office for counseling? He was there to get help because he was disciplining his children in exactly the same manner as his father had disciplined him. That didn't make the Social Services people very happy. That's precisely why parents need to consult the Bible for parenting tips instead of parenting like dear old dad.

Not only does the Bible give good advice about parenting, but it also allows us to peek into the lives of fathers who pathetically failed their children. We saw that in the life of King David. Now let's look at 1 Samuel chapters 2 through 4 and the story of a priest in Israel named Eli. He was a busy priest and occasionally got involved in counseling, much like myself.

Now Eli had a couple of kids named Hophni and Phinehas. (Who calls their kids Hophni and Phinehas anyway? Imagine what the kids at the local junior high called them!). Anyway, these two sons followed in their father's footsteps as priests. We're told that these two knuckleheads were "worthless men; they did not know the Lord." What we have here are two sons whose father is a priest, that are likewise in the priesthood but as *false* priests. They were religious charlatans! Did you get that? These slackers were in the business of religion for the fringe benefits. They really didn't give a rip about the Lord or His people. They were just sanctified thieves and hustlers.

But God had their number, and was determined to put these profiteers and womanizers out of business. God was also ticked at Eli for honoring his sons over Him. In fact, God was so angry that

His judgment fell on the entire family. God declared that both boys would die on the same day, and Eli would lose his priesthood. But you ask why does poor old Eli lose his priesthood over the actions of his sons? Good question! God gives us the answer in 1 Samuel 3:13. There we learn that God will "judge his [Eli's] house forever for the **iniquity which he [Eli] knew**, because his sons brought a curse on themselves **and he [Eli] did not rebuke them.**" In other words, God hates it when a father is not involved in the parenting of his children.

Absentee parenting doesn't honor God! If a dad sits back and just lets his kids do whatever they please, God gets real concerned. If children get away with doing evil and their father doesn't even lift a finger to correct them, teach them or protect others from them, God gets a real nasty headache. Hey fathers, did you notice the mother of these two problem kids isn't even mentioned in the scripture? To me it's rather striking that the kid's problems rested squarely on the shoulders of their disconnected, indifferent father. Sure enough, God made good on His Word as always. In chapter 4 we find out that both boys died in battle—and old Eli died of a broken neck after falling backward beside the gate. Ouch! End of story.

How'd you like that story, men? What did you learn from these two stories about King David and Priest Eli? Isn't the lesson simply that God wants fathers to be involved in the parenting process of their children from start to finish? To ignore their needs, or to distance yourself from the teaching and training of your children, is just unacceptable. In fact, we live in a culture that defines this phenomenon as the "absentee dad" generation.

But this problem hasn't just happened during our lifetime. The very first human family needed a father to get involved with his sons. You can check it out yourselves in Genesis 4. Adam needed to step in between Cain and Abel and help them work through their sibling rivalry. But he didn't. There's no record of him lifting a finger to help mediate his sons' disagreement with each other over the proper sacrifice to God. Rather, Adam was nowhere to be found. In their father's absence, Adam's son Cain actually kills his brother Abel.

We need to plug into the lives of our children. We don't need to smother them. Just be aware of what they are doing and what they are thinking. We need to be prepared to lead them through the many minefields they'll encounter while growing up. We need to have the courage to confront their sinful behavior and take the necessary actions to protect others from their wicked ways. We need to set aside the necessary time to teach them God's Word and God's way. Do you agree, or don't you?

Here are a few hints to start you on the path of involvement:

- First, stay abreast of what's happening in your kids' world. Read news magazines and books that help you understand what they're facing.
- Talk with their friends, visit their schools and learn what your children are dealing with.
- Pray and read the Bible to get God's instructions on how to lead them. Then teach them what God says about life. You can do this at the dinner table.
- Understand how peer pressure is affecting your child's dress, speech and attitudes. Be involved with how your daughters look in public, and how your sons are looking at other people's daughters. Teach them about personal appearance, correct speech and godly attitudes remembering that Christlikeness starts with what and how they think, not with what they do or don't do! Keep in mind that good parenting affects the heart, not just the behavior.

There's more to come! But for now, dads, think about the bad results of indifferent and uninvolved parenting. King David lost his son, Absalom was a human disaster, Eli's two sons were killed, Eli broke his neck and Cain slew his brother Abel. Sad but true! Seems safer to be a good parent!

Love you all,
Carter

Here's something to think about from *Life at the Lazy-U*...

TO: CARTER
FROM: STU – THE NEW PARENT
SUBJECT: Time! When is there time?

Greetings to you, Mr. Carter! Is it true that confession is good for the soul? I sure hope so because I'm going to try it! I appreciate your willingness to email me back, but be sure to pass your reply on to everyone in the Parenting Co-op. I don't think my problem is that unique.

Carter, this parenting thing really has me spooked. Your last email helped me understand the huge responsibility of being an involved father for Tanya and Rusty. But frankly, I'm at a loss about how to do that effectively. I know Stacy and the children are counting on me. However, *knowing* something is quite different than *doing* something about it.

Right now, I know I don't give the children the time or the attention they deserve or need. Yesterday was a perfect example. I came home from work to a wife that was frustrated out of her mind because our son, Rusty, had spent the entire day discovering new ways to annoy her. The minute I walked in the door I could tell that she was about to wring somebody's neck, and I could only hope it wasn't mine.

I asked, "Is there anything I can do to help you?" Then I ducked behind the kitchen table. Without missing a beat, Stacy demanded that I take Rusty off her hands and do something with him before she taped his mouth shut and tied him to the lawn mower. Basically, I think she just wanted me to get him out of her hair for a while so she could comb it. I was all right with that, so Rusty and I went outside and threw the ball around.

Can I confess something? I really didn't want to. I'll have to admit that it was fun for a while, but I was tired after a tough day at work. I was ready for dinner, if you know what I mean. As if that wasn't enough, after dinner Rusty wanted to play trucks, read a story and on and on it went for the entire evening. I was thrilled when Stacy said, "Tanya and Rusty, it's time for bed!"

Carter, it's like this almost every evening. For the first time in my life, I understand *why* men work late at the office and play a lot of golf. I've made this huge jump from basically being a self-centered, unbelieving single guy to being a self-centered, believing, married father of two. What an unbelievable leap! Now, most of my free time is taken up with my marriage and the rest of my free time the children suck up. I *do* have to work, you know. Plus, I like to relax a little before another day at the office.

I want to be a good husband and father but I realize now what a huge sacrifice that is. Please pray for me as I try to figure this mess out.

I bet you don't know about the latest development in our lives, but I'm not finished complaining yet. Don't misunderstand, I love Stacy. She's a wonderful mother. But I do feel that she has unrealistic expectations of me as a father. When I walk in the door, I think she wants me to stop everything else and give my total and undivided attention to her and the children. Has she forgotten how self-centered I am? It stresses me out just thinking about it.

I'd like to go somewhere sometime without the children. Have you ever felt like that? I've heard it said that parenting is a 100% fulltime job. Is that correct? I've also heard it said that marriage is a

100% fulltime job. Is that correct? My boss wants about $33^{1/3}$% of my days and I sleep another $33^{1/3}$%. You do the math!

How can I be all things to all people who are making these unreasonable demands upon my day? Everyone is sucking the life right out of me, and I don't have enough time to brush my teeth. I'm sounding pretty self-centered, aren't I? Sorry about that, but I need to get it out of my system. Honestly, I want to be a good husband and father—as long as I can continue to be self-centered. I'm just kidding. I wouldn't hurt Stacy and the children for anything in the world. So, some of your hardcore advice would be helpful.

Now, to make matters worse, here's the latest development in our lives. Ever since I became a Christian, I've wanted to put my Christianity into shoe leather. You know, to do some kind of ministry. There's a side of me that really wants to help others. Since my life was such a mess before, now I'd like to help others avoid the same mess. So, I've changed professions. I'm no longer in the health fitness business. I took a job in the family fitness business. I'm now serving as part of a ministry team that works with broken families.

My job description classifies me as a "resident assistant" in a foster child care facility within the Social Services system. While it's mainly an office position, I have a lot of contact with children and parents of many dysfunctional homes. It's a great opportunity for me to learn about family life through the mistakes of others. My family has already benefited from some of my experiences.

While I'm trying to put into practice what I tell others, I'm constantly confronted with my lack of willingness to work on my own family. I feel like such a hypocrite! That's what makes matters even worse. Here I am at my job, trying to help others work through their family problems and at the same time, suffering from all the guilt feelings because I'm failing to deal with my own family. As you can see, I NEED YOUR PRAYERS AND COUNSEL!

Stacy says, "Hi!" And I look forward to your next email.

Stu (Mr. Self-centered)

P.S. I had a question about the mother of Hophni and Phinehas. Now I know that these two sons were trouble from the beginning, but is their mother responsible for her behavior and her neglect of disciplining the children? Another question: Is it all right with you if I pass along your emails to my co-workers? They're very interested in our Parenting Co-op idea.

TO: STU and THE PARENTING CO-OP
FROM: CARTER
SUBJECT: The advantage of early detection

Well, Stu, it's true that confession is good for the soul. I appreciate your honesty. You've pinpointed the grass root problem for dads and moms in general. It's the problem of self-centeredness. Unless parents get their eyes off of themselves and onto the children, their parenting will surely suffer.

Being convicted about your lack of involvement with the children isn't comfortable, but it's certainly necessary. Every parent (I mean **every** parent) could do some serious soul searching on this important subject. Then, as you have done, get some help from someone and commit to making some fundamental changes in their family life.

Let me give you a few tips. Stu, here's Tip Number One: I like to recommend that parents establish "goal setting" as a regular way of measuring their parenting progress. It never hurts for any parent to set up goals or objectives to serve as a rudder or a compass to guide the family. How about setting a goal to develop better consistency in discipline, or a goal to throttle an angry voice, or one to limit the amount of personal TV time? Use your imagination.

There are plenty of other goals that can help grow your family. In fact, why not get the kids involved in the process? Maybe the children would like to help set some goals, and hold you accountable to your new commitments. As your accountability partners, they'll be better at catching you slipping back into old habit patterns than *you* will.

I try to remind myself how easy it is to deceive myself. I can easily believe that I'm doing a better job in my family than I actually am. Can you relate? My kids always held my feet pretty close to the fire. That made it hard for self-deception to creep in.

Tip Number Two: After leaving work, learn how to put it behind you and train yourself to relax and focus on your family. When you first arrive home, spend some quality time with Stacy. Let her know how much you love her. Share a little "party" together, like something to drink and a little snack, while you talk about each other's day.

Then it's off to the children. Demonstrate your affection to each of them and be sure to make good eye contact. Find out what they've been up to. Listen carefully, then share something with them about your day—maybe some lessons learned and what God's doing in your life. After a couple of weeks, everyone will enjoy your arrival.

Tip Number Three: Be creative! Remember to not just spend time with the children, but the *right kind* of time. Spend time teaching, training, having fun, laughing, joking, teasing, wrestling, playing catch, washing the car, changing the oil, mowing the grass, picking up after the dog, fishing, hunting, shoveling out the garage, disinfecting their rooms, cooking and having popcorn together.

Something surprising happens when you spend the right kind of time with kids. You're able to do a lot of other things by yourself without feeling guilty because their need for attention has been satisfied. Furthermore, kids need to learn to be alone, be creative and develop their own entertainment without demanding so much from their parents. They need the challenge of personal creativity and concentration without distraction. In our frazzle dazzle world, children need to learn to entertain themselves without outside stimulation and I'm not suggesting that computer games are the answer. It's unnecessary for parents to always drop everything and care for their every need. Plan your quiet times and times alone well in advance. The Bible tells us there is a time for silence. How does that fit with your family?

So at the end of the day, take a little time for yourself. Relax with just Stacy. Hmmmmm! Good! Recycle and renew, as they say! Learn to maximize those moments. Don't just get caught in the recliner with the remote in hand (unless, of course, there's a good sporting event or a cooking show for sissies you can watch. Don't worry, Stacy, I'm just teasing the old boy.) Recharge your batteries by reading, meditating or playing a game with Stacy.

Now let me try to answer your question about the responsibility of mothers in the task of parenting. Yes, mothers *are* responsible for their role in the family, as was the mother of Hophni and Phinehas. If a mother abuses her child, of course, she's responsible for that unacceptable behavior. If a mother screams and yells at her children, if she fails to properly discipline and train them, she *is* responsible for her personal actions. If she becomes a perpetrator of negative attitudes and actions in the family by nagging, complaining or having fits of anger, you bet she's one responsible woman.

But remember the Bible tells us the father is the head of the family, and the primary responsibility for the family rests on *his* shoulders. As a spiritual leader, he needs to protect the family from all abusive speech and actions, including those from the mother.

You understand there's a great deal of disagreement about the subject of male leadership today. Regardless of what some women say, it's by default that they provide leadership to the family—not by desire or choice. This is true. Mothers are taking up the slack because the fathers are simply more and more uninvolved. So often dads are guilty of family neglect and absenteeism. They've delegated the vast majority of the parenting responsibility to their wives. Over time they've gradually slipped out of their leadership position. But it was never meant to be this way.

Frankly, I've never heard a mother complain that the father of her children is spending far too much time loving and being involved with the children. Have you? Quite to the contrary! They don't want their husbands to just come in the house screaming and yelling, barking orders, demanding obedience and flipping on the TV. No, their desire is for fathers to get involved. Not just playing trucks, but getting involved in the tasks of discipline, training and teaching the children. Enough said!

Now let's go on to this subject of "early detection." I'll explain it this way. I believe I can safely say that most families have internal problems of one sort or another. These internal problems range from minor marital disagreements and parenting problems to much more severe issues. We live in a pretty sick and sinful world, and we're pretty sick and sinful people. It's no wonder our families struggle to get along. What do we expect? We put a sinful man, a sinful woman and sinful children in the same house and tell them to stay together and live happily ever after. It's just not that simple. I don't care what Hollywood says.

We all share the same tendency to ignore the initial signs and symptoms of problems. We lie to ourselves and to others (when in fact we are hurting inside) and delay getting the necessary help. We do a major cover-up by grinning on the outside, padding our successes and denying our failures.

From a counselor's perspective, I can tell you that most families who end up in my office arrive there far too late. Stu, it's like the families that will come to your foster care center for help. They've needed help for a long time but have continued to ignore the problem. They've missed the opportunity for early detection. They just go along telling everyone that all is well when, in fact, they're fast approaching marital and family bankruptcy. While couples know that the day of reckoning is right around the corner, they just keep putting up a good front as if everything is hunky dory. *Next* year, they'll worry about the problems.

Living like this causes us to focus more on covering up the problems than dealing with them. We become more concerned about what others think than what God is attempting to correct in our lives.

Go talk to your doctor. He'll tell you that early detection is of supreme importance when it comes to medical illnesses. It can be the difference between life and death. The same is true with the family. Early detection of problems in a family can be the difference between happiness, divorce and delinquency. I have a physical examination every year for this very reason. If I have a problem, I can get immediate treatment.

Men are good at avoiding annual medical examinations as well as ignoring family problems. When my loving wife calls some family failure to my masculine attention (ha!), I'm tempted to just dismiss the problem, grab my racquet and head for the gym. Men, we're guilty of not paying attention to the problems that are eating away at our wife and kids. How many of us put family matters off to another day? Maybe tomorrow we'll tackle the discipline problem with Junior, or next month we'll deal with our lack of communication. Until then, just keep a positive attitude and no one will ever know the difference.

You wanna bet? God knows. Just ask Eli's pallbearers. Eli knew early on that things were not right with his sons, but did nothing. He ignored the signs of early detection. Shame on him!

Say what? Shame on me! I know for a fact that I don't pay attention to Minnie and my children as I should, either. I think it's time to start paying attention. Our children need us to get involved in the discipline, the teaching and the training. Parenting is a fulltime assignment and one heck of a lot of work. It deserves your undivided attention. So shut off the TV and get with it, you rascal!

Speaking of early detection systems, my stomach's growling. I'm a bit hungry. I think there may be signs of prime rib in the kitchen. I'll check with Minnie, if you don't mind.

Carter

TO: STU and THE PARENTING CO-OP
FROM: CARTER
SUBJECT: Training parents vs. digging postholes

Thanks for the phone call, Stu! So Stacy likes the idea of early detection. Most women do. This whole matter of dads getting involved with the everyday matters at home is a hot button for the mothers of our children.

By the way, have you ever heard the joke about how many city-slackers it takes to drill a posthole? The answer is "a whole bunch." It takes one city-slacker to hold the drill and a whole bunch of others to spin the tractor! Well, let me tell you this was not far from the truth the other day. I basically lived out this little joke. I needed to dig a few postholes, so I decided to invite some teenagers out to the ranch for a workday.

Even though they didn't know a lot about fencing, I figured I could teach them how to dig a posthole in about four minutes. "It's so simple," I thought. "Dig the hole, take all the dirt out of the hole, put the post in the hole, put the dirt back in the hole and finally, tamp the hole tight."

About three minutes into my explanation of the game plan to my city friends, I realized that I had, in fact, miscalculated their ability to comprehend the details of posthole digging. (They'd probably never seen anything like it on a computer game.)

Well, I thought, first things first. I'll introduce them to the tools necessary for digging a posthole, and then demonstrate how to use them. The first item on the list was a posthole digger, or "dirt tweezers," as it's referred to at the ranch. (A posthole digger actually looks like a very large tweezers used by the Jolly Green Giant to pull his nose hairs.)

You don't need to be very smart to use these dirt tweezers. You simply put your hands high up on the handles and drive the diggers into the ground. Then you spread the handles outward, lift the dirt tweezers out of the hole and move it to the right or left away from the hole. Then you bring the handles back together. This allows the dirt to dump out of the dirt tweezers. Then you repeat the process, with the objective that you hit the same hole you started.

This was a problem for my new friends. Ideally, the same guy digs away at the hole for the first couple of minutes then someone relieves him and takes over. I say ideally! As it worked out, these city-slackers were good for just one or two attempts at hitting the hole. After about 30 minutes, our hole was 27 inches wide and about nine inches deep. One teenage slacker was repairing his shoe with some duct tape after slamming the dirt tweezers down on his foot. I thought that only one near-amputation in that group was a pretty good statistic.

After lunch, we reached the proper depth of 2 ½ feet. Sadly, I had a hole wide enough to park my stock trailer in. For a post, I wanted to use an eight-foot railroad tie. These railroad ties weigh upwards of 100 pounds. It takes one man, or five city-slackers, to handle a tie. So I went ahead and dropped the post into the hole, hoping we could maybe finish before suppertime.

Getting the post to stand straight up would have been a lot easier if they would have listened to the kid with the purple hair. He didn't think that the level should be set on top of the post, but rather placed lengthwise down the side of the post. Pooling their IQ's, they decided that he was right. Since there are three bubbles on my level, the problem then was in deciding which bubble on the level should be used. They figured they'd use the bubble at the bottom of the level because it's closer to the ground. Just as well. They were sitting down most of the time anyway, and the lower bubble is easier to read when you're sitting down.

Now it was time to put the dirt back into the hole and tamp the dirt tight. One thing for sure, they didn't like my tamp bar. I don't know why! It's a collector's item. I made it out of an old drive shaft from my broken down pickup. Since it weighs a ton, it really pounds the dirt tight in the hole. This assumes, of course, that the user of the tamp bar can hit the hole and has enough muscle attached to his arm to lift it.

These city-slackers God gave me for the day didn't have a muscle attached to their arms. What actually moved the tamp bar up and down was their excessive complaining, combined with obscene gestures with their tongues. Kneeling next to the hole is the best position for using this type of tamp bar, but my young friends didn't want to get their knees dirty. Besides, it was too uncomfortable to bend down that far. Even I could understand that dilemma. Since they wear jeans about 14 sizes too big, and since the crotches of those jeans hang clear down to their kneecaps, kneeling was next to impossible. However, I found that a little cold water down the canyon that appeared at the rear of their jeans was helpful in getting them to pull their pants up where they belonged.

We finished putting in four posts that day. My city-slacker friends were sure glad to sit down at the dinner table for some steak that night. You should have heard the talk around the table. You'd think they were fence post professionals and A-1 ranch hands. I gotta hand it to them, though. They didn't know the first thing about dirt tweezers, or how to tamp dirt around a post but they were sure willing to learn. I was proud of their determination and perseverance. Not only had I made some new friends, but I also learned some new vocabulary: "Dude!" "Awesome, Dude!"

They were pretty excited about their new battle scars (blisters on their hands, slivers in their knees and new little tiny muscles dangling from their biceps) because apparently those will impress their girlfriends. I think I'll try that technique on Minnie.

Hey Minnie! Minnie! Minnie! Do you want to feel my new muscles dangling from my biceps? Say what?......Go where?...... Do what?......

For some reason, Minnie doesn't seem that impressed with my new muscles. Well, I guess that's marriage for ya!

Now down to business. I want to use this little story to teach everyone a little lesson. Our wives may not want to feel our tiny little bicep muscles, but one thing is for sure. They're very impressed when their men dig into the challenge of being the best dads and husbands in the world. You see, becoming a father is a very frightening thing.

How many of us knew a thing about parenting when our first baby arrived? I didn't know the first thing about being a daddy, feeding the baby (which I wasn't good at), changing the diapers (which I refused to do), unfolding the stroller (which required more IQ than I could muster up), operating the car seats (which drove me crazy), dealing with barfing—"hurling" according to my new friends (which generally made me nauseated), winding up the automatic swing (which made me seasick) and getting up several times in the middle of the night to nurse the baby (which I didn't have the right plumbing for). Now I'm numb to all these things (except changing diapers) because I am a seasoned dad and grandpa.

As I look back on my parenting, it was one lesson after another. Learning, growing and expanding my parenting skills. None of it came naturally for me, but I learned just like my city-slacker friends had to learn about postholes.

Whether you are digging a posthole for the first time or parenting your first child, there are tools that make the job much easier. Over the next several emails, I'd like to introduce you to some of the tools that make the parenting process an exciting adventure for both Mother and Father.

Before I sign off, the Bible gives us a word of wisdom right at the get-go of parenting. In the Book of Proverbs 22:6, the wise man tells parents to "train up a child." In other words, kids don't raise themselves as much as lazy parents might think so. Children need to be *trained* by their parents in order to grow up successfully. Training is methodical, intentional, continual and time-consuming. This is where so many parents fail. They often think that training a child is a part-time occupation or one you do when you feel like it. Wrong!! Unsuccessful parents generally don't have a strategy to their parenting, but rather attempt to train their children using any method that makes sense at the moment. This *really* doesn't work, nor is this training! You need tools for this job of training and I hope to give you some suggestions. Are you ready to go to work?

I'll send out another email next week. In the meantime, get some gloves and pull up your pants. There's a lot of hard work ahead for the growing parent. By the way, parenting, like tamping a posthole, works better if you're on your knees—God *does* answer prayer.

Later "Awesome Dudes"!
Carter

TO: CARTER
FROM: AJ
SUBJECT: Fishing isn't real fishing
until you bring Carter along!

After reading your last couple of emails, I thought you might just want to play horse. What do you think? I'll be the front end, and you just be yourself!

I couldn't believe it. How do you get off ripping on dads that way? The ladies are more involved, but they sure don't know how to handle kids. They let the kids get away with everything. Maybe you should spend some time ragging on them. (I can hardly wait for your next email.) Well, enough of that discussion.

I haven't contacted you since your vacation to Texas but wanted to remind you to practice shooting your gun before you come to hunt pigs again. Your aim is awful! You couldn't hit a wild pig in the barn, let alone one on a dead run across the Texas desert. Good thing your bullet hit that cactus, or it probably would have drilled my ATV. Are you this good at elk hunting? Maybe in October we can find out.

By the way, why didn't you tell me you might get seasick out on the open water? Just wanted you to know that I felt sorry for you, but I was having so much fun catching fish I couldn't stop to loosen your belt. Look at it this way: at least what you were doing had some positive effect—chumming the fish. Sorry!

Did you enjoy your bath in the ocean, by the way? When you got off the boat you were as white as a sheet, and your clothes were spic and span. You looked perfectly DEAD!

Carter, I'm just getting even for all the razzing you gave me over the menu. I happen to like hot dogs when fishing and hunting. I'll say one thing: steak and mashed potatoes mixed with hot coffee and ice cream did sound pretty good at your hunting camp.

On a more serious note, you asked me a very pointed question after we left the marina and wanted me to wait at least a week before answering. It's been ten days now and you've probably forgotten the question. Anyway, the question was, and I quote, "Do you want me (Carter) to help you and Jenny with your marriage and family problems?" Well Carter, you're fun to hunt and fish with but the answer to your question is "NO." Especially after your last two very biased emails about the men.

Really, I don't want counseling from you or anybody else. I have to do the anger management counseling through the court order but when that's finished, I'm done with counseling. I'm already getting plenty of counsel from Jenny that I don't want or need as well as from her nosy sister, Sue, who needs to mind her own business. Carter, I don't want to be a hard nose but this is my personal stuff, not community stuff. OK?

What makes me angry is that everyone's blaming me for the problems around here. Remember that kids will be kids and they suffer the consequences for being stupid and rebellious, not me. To make matters worse, Jenny even wants a separation as if I'm the problem instead of the kids. She's pretty likely to get it because I'm tired of screwing around with this mess.

From now on let's talk fishing, NOT FAMILY. Is that a deal? And take care of your aim. It sucks!

AJ

TO: AJ
FROM: CARTER
SUBJECT: Go ahead and paddle your own boat

AJ, thanks for the wonderful trip to the gulf. I'll never forget the fishing and throwing up. Hunting pigs by ATV was a total blast. Is that legal? When I lay quietly on my bed, I still get the sensation of being at sea, bending over the rail feeding fish—or bouncing around on the handlebars of an ATV. I don't know which it is, but it's real. I've recovered now, no thanks to you, my slacker friend. Seriously, thanks again for the fun!

So you think I've been picking on the guys. You haven't seen anything yet. The only reason you're bristling over my email is because I hit the nail right on the head. Your head! Sorry if I offended you, but I figure God gave you those broad shoulders for something more than just supporting your oversized head. Relax, man, and know that I love you a lot. (By the way, I like it when you bark at me! It lets me know you're alive deep down in your soul.)

I appreciate your honesty about counseling with you and Jenny. If you want to "paddle your own boat" then it's your call, and it's OK with me. You're right! It's your family, your kids, your wife, your problems, your mess and if you're not careful it'll be your LOSS! I'll be available if you want to talk, but in the meantime I'll respect your wishes.

I'd like to continue sending Jenny my emails about parenting if that's OK. She seems discouraged about parenting, and possibly my emails will encourage her in the future. If it's not OK let me know, and I'll send them anyway.

Now AJ, I'm not counseling you but wanted to pass along one parting observation about our pig hunt. Those pigs were running as fast as they could because we posed a life or death threat to them. If they slowed down too much, we were going to kill them. They did everything possible to avoid us. Right?

So why are *you* running, AJ? Nobody's out to shoot you! From what I can see, we all just want to be friends and do what friends do—help each other. None of us wants to highlight your problems as if you're the only one with a corner on problems. We've all got some. If you'll remember correctly, I let you help me when I was barfing all over everywhere. Didn't I? You put a cold washcloth on my forehead, didn't you? It was OK with me, right? You kept checking in on me to make sure I wasn't dead, and even cleaned up after me when I didn't get to the rail fast enough. Right? Furthermore, you told me where to fish and what to fish with, when I was able to walk.

What makes it OK for you to help me when I'm suffering or needing guidance, but wrong for me to help you when you're suffering and in need of guidance? I'll tell you what makes it wrong. Your ego, that's what! You're of the opinion that you don't need the help of others because you can take care of yourself. Isn't that right, AJ? Just remember, dear friend, that you put your pants on one leg at a time just like the rest of us egocentric males.

If you really want to help your family, then you'll throw your pride overboard, humble yourself and admit that you could use some help from a pretty lousy fisherman. In fact, I understand he's got some steak and taters to give you if you'd just quit running. It's worth considering!

Next time we go fishing bring a bucket, will ya?

Carter

TO: GERRY, SUE and THE PARENTING CO-OP
FROM: CARTER
SUBJECT: Before we get the tools,
let's understand the job better

Sue, I got your phone message. Thanks, and I'm sorry about AJ and Jenny. It seems appropriate that we sit back and respect AJ's wishes, and trust God with the results. Always remember that God can get AJ's attention in a heartbeat and God's Word "…will not return to Him empty without accomplishing what He desires and without succeeding in the matter for which He sent it." We have a great God!!

Jenny must put first things first, and her spiritual condition is first. Unless she grows in her spiritual understanding and becomes more acquainted with what God is doing, we're almost at a standstill. I share your concern, and it's possible she will leave AJ and the kids and won't return. I've seen it happen before. But let's pray that God will intervene and change her heart.

In the meantime, we need to be proactive. Let's give her some options besides bailing out. The next time you talk with her, you could go over some Bible verses that will give her some hope. Show her Hebrews 13:5,6, that says, "…I will never desert you nor will I ever forsake you" and "the Lord is my helper, I will not be afraid." Remind her of her vows "to love and cherish, for better or for worse" even though these times are certainly on the for worse side of the equation. Tell her how God has changed your life and marriage. This just might give her a reason to hang around a little more.

Tell her how difficult life becomes for those who reject God's plan to salvage broken marriages and hurting families. The Bible does tell us that the "way of the transgressor is hard." I suppose it's hard because it's so crowded with unbelievers. Let's pray that the Lord will bring both of these friends to salvation.

Gerry and Sue, you gave me an important reminder that shows me how insightful you are: *nobody would go into the tool shed and grab a whole bunch of tools before they knew what job was going to be done.* In my last email to the Parenting Co-op, I told you I was going to provide some tools but failed to help you understand the extent of the job we've all agreed to tackle. That makes about as much sense as telling my sons to get up at 5:30 AM, go down to the barn and load up on tools before telling them what the job was for the day. If we're working calves, they'd need to get the branding irons, hair clippers, de-horning equipment, vaccination syringes, and the scalpel for castrating the bull calves. They'd also need some cooking oil, a fry pan and flour for cooking the Rocky Mountain Oysters, which make a real nice snack after wrestling calves all day. But if we're fixing fence, totally different tools are called for. They'd need the dirt tweezers, shovel, fence stretcher, tamp bar, fence pliers, staples. Gloves would help protect their hands but they always forget those.

For our purposes in this co-op, the job ahead is parenting. Let me repeat that. The job is PARENTING! In my last email, I shared Proverbs 22:6. It says to "train up a child in the way he should go."

Now let's review those words. Who is to do the training here anyway? Grandma? No! How about the baby sitter? No! Well, what about the staff of Sunday school teachers? No! How about the school? No! What about a child's friends? No! Maybe the sheriff's department? No! Well then, *who in the world is to train the children*?

Let's get one thing straight, right here and now. *A father and a mother are responsible for training their children. Nobody else!* Parenting is a combined effort of a concerned, loving, involved and determined dad and mom. These days, so many other sources compete against parents for the opportunity to train and care for their children. From day care centers to extended family members, many parents are guilty of shifting their parental responsibility onto the backs of others while they carry on with their own self-centered, personal interests. Even our government thinks it's a surrogate parent, for crying out loud!

There's no question that others occasionally assist parents in the upbringing of our children. Everyone benefits from friends and family who reinforce Mom and Dad's role with the kids. It's great for these dear people to give Mom and Dad a break. But make no mistake. The job description says it's the parents who are to train their children, not others.

Is it time to go and get some parenting tools? Not yet!!! Well then, what's still missing at this point? Come on and think! What's still missing before we go and get some equipment?

Here's the point. "Parenting" is a very broad job description. It's a lot like the term "ranching." Within the term ranching there are many different types of ranches. Ours is a cow/calf operation. Others are yearling operations. Ours is a Hereford ranch. Others have Angus, Limousine or Longhorn cattle. Some ranches run buffalo, and other ranches have elk herds. I've even heard of emu or ostrich ranches.

Each ranch is very different and very specialized. Each one needs careful management in order to maximize profits. Some raise alfalfa hay, others grass hay, and still others harvest grains. You couldn't manage these different ranches using the very same method, could you? Obviously not! They're all very different and need to be individually understood.

If you build a barbed wire fence at a quarter horse operation, chances are you'll cut the heck out of a bunch of horses before you can say "jackrabbit." On the other hand, if you use smooth wire to hold in a herd of Angus cows, you'll be chasing them all over your neighbor's garden. Building a nice four-foot-high barbed wire fence might be the ticket for keeping your yearling steers at home, but it won't do a thing to stop elk. If you feed the same food to ostriches, pigs and buffaloes, you could end up with big birds that oink and buffaloes that lay jumbo-sized eggs! Whoa!

As there are different types of ranches, there are also different elements that must be considered when it comes to parenting. One size *doesn't* fit all in ranching or parenting. We must begin to think in terms of the specific needs of a child or family. What works for our family may not work for your family and vice versa. Families are all different.

Minnie and I have four children, one of each kind. In other words, all our children are different and have very different needs. What works with one of our children doesn't necessarily work with all of them. While one of our children might easily be held in with a four-foot fence, another one might need a ten-foot fence. One might benefit from barbed wire, whereas another child might need smooth wire. The discipline that we dish out to one of our children might be highly inappropriate for another. Every one of our children is different and needs very specialized attention. This is one of the mistakes parents make. They apply the same procedures of training and discipline to all their children, regardless of how different they are from one another. This is the wrong approach, and results in frustrated and disobedient kids. If you don't believe me, just try putting a square peg in a round hole.

In the Proverbs 22:6 passage, the words "should go" direct us to this important principle. The words "should go" speak of a child's

individual makeup. In other words, a parent is to "train up a child" in the way he "should go" or *according to that child's individual gift or bent*.

Do you know that your child came into your family with a pre-determined bent? You bet! Just notice Psalm 139:13-17. The psalmist reminds his readers that (I'm going to paraphrase a bit), "God formed your child's inward parts like a tapestry while that child was still in the mother's womb. God formed your child's skeleton in that protected place. God's eyes watched over the embryo, and in His book, all of your child's days were written and ordained when there were none of them."

You see, our children are delivered to us by God after He has established their individuality and uniqueness. God does this before they're even born. It follows then that as parents, we're to apply the tools of training and discipline to our children *understanding their individual makeup and uniqueness*. That means *every child is entitled to his or her individualized parenting*.

It would be wrong for me to discipline my oldest son the exact same way that I do my younger son. My oldest daughter is a totally different personality than my younger daughter. It would be frustrating to both of them if I trained them in exactly the same fashion. From the moment they were born, they were very different. Let me illustrate it to you this way from a hospital delivery room:

- Our first son made his entrance as a very amiable baby boy. He emerged slowly into the doctor's warm hands, looked pleasantly at Minnie and me, and smiled at the doctors and nurses. "Hi, everyone," he said. "I love you all. I'm going to be a good baby. You all are going to like living with me. Is there anything I can do for you, Mom?"

- Now our second child was an exceptionally conscientious and observant child. As she peeked into her new world in the delivery room, she noted every detail. After a few moments, with a serious look on her face she said, "I'm a little concerned about the quality control in this delivery room. I notice some of the instruments haven't been put back in their proper places. And was it really necessary to use those forceps? Doctor, how long has it been since you received your medical degree? What was your specialty? And by the way, who tied my umbilical cord? It needs to be a little tighter, and it's a little off center."

- In contrast, our third child was an emotionally dominant baby boy. He was barely over his anger about being slapped on his behind when he scanned the delivery room and said, "What's the deal here? Who's in charge? Where are my bags? I've got places to go and things to do. Let's get moving! By the way, which one of you slapped me? Dad, get the attorney on the phone!"

- Our last baby was a little girl who reveled in being relational. She entered the delivery room and excitedly said, "Isn't this great? Look at all the people who are here for my birthday! Where's the cake? Let's have a party! Don't worry about cleaning up the delivery room, let's just have some fun together!"

Can you see how different they are? It's been that way since Bible times. From way back, God has been making siblings different from each other. The first known brothers were Cain and Abel. They had the same parents, but it seems Abel was much more sensitive to God, whereas Cain was more self-willed. And what about Jacob and Esau? The Bible tells us that Jacob was a bit of a sissy, while Esau was a hunter and a man of the field. David's two boys, Solomon and Absalom, were marked with differences. Absalom lived by his looks; Solomon lived by his brains.

My point is simply this: some kids are born with a happy disposition and others are negative. Some are optimistic and others pessimistic; some angry, some easygoing. So don't try to make your children all the same. Do your level best NOT to compare them to each other, but parent them as individuals. Comparing one child against another is so destructive. Your child is an individual, and wants to be treated like one.

As parents, we are responsible to understand the differences between each of our children and parent accordingly. We need to know who they are and what makes them different from everyone else. We must discover how they individually learn, what frustrates them, what unique kind of discipline fits them and what angers them.

So, how do you begin the process of studying or learning more about your children? Proverbs 20:11-12 says, "It is by his deeds that a lad distinguishes himself if his conduct is pure and right. The hearing ear and the seeing eye, the Lord has made both of them." In other words, *talk* with them, *listen* to them and *observe* their attitudes.

Take them to the library or places of special interest to learn what they like to read about. Ask yourself if your child is more emotional or thoughtful than other kids. Also, if "water seeks its own level," then what kind of friends does your child like to be around? If one of your kids relates better to you than to his mother, then what does that tell you about the individual needs of that child? Does your child like to read books or goof around? Does your child work well alone, or are friendships very important to him?

Learn what's unique about your child. That's the assignment before you pick up the first tool and start the job of parenting. Yes, some of this we learn as we go along but we must not forget its importance as we go. KNOW YOUR CHILD is the first step in successful parenting. We'll discuss this more in future emails.

Bottom line: don't try to make your kids be like you. **They're individuals!** Allow them to be themselves and train them accordingly. If one of your children is sensitive, you'd better be careful that he doesn't interpret being sent to the corner as your personal rejection of him. Before you have a child write "I won't cuss out Mom" 10,000 times or send the child to his room to act out his anger, you'd better make sure what you're doing is in the best interest of the child in the long run. For some children, an ice cream cone or a trip to the park is a better way to discipline. Think about it!

Let's review what we have in place. Parenting is the job we've signed up for, and **knowing our children** is the first step in that process. I call this *individualized parenting.* Maybe now we can talk about some tools that will help in the process of getting our kids out of the house in good shape "so that when they are mature, they will not depart from their training."

Till a later date!
Carter

P.S. By the way, what's for dinner? I'm hoping for a high cholesterol, high protein and high calorie meal. My wife has been on this diet thing and it's like living in a refugee camp. Pray for me.

TO: CARTER
FROM: JENNY
SUBJECT: Where did we jump track?

Carter, it was terrific to get to know you and Minnie while you were visiting the state of Texas!

Having dinner together at Stu and Stacy's was a lot of fun. Thanks for including us! AJ doesn't care much about getting together with other couples, but he told me later that it was a hoot. Of course, he enjoyed making fun of your fishing and hunting experiences, and good old Stu just chimed right in with his own teasing. I must say you were a pretty good sport about the whole thing. Frankly, AJ doesn't have a lot of friends but he seems to connect with you and Stu. That's encouraging to me.

However, it hasn't helped our marriage one bit. As I sit here alone tonight reading your latest email, I'm trying to figure out where we went wrong. I want to get my children back home! But Social Services tell us we need to get some better parenting skills before any of that can happen. I don't see how that's even possible, because AJ refuses to talk with me. He thinks only of himself. Why else would he be withdrawing more and more, instead of facing the problem?

But what else can I expect? That's who he is! He's not been a husband or a father for a long time. Of course, my nagging and constant complaining haven't helped the situation either. Stacy's been showing me in the Bible how Israel was such a nagging and complaining nation, and how much God hated their complaining. They were never content and she says I'm somewhat the same. But Carter,

I've just wanted so much more from our home life and thought that enough nagging and complaining might eventually convince AJ to change. I guess I wanted a family that lived in harmony instead of a family like my parents'. I wanted to laugh and grow old together with AJ. I was hoping to take fun family vacations without all the screaming and arguing. Oh well. Another dream down the drain!

You emailed everyone about "early detection." Since the early part of detection is gone for us, I'll try to come up with some later detection ideas. Since we do need a better understanding of our parenting, I'm making a list of parenting patterns that might be helpful so you can better understand us. Maybe our detection is better late than never.

Here goes:
1. Both of us are easily frustrated with our disobedient and disrespectful children. Actually, we're frustrated *period*! Since our kids are older, discipline always seems to be a battle of the wills. It usually leads to screaming and outbursts of anger.
2. AJ and I never discuss our parenting. In fact, we don't discuss anything. We take our marriage problems out on the children.
3. AJ is very strict and I'm more lenient. The children are afraid of AJ, but he feels that I'm a pushover. Maybe I feel sorry for the children because he's so hard on them. Sometimes it seems I need their affirmation, since I don't get any from AJ.
4. We discipline by time-outs, taking away privileges and grounding. Neither of us is very consistent with any discipline. We ground one of the kids for a month, then cave in three days later. It's just too much of a hassle.
5. AJ is gone a lot, and the parenting falls on me. I resent it and get angry over his absence.

6. Even when we do things together, we aren't together. Can you understand this? Nobody is happy with anybody!
7. We discipline for the moment, without considering what to do for the long haul. *Getting control of the situation was always more important than figuring out how we could prevent the situation from happening in the first place.*

I guess every parent can relate to some of the things on my list, but I feel we've missed the boat on all of them. I wonder if it's even realistic to think that, at this stage, we can turn this mess around. Carter, can AJ learn to be a better dad? Is it even possible for me to be a better mother and wife? Remember, I'm no spring chicken!

Maybe all this later detection has just confirmed how mortally wounded our family is. Is it better to just bury it and move on? Why not just put this family out of its misery?

One other thing, as I read your email, God seems to be a very big part of your parenting. Where has He been in my family? Does He even care about what's going on down here in Texas? Gerry and Sue are Christians. Do they have guarantees that their children will turn out fine? What about Stu and Stacy? How does God fit into parenting anyway? That's my question.

Carter, I know you can't answer all my questions at once. Nor do I think there are even answers to all my questions. But I do look forward to receiving your emails, because they are a speck of light in a very dark tunnel. I think they're even more helpful than phone calls because I can read them over and over again. I also set them on the coffee table so AJ can read them as well. Maybe God will give him some new eyeglasses.

Love to you and Minnie,
Jenny

TO: JENNY and THE PARENTING CO-OP
FROM: CARTER
SUBJECT: Think Sacrifice and Relationship

Jenny, thanks for being so vulnerable. I know it will encourage all the others in our little group. I can assure you that we all love you. We've experienced failure with our children as well. So hang in there! As I read through your list, I could relate to all of them. My personal parenting history is marked with regret and failure as well. I'm glad you're in the Parenting Co-op since it's made up of a bunch of struggling parents. What makes our group special is that we all want to be better parents, and are not embarrassed to face our failings. That's pretty rare.

Let's first discuss your list in a very **general way** because in the future I'll be sending emails that deal more specifically with it. When you look at the seven points on your list, it tells me two very specific things about your parenting style. The first is that your parenting is driven by self-centeredness. Secondly, your parenting lacks sound relationships. The first you can't do with, and the second you can't do without.

Self-centeredness kills everything that is good and necessary about parenting. It must be done away with. You can't parent successfully if your focus is on self-interest. Simply put, if a mom and dad can eliminate their self-centeredness and sacrificially build healthy relationships with their children, then parenting becomes a piece of cake. It might be upside-down cake, but it's cake nonetheless.

Generally speaking, parents are very self-centered and lack meaningful relationships with their children. Often parents know very little about personal sacrifice and selfless relationship building with their children. I want to be careful here because you might misunderstand my point. I know parents who would say, "We sacrifice all the time. We're not self-centered! Look at all the money we spend on these lousy kids. We buy their food, wash their clothes and put a roof over their heads! If that isn't sacrifice, then what is?"

Let me remind you of something. Some of the most abusive homes I encounter have all these material things, and often more. What I'm talking about is selfless relationship building. I'm talking about relationships that are carved out of selflessness, not self-centeredness. There's a big difference. I'm describing a mom and dad who are willing to give up *what* they want to do, *the way* they want to do it and *when* they want it done in order to give time and energy to building meaningful relationships with their children on their children's terms. These are the kinds of relationships that draw your children to you so they want to be with you, love you and follow in your steps. Do you and AJ have this kind of relationship with your children? It doesn't sound like it to me. How about Gerry and Sue? What about Stacy and Stu? If you don't, then *that's precisely where you need to begin.*

We've already talked about the importance of knowing your child in good parenting. Step #2 is changing your relationships. Folks, the backbone of successful parenting is relationships—selfless, sacrificial relationships. The families whose children are doing well are families with good relationships between the parents and children. I don't care if they're Christian or non-Christian families. Those children who are struggling generally have poor relationships with their parents. It's as simple as that!

There's nothing novel about this. It's just as true with God's kids and our relationship with Him. People who are living for God generally have a good relationship with Jesus Christ. On the other hand, people who are living in sin generally have a very poor relationship with Jesus Christ. The more I witness His loving sacrifice, the more I want to follow His teachings in obedience.

Jesus Christ demonstrated how you go about building loving relationships through sacrifice and selflessness. The results of His sacrificial love are summed up in the Bible in two verses. The first is, "We love him [Jesus], because he first loved us." (1 John 4:19, KJV) The second is, "If you love Me, you will keep my commandments." (John 14:15)

As with a Christian's relationship with Christ, children generally respond to a parent who sacrificially loves them. Along with the child's love comes a willingness to obey. When children love their parents, they will more naturally strive to please them. Obedience comes much easier. The reverse is true as well. When children dislike or disrespect their parents, then disobedience and rebellion are not far behind.

Jenny, I want to briefly answer your questions about God's presence in our families. Where is He? Does He care? Are Christian parents guaranteed their children will be OK? Jenny, there are no guarantees—other than the fact that God is our loving and caring Heavenly Father. Right now God is demonstrating that He does care a great deal about you and AJ by bringing friends like Stu and Stacy, Gerry and Sue and Minnie and me alongside to love you. From eternity past, God has been orchestrating our Parenting Co-op knowing the needs of your family.

The issue is simply this. God occasionally allows us to go our own way. We reap great consequences from our disobedience and self-centeredness. God gets our attention through suffering. When things are going well, we ignore God's call upon our lives. But when distress comes calling, we have an unusual opportunity to get more acquainted with the Creator of the Universe. Has He got your attention yet?

I hope that's helpful. There'll be plenty more to follow on this subject. In the meantime, I want you to go back over your list. Look for self-centeredness in the way you parent. Then evaluate your relationship with each child. In doing this simple exercise, maybe you can identify where you got off track.

We'll be considering in the future how you can rebuild your relationship with God and your family.

Later, Gator,
Carter

TO: CARTER
FROM: GERRY and SUE
SUBJECT: "Can two walk together unless they be agreed?" Amos 3:3

Well, you'll probably be thrilled to learn that Sue and I had quite the discussion (maybe an argument) over your last email.

Jenny's not the only one that went back over her list of parenting problems! Sue and I did the same thing. After we finished, our conclusions were very different. I think I have a great relationship with Clayton (he's nine now, can you believe it?) and Jessica, our six-year-old sweetie. But catch this: Sue feels I'm more like an *employer* rather than a *father*. I WAS SHOCKED!! It seemed so unfair, after all I do with the children. We wash the car, watch football on TV and always go to church together. I wonder at times what she expects?

Anyway, it's not like I don't want to be a better father so I told Sue I'd follow up with you. Carter, I see what's happening to AJ and Jenny and it scares the life right out of me. What a sad thing to realize that your children want nothing to do with you. After meditating on your email, I notice that so many of the children at our church are disrespectful of, and distant toward, their parents. Let me give you an example.

We were invited to have Sunday lunch with a family from our church. Good people, committed to church life. The meal was fabulous! Roast beef, smashed potatoes, and I even had some cherry pie for dessert. Very nice! But I couldn't help but notice the not-so-nice relationship between our hosts and their children. While the children had perfect table manners (controlled by angry looks from Mom and Dad), there wasn't one bit of laughing or casual touching between them. In fact, they acted as if they were perfect strangers. They didn't speak to each other, tease each other or communicate with each other the entire meal. Rather, there were looks of disgust and frustration from both parents and children. I sensed that all of them could hardly wait to get away from each other.

When I talked with Sue that night to double-check my observation, we agreed that something very important was missing in that family. They didn't have healthy relationships. Carter, could you help us get a better grip on this relationship thing?

Gerry

P.S. How does a slacker like me have a relationship with a dirt bag like you, anyway? Well, we play together, talk together, work on our spiritual lives together, we are growing fat together, fish together (sometimes) and grow old together. Do we have a good relationship? Seems like relationship is based on a lot of "togethers," huh? (Am I answering my own question here?)

TO: CARTER
FROM: JENNY
SUBJECT: Rebuilding a Humpty Dumpty relationship

Carter, as you know, our relationships around here are pretty pathetic. AJ's mad at me, I'm sick of him and the kids have had enough of both of us. Like the old nursery rhyme says,

> "Humpty Dumpty sat on the wall,
> Humpty Dumpty had a great fall,
> All the King's horses and all the King's men
> Couldn't put Humpty together again."

This is how I view our relationships. The question for Humpty Dumpty Relationships is, can they be put back together again when "all the King's horses and all the King's men" (the Parenting Co-op) are trying but nothing seems to be happening?

On a more positive note, your email made perfect sense to (guess who?) AJ! I caught him reading it after the five o'clock news. I kidded him, "Couldn't stand it, could you?"

AJ shot back, "It's comments like that that have ruined our relationship. I want to have better relationships with you and the kids but frankly, I can get along better with my horses and even rattlesnakes than you guys. Horses don't smart off and even rattlesnakes show me some respect. You and the kids never do what I say without complaining, and none of you have one ounce of respect for me."

I responded, "That's all pretty apparent. Why do you think the kids are gone and I don't care anymore? You spend more time with your horses than you do with us. When you go fishing, you always go alone. What do you expect? Why would any of us respect a man who just barks orders and snuggles up to his remote every night anyway? Why don't you go *live* with the horses for a while?"

Well, that ended that. Carter, I couldn't help myself. I'm emotionally shot and don't have the strength to massage his frail ego. I just want out!

There's something else about that email. It slices through all the external problems, right to the heart of our broken family. It's become apparent that our family turmoil is merely an expression of our fractured family relationships. We're all filled with self-centered thoughts and actions. Our relationships have become self-serving, self-righteousness, self-loving, self-willed, self-absorbing and you name it. Is it any wonder we can't get along?

I'm beginning to understand something very important. If we want to turn our family around, our relationships must change. You may not believe it, Carter, but AJ and I were once very happy. We even enjoyed the children, but our relationship has disintegrated over time. Now we focus more on external matters— do the dishes, mow the grass, clean up your room, take out the trash—and we've lost our love for one another. Isn't that pathetic?

AJ is meeting with the kids later this week. It's a supervised visit at Social Services, and I'm hoping that your email will have an effect on the way he conducts himself. Anyway, we ended up going to the dinner playhouse with the tickets you and Minnie sent. Thanks so much! You and Minnie are so thoughtful. It's been months since the two of us were together alone. Frankly, it was very uncomfortable for both of us, but at the same time it wasn't too bad either.

I'm trying to think "relationship, relationship, relationship." But where do we go from here knowing that Humpty Dumpty is broken into a million pieces? Who can put Humpty Dumpty back together again?

Looking forward to more emails,
Jenny

TO: THE PARENTING CO-OP
FROM: CARTER
SUBJECT: Relationship Building #101

Children aren't horses, so don't misunderstand this email.

Most people are more successful at training a dog to roll over, a gerbil to eat carrots, a cat to use the litter box, a seal to jump through a hoop, a pig to open a door, a horse to stand on its back legs and a llama to spit straight than training their own children.

Why is that? Isn't it because they often have better relationships with their animals than with their own children? Training an animal actually has its similarities to parenting, especially when it comes to building a relationship. Like with training animals, if you don't parent correctly, you're likely to get kicked, bucked off or find kitty litter all over your pillowcase.

Take a horse for example. Here are some important principals to follow when working with a young colt (or filly).

1. Remember, it's hands-on work. Lots of brushing and combing—touch is very important!
2. Keep track of the colt's head. You want him to follow you.
3. Eye-to-eye contact is a key to your success.
4. Validate his gradual progress. Let him know you're proud of his performance, even when it's been a tough day.
5. Jerk his halter if he acts up. He needs to feel your leadership.
6. Go slowly with his training. It doesn't happen in one day.
7. Train every day. Consistency is the goal.

8. Never yell, scream or act ugly or mean. He'll fear you instead of respect you.
9. "Feed him some parties." Give him little treats that say, "You and I are buds."
10. Spend a lot of time with him by your side, so he learns to trust your every move.
11. Make sure his equipment fits him, and not one of the other horses in the field. Personalization optimizes performance!
12. Don't overfeed him. Too much grain will make him sick or fat.
13. Be very clear with your expectations. Follow through until the colt performs properly.
14. Learning to wear a saddle is a process that doesn't happen overnight. Remember, your colt is an adolescent at two years old.
15. Clean up after them gladly.

Now Gerry, in like manner, building a relationship with your children requires

1. Hands-on work. Lots of hugs and kisses.
2. Understanding what the child is thinking.
3. Eye-to-eye contact.
4. Validating their performance. Tell your children you're proud of them!
5. Jerking their chain (healthy discipline) when they act up.
6. Going slowly with training. Patience is a virtue in parenting.
7. Enjoying each other every day by spending time together.
8. Never yelling, screaming or acting ugly or mean. It only scares children, and you want your child to respect you for who you are—not for how loud you yell.
9. Having lots of special, fun times together that say, "You and I are buds."

10. Walking together, playing and working together, laughing together. (See, Gerry, you were right about all those "togethers"!)
11. Accepting your children for who they are as individuals, and responding with personalized parenting.
12. Eating together.
13. Communicating your expectations clearly so they understand how to stay on task—and doing that with consistency.
14. Building a relationship today in light of the needs of tomorrow.
15. Cleaning up after them gladly.

But here's the big difference between horses and children: *unlike horses, children are spiritual people.* Children need to learn about spiritual things as well. You must learn to build a spiritual relationship that impacts the *hearts* of your children, not just their behavior. Throwing a lot of Bible verses at them or forcing them to sit still in church while the good reverend gets his weekly vocal exercise doesn't necessarily build a spiritual relationship. Part of our spiritual relationship building with our children is similar to the process we outlined above. Here are some more comparisons:

1. It's hands-on work. Serve the child, and let him see Christ in you.
2. Understand the spiritual needs of the child, and personalize spiritual education to fit your child.
3. Exercise eye-to-eye contact about spiritual matters. Don't just expect the church to do it.
4. Validate spiritual performance.
5. Encourage spiritual interest. Expose the child to the needs of others through your personal involvement with others.
6. Be proactive about promoting a biblical worldview. Help them deal with postmodern thinking, and how to bring it to accountability with the Scripture.

7. Go slowly with spiritual things. Be patient, and allow your children to formulate their own beliefs. It's OK if they don't always agree.

8. Involve your children in spiritual things (mission trips, hospitality, serving seniors, etc.). They need to experience the mission of the church of Jesus Christ.

9. Never yell, scream or act ugly or mean. That's hypocrisy.

10. Fellowship with other Christian people. Kids are influenced by passion-driven Christians.

11. Enjoy your relationship at all times. The early part of Deuteronomy 6 says we need to keep God and His agenda in front of our families as we go through each moment of everyday life. That doesn't mean every minute is a Bible study. But it does mean every experience is an opportunity to show how God connects with us.

12. Define your child's unique spiritual giftedness. He wants to know how he fits into God's family.

13. Read spiritually-centered things together. Stories, biographies, devotionals, and the Scriptures come alive when you read them together.

14. Communicate God's expectations for your family.

15. Build consistency into your spiritual relationship.

16. Pray for your children. Pray with them, too.

Okay, I'm on a roll now. So here are some questions you might ask yourselves as you evaluate your relationship with your children. You can use these as a means of grading your relationships. Just be honest and answer each question with a number from 1 (absolutely not) to 10 (absolutely so). After you answer all 15 questions, add up all the numbers and divide by 15. That will give you an average "grade" for your relationship. The higher the number, the better your grade. Also, these questions will help you work specifically on certain areas of relational weakness. So here we go!

1. Do the children like to work alongside of you?
2. Do you have consistent fun together? (How consistent? Daily? Weekly? Monthly?)
3. Do the children want you to meet their friends? In other words, are they proud of you?
4. Do the children feel relaxed with you?
5. Do they respect your parenting and respond to your discipline?
6. Do they seek your opinion?
7. Do you allow them to make some of their own decisions?
8. Are you generally congenial?
9. Are you generally flexible?
10. Do your children feel emotionally safe around you?
11. Are you connecting with your children?
12. Do your children want what you have spiritually?
13. Do you and your spouse operate as a team?
14. Do you foster individuality in your children?
15. Is your home a fun place for your children *and* their friends?

Now wasn't that fun? What's your average? If it's below 8.0, then you've got a New Year's resolution in the making.

Explore this question with me: Why is it that when I get bucked off a horse I always blame the horse? Shouldn't I ask why he doesn't want me up there? (Maybe he doesn't want anything to do with me.) Isn't this a training issue? Maybe I should go back to Items 1-15 on raising a colt.

Carter

TO: STU
FROM: CARTER
SUBJECT: Let's go hunting for an opportunity

Howdy Stu, you no good slacker! How in the heck are you and Stacy doing anyway?

Your hands gotta be pretty full with those little rugrats running all over the house. Remember, God gave children to young parents rather than waiting until you're old and gray because it takes more *energy* than *brains* to raise children. I think back on those days of hide and go seek, reading books over and over again, playing catch, going on imaginary hikes, playing dolls, dressing up funny, going fishing for ten minutes and throwing rocks in the lake for the next six hours. It wears me out just thinking about it. I'll pray more for all of you when I get up from my nap.

Stu, you know I like to hunt. Right? There's nothing like stalking a nice bull elk and having it end up as meat in the freezer. Well, I've got a hunting proposition for you. How about you go hunting for an "opportunity" instead of an elk? This will be a real hunting challenge!

Here's the deal. We both know that God uses us humans to accomplish His divine purposes down here on Planet Earth. We pray, and often God chooses us to reach out to others. Right? While I've been praying for AJ and Jenny, something keeps popping up in my mind and heart. It's simply a ministry opportunity, and it concerns you.

Stu, what are the possibilities of you reaching out to AJ and his children through your connections at Social Services? I understand that AJ is having a supervised visit with his children shortly, possibly even this week. Could you pull some strings through your work to get involved with AJ and the kids? Here's what I've been thinking:

1. Do you know if you could take over the supervised visits or maybe just be involved in those visits?
2. Could you do the anger management assessment for AJ?
3. What about counseling the children?
4. Could you find a way to build a relationship with this family through your work, or is that even legal?

Stu, I feel there's an "opportunity" out there somewhere. Do you want to go hunting for that opportunity? What do you say, Bwana? Let's ask God to arrange things for you.

Carter

TO: THE PARENTING CO-OP
FROM: CARTER
SUBJECT: When does the black dog quit biting?

Does anyone like biting dogs? I sure don't. Nevertheless, I ended up with one at the ranch. It was a black dog that wanted nothing to do with humans, especially a Carter human.

I milk three cows by hand, like clockwork, every morning at 5 AM and every evening at 5 PM. At those times you'll find me straddling a one-legged milking stool with a stainless steel milk pail between my knees. I often remind old Bossy about her disposition, and how it would be easier for both of us if she'd hold still and quit kicking me. Right alongside of me are three crying barn cats and one Australian Shepherd cow dog named Panda wanting a squirt of warm milk from good old Bossy.

One morning I noticed this mangy looking black dog hanging out down by our creek. I tried to get a little closer to this straggly ball of knotted black fur, but he wanted absolutely nothing to do with me. He'd run off down into the creek and hide when I got too close. For better than a week, Cowboy Carter tried to build a relationship with Black Dog. He obviously was a victim of an abusive owner (not Carter but the black dog), and wasn't the least bit interested in making my acquaintance.

I felt sorry for this distant pooch. I started exploring ways to build a little relationship with this scrawny rascal. Being a little smarter than a dog (I don't think Minnie would agree with such an outrageous statement), I started putting a bowl of warm milk down by the creek after each milking. It was the natural thing to do when you combine a cold morning, warm milk, a hungry mutt and a smart cowboy. Next step was to move the bowl a little closer to the barn each morning and evening. We were falling in love!

It wasn't but a couple of weeks, and the black dog was sitting at the barn door waiting for breakfast. But I couldn't touch Black Dog, or he'd be gone like a shot and I'd be down to nine fingers. So I thought to myself, "Why not squirt milk on my hand and on my boot?" Sure enough, this mangy black hound started licking my outstretched hand and it wasn't very long after that the mutt was joining the rest of the critters, waiting for a warm squirt from Miss Bossy.

After much consideration, we gave the mutt a name: Black Dog. He lived with us for another eight years before becoming a highway fatality. By then, that scraggly dog had become one of my good friends.

I learned a few things from that experience.

First, *broken relationships can be rebuilt.* You must have the desire and make the commitment of time and energy to make it happen, but they *can* be rebuilt.

Second, *it takes creativity, courage, and the discipline of time and patience to restore hurting relationships.* You need a good strategy. Incidentally, it doesn't hurt to have a cow and some warm milk (if you get my drift). You need to stick it out if you get bitten or fail along the way. Don't be slackers here—it takes a lot of work to build a new relationship!

Third, *you have to consistently and proactively reach out with personal touches to rebuild relationships.* Black Dog needed the personal touch of a squirt of warm milk. He needed it twice a day like clockwork. If I was to have any relationship at all with that pooch, I needed to reach out to him—**not the other way around**.

Fourth, *you need to seek understanding, and risk vulnerability, to rebuild relationships.* It *does* help to understand why a relationship is broken. Then you have a better idea of how you must act, and what you must do, to make it better. It's crucial that you take the risk and make yourself vulnerable if your relationships are to improve. It's a stretch for all of us to risk being insulted or injured while working on relationships. But the risk is worth it, especially in our families.

See, black dogs usually don't bite unless you give them a reason. It's the same with your children. Watch some other parents handle their children. You'll understand why their children bite, growl or run away. Those children are more respected at the neighbor's house than in their own. It shouldn't be a great surprise that our children often enjoy spending more time at the neighbor's house, should it? They get **MILK** there! (Hint, HINT!!!)

I want to add this very important note: the Bible reminds us that God has fixed our broken relationship with Him. Romans 5:8 says that even while we were yet sinners, Christ died for us. Don't miss the point! *God wanted a relationship with us so badly that He sent his very own Son, Jesus Christ, to die for us.* If you want to understand how to fix broken relationships, read the Book of Romans. There we read that we are sinners separated from God and under the penalty of death, but God redeemed our relationship through His personal sacrifice.

Human relationships demand personal sacrifice, too. But here's the dilemma. You cannot expect to rebuild relationships without personal sacrifice, and you can't be personally sacrificial until you deal with your self-centeredness. *And* you can't deal effectively with your self-centeredness without the Holy Spirit dwelling in you, and the Holy Spirit cannot come into your heart unless you receive Jesus Christ as your personal Savior.

So what's next? Maybe receiving Christ as your Savior is next for some of you. On the other hand, if you're already a Christian, maybe it's time to apply the Word of God to your life and stop serving yourself.

I wonder if I could put a personal comment to AJ and Jenny here. AJ and Jenny, all of us in the Parenting Co-op love you both and desire the best for your family. Jenny, you remind me of my good friend Black Dog when I first met him: hurting, alone, afraid and self-absorbed. AJ, you remind me of his former master: abusive, angry, controlling and self-willed. To repair your broken relationships, you both need Christ in your life. That relationship is essential to completely and totally eradicate your self-centered actions and attitudes. Folks, you're not alone in needing His help to deal with self-centeredness—we're all in this together!

Well, my brain can do only so much before turning into mush. Furthermore, Minnie's telling me I have a better relationship with my computer than with her. Now that's really cruel! My computer doesn't cook supper! What is she, CRAZY? Hey Minnie, what's for supper?

Carter

TO: CARTER
FROM: STU
SUBJECT: What you sow, you eventually reap!

You sorry old cowboy! Even a dog doesn't stand a chance when trying to avoid an encounter with you. Poor thing!

How are you and Minnie doing? Minnie tells a very similar story to the one about the black dog, you know. It's a story about how you two met. She said you were down by the creek fishing, and she wanted to get a little more acquainted with you. You were a mangy looking fellow who looked as if you didn't have a friend in the world except your fly rod. She took pity on you and put some steak and taters out in the field. Sure enough, pretty soon you smelled something cooking. Before you could say "Jack be nimble," you were sitting right next to the picnic basket licking her fingers. Is that true? You always told me she was begging you to marry her because so many ladies were chasing you. Are you sure you got your facts straight, Romeo?

Anyway, Carter, I wanted to add just a footnote to your last email. You know Stacy had two children when I married her. Before we got married and shortly thereafter, the kids and I enjoyed each other and had great relationships. But now in a very short time, I see the children responding to me negatively because I haven't continued to invest enough time in strengthening our relationships. I confess I'm too busy with other things, and our home suffers as a result.

Carter, I don't think I'm alone in this. Honestly, these other things are more satisfying, more challenging, more exciting, even more relaxing than being at home. For example, I followed through on your hunting idea. I hunted down an opportunity with AJ. I'm really excited. AJ and his sons are in a basketball league for dads and sons sponsored by the Community Center. AJ's caseworker recommended they participate in it along with AJ's counseling. The league needed a referee, and guess who that's going to be? I've never refereed before in my life, but here we go.

I'm excited about that opportunity but there's also something discouraging about it. Building friendships with AJ and his kids seems more challenging and interesting than building relationships with my own kids. What's wrong with that? Carter, when a dad's work, ministry, mission or whatever seems more intriguing than building relationships with his own flesh and blood, something's WHACKO! Right?

I'm ashamed of what I'm writing, but it's true. I bet AJ and Gerry can sympathize with me. Did you ever feel this way when you were parenting? How did you balance it all?

Tighten your own cinch.
Stu

TO: STU and THE PARENTING CO-OP
FROM: CARTER
SUBJECT: Prioritizing vs. balancing

Life is often referred to as a "balancing act." We must balance the budget, our diets, our tires, our portfolios and our checkbooks. We need to balance recreation with work, balance exercise with rest, income with expenses and balance time with the kids and time with our spouses. With all the normal, everyday pressures we face, it's no wonder we often lose our balance in the process!

This past winter, I was fishing with my sons and grandson up on the North Platte in windy Wyoming. I need several things to be in balance to have a successful fishing outing. This wasn't one of those days.

To begin, the weather was out of balance. It was colder than a well driller's wallet. It was 22 degrees with a 25 mile-per-hour wind. Balanced weather is 80 degrees with no wind. The drive was out of balance. We drove longer than we fished. That's just wrong! Even the flies were out of balance. There were none! I had more flies in my fly box than I could find on the water.

My eyes were out of balance. The **eye-lets** on my rod were frozen shut and so were my **eye-lids.** That's out of balance! I couldn't see and couldn't cast. To top it off, the time I spent fishing was less than the time I spent walking around in the willows trying to keep warm. No balance there!

The guy across the river was a perfect illustration of my whole day. He had a 3½-inch icicle hanging from his right nostril. His legs and feet were as stiff as a board. Worst of all, when he tried to take a step, his legs didn't cooperate. He lost his balance and went swimming. Poor guy! He ended up in the ice-cold river up to his neck. When he finally got his balance, he looked like a 250-pound green Popsicle. The cigarette that had been his only source of heat was now making its way down the river. He was all right; he'd just lost his balance.

Now folks, I want you to read the next couple of paragraphs very carefully. When we talk about spiritual matters and family relationships, we shouldn't think in terms of balancing them with the other busy areas of our lives. Did you catch that? Let me say it another way: *don't attempt to "balance" spiritual matters and family relationships with the other responsibilities you have.* It doesn't work like that.

What we need to do with spiritual matters and family relationships is to *prioritize* them above everything else, not *balance* them along with everything else. Remember Matthew 6:33: "Seek first the Kingdom and His righteousness," *not* balance the Kingdom with a bunch of other things!

I know we're all very busy, but much of our busyness is of our own choosing. We elect to immerse ourselves in TV, recreation, exercise and computer games. We buy expensive homes and automobiles that drain our finances as well as our time. Christian people commit to every possible church activity and opportunity, often at the expense of family relationships. Consequently, our spiritual lives and family relationships suffer.

So it's not about balancing. Instead, it's about *prioritizing* personal spiritual growth and family relationships above these other commitments. Prioritizing might mean that some commitments at church should go. It might mean that some of my personal exercise or recreational commitments need to change to *family* exercise and *family* recreation. It's even possible we might need to sacrifice some TV in order to play with the children, or help with their homework. To simply balance spiritual growth and family relationships along with everything else is to minimize their importance. You can't fill up your life with all kinds of personal activity, throw in a dash of time with the kids, mix it all up and then expect those ingredients to balance themselves. It doesn't work that way.

Always remember that other activities are in *addition* to family and not in *substitution* thereof. We can **balance** all of the other activities we're involved in after we **prioritize** the family and our spiritual lives.

Give all the kids a hug for Minnie and me.
Carter

P.S. This guy doesn't understand prioritizing, does he?

TO: THE PARENTING CO-OP
FROM: CARTER
SUBJECT: Here today—gone tomorrow?

I was lying in bed this morning, thinking about how old I'm getting.

I celebrate my 60th birthday in a few days. Minnie just called me at the office and we decided to go out for something special to eat for my 60th birthday. She wants some yogurt and broccoli. That's *special*? Whose birthday is it anyway? After some convincing, we'll be going out for some STEAK and TATERS! Now that's what I call special!

All this birthday bologna has me thinking about the old saying, "What's here today is often gone tomorrow." For some things like diarrhea, the flu, old automobiles and flat tires, here-today-gone-tomorrow is a reason to rejoice. But for some other things…well, for example, who wants to say goodbye to their youthful energy, bulging biceps, strong physique, financial security or their occupation? I sure don't like the sound of that!

Then there are some things that are here today but never leave. God's Word lives and abides forever! Aren't you thankful for that? Jesus is the same yesterday, today and forever. You know, there's something else that's here today and never goes away tomorrow. Do you know what it is? It's CHILDREN! Yes, your children are here today and will never go away. They might go off to college but they don't go away. Even though they get married and move to another state or country, they still don't go away. In fact, if your children precede you in death, they still don't ever seem to go away.

I can prove it with just a few little trite statements:
- Children may be out of reach but never out of our thoughts.
- Children may be out of sight but never out of our hearts.
- Children may be out of touch but not out of our prayers.
- Children may be out of our presence but never far from our memories.

You can get rid of a bad car and sell a lousy mutual fund, but your bad kids never go away either. You're just stuck with them! As parents, we live out the rest of our lives with the consequences of our parental relationships. If you have healthy relationships as a family, you'll enjoy your children your entire life. You'll watch proudly as your children go through school and beyond. Your children will love being with you. Your family traditions and gatherings will be pleasant and fulfilling. On the other hand, poorly managed family relationships will haunt you the rest of your life. No calls, no fellowship together, no caring, just heartbreak. You can't just get rid of your children. Your mind and heart won't allow it to happen.

Every day as a parent you choose what's really important. Today you decide what your future relationship will be like. Prioritizing relationships has lifelong advantages. Remember HERE TODAY – HERE TOMORROW!

Aren't you glad you got me forever? Don't laugh!

Carter

P.S. You don't want to know what Minnie just said. It was something about good riddance to bad rubbish. She must have been talking about our children. I know what you're thinking! You thought she was talking about me! Wrong again.

TO: CARTER
FROM: GERRY AND SUE
SUBJECT: Is there such a thing as fearful parenting?

Carter,

I thought you'd be proud of me for this stunt. Just the other night, I hid in the closet in our bedroom behind Sue's dresses and shoes until Sue came in to change into her negligee before bed. While she was pulling her sweater off over her head, I slowly reached out from between the shoes and placed my cold hand gently on her bare foot. Now Carter, I never intended to scare Sue to the point of hyperventilation. And I don't know what was worse: sleeping on the couch, or waking up to the sound and pain of Sue pulling duct tape off my hairy legs. OUCH!

When it comes right down to it, I guess we're all afraid of one boogey man or another. When Sue and I sit down to talk about parenting, you know what really scares us? THE CONSE-QUENCES! THE RESULTS! THE DAMAGE THAT'S DONE TO OUR CHILDREN from neglectful parenting! What happens if our children get into trouble? What if they start cussing, drinking, doing drugs or reject Christ? Those are the things that scare the pants off us.

When we look at the mess AJ and Jenny have with their family, it's no wonder Jenny's filled with grief and AJ's hiding behind his fishing pole. We'd be doing the same thing! Jenny just sent us an email last week. She wrote, "My kids are all messed up and it's all because of their lousy parents. It's no use. AJ and I are the ones responsible for this."

Now that's real scary for us. Consequently, much of our parenting is "fear-related" because we don't want our kids to get into problems that will affect their whole lives. Do you understand fear-related parenting? We don't want them hanging out with other children who are bad influences on them. The neighborhood kids cuss, talk about sex and smart off to their parents. We'd just as soon never let our kids ever see them because we're afraid.

On top of it all, we're afraid of what our Christian friends might think if our children don't follow the typical Christian model. You know what I mean. Because of all the outside threats and the inside fears, we yell, demand and threaten the kids. "Don't do this! Don't do that! Don't do this or that or else! What will others think of this or that? If you do this or that you'll embarrass us all." It's so pathetic. Neither Sue nor I want that kind of relationship with our kids. We want some fun and freedom, but we feel pressure from our fears.

Carter, we are constantly bombarded with negative influences that threaten our children in this postmodern world. Relativism sneaks in, moral values get more obscure, and our kids are the targets. Clothing stores sell less fabric and more exposed skin. Advertisers sell with sex. Our kids are just a click or two away from all kinds of evil opportunities on the Internet. The culture around us is awash in alcohol, drugs, sexual permissiveness, foul language and empty values. You name it and we're afraid of the consequences to our tender little ones. So what do we do? We try to insulate them with handpicked friends like other protective parents. We even segregate them in order to guard their innocence.

When you raised your children, times were different. The only thing your children could do wrong was toilet paper the neighbor's barn or burn a sack of cow manure on his front porch. But look at the mess we've got as parents in the 21st century. Is it any wonder that parents want to home school, or enroll their children in charter schools or Christian schools? Does it surprise you that parents don't want their children out of their sight and erect fences so high that a giraffe can't see over it and devils can't climb through it (especially the neighborhood devils)?

What do you think of this, Carter? Don't you think it's about time for you to stop mooning the recliner and get back to writing another email?

We gotta run. The ice cream man is coming down the street and the kids are heading outside to meet him. By the way Carter, have you read about the ice cream man who sold drugs to the children that came to him for Popsicles? Is it any wonder that we don't want our kids out of our sight? Now I get to interrogate the ice cream man or Sue won't let the children have a Popsicle. What's next?

Gerry and Sue

TO: GERRY and SUE
and THE PARENTING CO-OP
FROM: CARTER
SUBJECT: How big is your God?

Folks, it's time for a reality check here. How would you like to clean the neighbor's boots after he tried to stomp out the burning bag of cow manure on his porch? My dad caught me and another kid pulling that trick on Elmer Slickholtz from the feed store. It took about an hour to get all the manure off his boots and a couple days to heal my backside. See! Parenting was just as tough back then because every parent must deal with a lot of "manure." Yours is just a little different type of manure.

Let's get a little perspective about the fearful parenting syndrome for a bit. Gerry and Sue, there'll always be lots of dos and don'ts because parents don't want their children to grow up to be "this or that." It's true because we know that if our kids grow up to be this or that (God help them) then they'll end up doing "whatever to whomever whenever" no matter how foolish it might be. Right?

Since this is the case, let's think about this whole subject a little differently. I don't want to minimize your heartfelt concerns, because they're very real. Yes, children are subjected to all kinds of temptations and it concerns all of us a great deal. However, I'd like to build a more positive perspective to give you confidence when dealing with the negative influences (known and unknown) in your children's lives. So here we go!

In my parenting, I found it helpful to keep focused on two very important principles. These principles come directly to us from God who not only created children in the first place, but also loves them dearly.

- **Principle Number One**: God is the Sovereign of the Universe, all-powerful, all-knowing, everywhere present and does as **He pleases** in our world and in our lives. He is in complete control of every aspect of our lives. He is a great big God, not a tiny midget God.

- **Principle Number Two**: God uses parenting as His sovereign means to train, to teach and to discipline children for His glory.

This is the third step in successful parenting. (Remember, knowing your child was the first step and building relationships was the second step.) You see, unless we understand the Sovereignty of God in the parenting process, our parenting will take on a very controlling, fearful, negative and defensive quality. We must understand that parenting isn't a formula like

A (Dad) + B (Mom) x C (parenting technique) = Good Children

because that leaves God's determined will for your child out of the equation. As parents, we must trust God and pray that He will touch the lives of our children because if He chooses to not influence our children for good, then our children are flat out of hope. As parents, we can't cause our children to be born again, can we? We can't cause them to grow spiritually, interpret God's Word or make spiritual decisions because that's the work of the Holy Spirit isn't it? Yes, we can plant and water but only God can bring true spiritual increase, right? **Parents can't fix what God has no intention of fixing.** Do you understand that? When we trust God with the *process* as well as the *finished product*, then our parenting is not fear-driven but rather is trusting, positive and offensive in nature.

Let's relax as parents and enjoy the ride. Trust God with the end result and do the best you can as a parent in the process and don't be so paranoid. Parenting is fun as long as God is greater and more powerful than the Devil or the neighborhood villains. When your kids misbehave and do things that displease you, just understand that God knows what's happening with His kids. Do your best to parent them and leave them and the results with God.

Go have a Popsicle with your kids because God knows the ice cream man and what he's up to. And take a careful look at the attachment on this email for some details on these two principles as they relate to parenting.

Love to you all,
Carter

Parents: Do You Believe God Is This Big?
Two Principles to Remember so You Can Relax

I. God is Sovereign over all things, including parenting.

A. God is the creator of the universe. Genesis 1 tells us that God did as He pleased in creation. On the various days of creation God divided the waters, hung the stars, separated the day into two parts using the sun and the moon and created animals and fish just like He desired. **Do you believe God is this big? I do.**

B. God is over all animals and uses them as He pleases. He ordered a whale to give Jonah a ride, pigs to run off a cliff and a donkey to speak. **Do you believe God is this big? I do.**

C. God controls even inanimate objects like the wind, the sea and the growth of a tree (sounds a little poetic). When God speaks to the wind it stops blowing. God spoke and the Red Sea split apart so the children of Israel could pass through. He set a bush on fire but it didn't burn. Truly, God is great and controls all things. **Do you believe God is this big? I do.**

D. God knows everything about our parenting. He's aware of our abilities and weaknesses. He is involved in both the process of parenting as well as the end results of parenting. Take note of this: *good parents sometimes raise very disobedient children.* In like manner, bad parents sometimes raise children that turn out pretty good. Can you figure that out? Why does that happen? Why don't all children from Christian homes put their faith in Christ? Why is that? Simply because God does as He pleases with the lives of our children. **Do you believe God is this big? I do.**

E. God has a divine plan for my children that I'm not privy to. I don't set the agenda for my children. God does! Judas Iscariot's mother didn't raise Judas to be Christ's betrayer. God had pronounced that Esau (the older son) would serve Jacob (the younger son) before the twins were even born. What could Isaac and Rebecca (parents) do about that if they wanted to? Absolutely nothing because God had a divine plan for their children before they were even born. Go back and review Psalm 139. Read in verses 1-6 that God is "all knowing" (or as theological students say, "omniscient"). Then in verses 7-10 he is "all present" or "omnipresent." Finally, in verses 13-18, creating each little child, He is "all powerful" or "omnipotent." Our God is a GREAT GOD! **Do you believe God is this big? I do.**

F. God loves my children more than I do, and He has entrusted them to my care to be parented according to biblical principles. However, I'm not responsible for the outcome of my children but for my parenting them in a way that's pleasing to God. Did you get that? Maybe you better read that last sentence again. Consequently, we need to see parenting as stewardship. We care for God's kids on His behalf, parenting them as we see fit and leaving the results to His sovereign design and plan. **Do you believe God is this big? I do.**

G. If it is God's divine plan to keep my children away from a drug-dealing ice cream man, then that's the way it will be. Yes, my parenting will tell me to protect my children from drug-dealing ice cream men but I must understand that ultimately, God must protect my children from drug dealers. As a parent we must trust God with our children, and not run around paranoid all the time as if *we're* God. **Do you believe God is this big? I do.**

II. God uses parenting as His sovereign means to train, to teach and to discipline children.

A. Parenting should be offensive, not just defensive. In other words, **God uses parenting that is proactive, not just reactive.** Parenting should be looking to the future, not just looking around; looking to God, not just looking over our shoulders for villains. Remember what the Bible says: **"Greater is He that is in you than he that is in the world."** Good parents are interested in preparing the child for the future, not just damage control in the present. This offensive approach to parenting includes:

1. Pro-active teaching
2. Consistent training
3. Personalized guidance
4. Parental modeling
5. Character development
6. Positive discipline
7. Spiritual education
8. Training a child's freedom to make their own decisions
9. Planning and strategy
10. Add your own here…

While all these parenting tips are very important, they do not guarantee that your children will grow up to be solid Christians and effective citizens. There are no guarantees in parenting. Sometimes, parents carry all the responsibility for the outcome of their children and forget that God is a Sovereign God who calls all the shots according to His divine plan and purpose. **Do you believe God is this big? I do.**

Parents have an enormous responsibility to parent correctly but the outcome with their children rests in the hands of a loving God. This is why parents often respond to parenting fearfully and carry an enormous amount of guilt. They feel that from start to finish they are responsible for the finished product when, in fact, God takes that responsibility on Himself.

Children will have temptation and will often fall into sin. That just happens to be part of their spiritual journey. However, **nothing happens to your child that isn't allowed by an "all powerful and all knowing God." Do you believe God is this big? I do.** Trust me! God isn't in heaven sharing our headache and anxiety over the behavior of our children. Quite to the contrary, He is in complete control of the situation. We forget that God chooses, predestines, elects and determines outcomes "according to the kind intention of His will ..." not ours. That doesn't mean that your child will never take drugs, but that God has bigger plans for your family than your child taking drugs.

So many things are "outcome based." The outcome side of parenting for parents is that in their parenting, they exercise stewardship which is pleasing to God. The outcome side of parenting for our children is that God, and *not* their parents, is in control.

Remember, our job is to raise God's kids to live skillfully, with discernment and with reverence for Him. **What happens in the end is God's business, not ours.**

TO: CARTER
FROM: AJ
SUBJECT: Get your sorry rear to Texas!
It's time for some fishing!

From the very beginning, I knew something was pretty weird about you. Stacy had warned Jenny about your rough edges and your "in your face" style. I figured the fishing and hunting trip down here in God's Country (as I call it) or the armpit of the world (as you call it) would soften you up a bit. I can see now that I was merely dreaming.

Well old buddy, I want to get you up to speed on a couple of things. I know you'll probably think this is a "God thing," but you'll never guess who's refereeing the Father and Son Basketball competition at the Rec Center. Crazy Stu, that's who! Since I'm in trouble with Social Services, they recommended/suggested/demanded that I join the boys for some basketball therapy. I guess Stu was available, through his job, to assist with the program.

The boys (Troy and Tyler) and I shoot some hoops together every Tuesday evening and play a game on Saturday morning. It's a strange league, but all the dads and their kids play just for the fun of it. It really doesn't make any difference how old your boys are. The teams are a hodgepodge of dads and sons put together by the community center staff, making it more competitive. Win, lose or draw, we have a great time. In fact, Stu joined us for lunch this past Saturday and guess what? We started talking about fishing and it wasn't long before he was excited about going. Slopping around in the Gulf of Mexico fishing for some lunkers sounded pretty good to a couple of fishing-starved guys.

All these great plans were forming in my head, then the subject changed. Let me tell you how to turn a good lunch into a bad lunch in about 15 minutes. Everything went south when Stu asked Tyler if he liked fishing. Tyler's chin bounced off the table and he said, "I've never been fishing with Dad." Boy, did that open a can of worms! Troy chimed in and before you could say "Drop anchor!" I was the worst father in the world.

Normally, the conversation would end in a heartbeat after I'd tell the boys to shut up and finish eating. But not this time. I tried to be polite and change the subject gracefully, but Stu kept fueling the fire by asking questions like:
- Why are you angry with your dad?
- Are you afraid of your dad? How come?
- Do you think your dad loves you? How can you tell?
- How would you like your relationship with your dad to improve?

I don't ever remember being so uncomfortable and getting indigestion so quickly. By the time they answered the questions, I felt guilty, angry and sick to my stomach. At first, I didn't give a rip what the boys thought. I couldn't have cared less what Stu thought about the whole mess. I wanted to tell the boys to grow up, be men and knock off the moaning and complaining. I could feel the heat building in my brain. I was getting madder by the minute.

Then Stu asked them about basketball. Tyler piped up, "The only reason Dad's playing basketball is because it will look better to the judge. He really doesn't care about anybody but himself. You don't think he wants to spend time with us, do you?"

That accelerated my heartburn! "Lousy kids!" I thought. "I put food on the table and a roof over their heads, and all they do is whine and complain."

To make matters worse, Stu just sat back, continued to fuel the fire, and watched the fireworks explode. I couldn't do anything but fidget in my chair. Then he made a remarkable statement that's been bugging me ever since. I'll try to quote him.

"Well AJ, you're leaving quite a legacy! The boys are angry, hurt and really don't care anymore. Jenny's about ready for divorce, and none of them seem to respect you. You're selfish with your time and energy and you do only what pleases you. What do you expect from them? You're too stubborn to change voluntarily, so the courts have taken over. Way to go, BIG GUY! Now it's about fishing. **Who did you say was going, AJ?"**

I wanted to deck Stu. I sat there for about one minute in dumb silence, thinking about the last 20 minutes worth of chewing out by my two kids and a so-called friend. But before I could grab my tongue, out came the words "We're all going! So what do you think, boys?"

There you have it. Stu and his family, Jenny and the boys are all going fishing with me after basketball next Saturday and Sunday. That is, if the courts will allow it.

I got one other thing. We got the Gift Certificates to the dinner playhouse that you and Minnie sent. The meal was terrific, and the show held our conversation to a minimum, which was probably a stroke of good luck. Thanks for being concerned about us.

AJ

P.S. I just talked to Jenny about the trip before pushing "send" on my computer. She reminded me that the courts won't let us take the boys anywhere unless the visits are supervised. Maybe they figure someone is going to drown. So I guess only the four of us are going plus Stu and Stacy's kids.

JENNY: Who's there? Minnie, are you online? Carter, is that you?

CARTER: It's Carter here. Good evening, Jenny. What's a nice lady like you doing on your computer at 11 PM?

JENNY: Well, I might ask the same question of you, young man. Carter, I've got a lot on my mind tonight and I was hoping to chat with someone.

CARTER: You've either been drinking or your mind isn't thinking too clearly at 11:15 PM. I'm not a very young man, you know! Actually, I've been working on a sermon and returning some email. Minnie's in bed reading a book on how to whip your husband into shape and says HI! What's on your mind, my dear?

JENNY: I'm having a pretty difficult night. But before I get started I wanted to thank both of you once again for your generosity. AJ and I had a very nice evening at your expense. Carter, AJ has taken a liking to you and Stu. He appreciates your honesty and non-judgmental attitude toward us. He feels that your confrontational style is the way men like it. Telling it like it is and being "in your face" saves everyone a lot of time, and you can talk more about hunting and fishing. Maybe someday AJ will want to hear your counsel. In the meantime, the emails will have to do.

CARTER: You're more than welcome for the gift. Even couples with marriage troubles need to eat out now and then. Every once in a while we collect the money from the couch cushions and send it to someone we love. We're both getting too old, and we can't take it with us. Glad you enjoyed your time together. As for AJ, I enjoy his company as well. He's a good guy who's been going down the self-centered road far too long. He's gotten a lot of bumps and bruises along the way and also ruined his family in the process. I hope God will straighten out his thinking, which in turn will straighten out his behavior and eventually his family.

JENNY: Well, Carter, I don't want to run you off but I had a couple of questions to run by Minnie. Would she be willing to get out of bed and join me for a while? I need a woman's opinion.

CARTER: Oh sure, Jenny! Make me feel bad! You don't want to chat with a hardheaded, stubborn, insensitive, and egotistical old cowboy. You'll settle for anybody, won't you? I'm offended! Just kidding! Love ya, dear, and I'll get Minnie. Be patient. It could take her 20 minutes to comb her hair, brush her teeth, put on lotion and touch up her lipstick. She never goes public looking like she just climbed out of the sack.

MINNIE: That Carter is such a pain in the old whatever. I should've left him 30 years ago and got a fresh start. Ha! So what's up, girl? The night is young.

JENNY: Thanks for being willing to chat, Minnie. I promise I'll try to be brief. I was thinking about the day Troy was born. It seems as if all of life culminated in one painful yet exciting event. AJ and I were so thrilled, we'd forgotten there would be things to do. Diapers to change, doctor's appointments to keep and a crying little baby boy to feed. Inexperience ruled, and before long we were caught right in the middle of a chaotic meltdown. Adding two more children severely increased my workload, then AJ disappeared somewhere into the woodwork. Looking back, I often wonder where he went. Anyway, it seems the man I once loved is now an adversary of sorts, and the children I dreamed of are now a living nightmare.

You know, AJ and I hadn't been out for dinner together in months and months until you and Carter sent us the gift certificates. Thanks again, Minnie! AJ never wants to part with his hard-earned money unless it's something for his boat. But anyway, that little night out also served as a reminder of all we've lost between us as husband and wife. We just sat and stared at each other. I'll bet we didn't say half a dozen words the entire meal. It's not that we don't have things to talk about; we just don't know how to talk anymore without fighting. Isn't that sad? Maybe our kids have ruined our marriage; maybe our terrible marriage has ruined our children. Either way, my life feels irretrievable! All I see in the future is divorce, financial struggles, court battles, problems with the children and sadness.

I don't feel I can face it. It seems so futile. Minnie, I don't have the emotions for it anymore. I just don't seem to care. Maybe it's better to close the book now instead of living out this nightmare.

MINNIE: Well girl, first things first. Let's both go and get a cup of warm tea and a nice little cookie before we go any further. I don't feel prepared to make a decision about your whole future without some tea. Back in five minutes.

MINNIE: Back again.

JENNY: I'm ready. There's nothing like a little tea and a chocolate chip cookie to put things into perspective.

MINNIE: You won't believe what I just saw in the kitchen. My heart nearly jumped out of my nightie. I rounded the corner on the way to the teakettle and there sat Carter on the counter in his underwear with a stick of licorice hanging out of his mouth, his hair sticking straight in the air, reading a devotional. I said, "What in the world are you doing, old man?" He said, "I'm trying to keep from falling asleep so I don't choke to death while eating this piece of licorice." Oh well.

Jenny, so many women feel the very same way you do. In fact, I sure identify with your feelings. When Carter and I were in the midst of family and marital problems, I couldn't see any way out either. Life looked so empty. I just wanted to get in the car and drive off into the sunset. Carter and I had let so many things eat away at our marriage. He had his life outside of the house, and I was stuck inside. It was so frustrating to me. Since our relationship was in trouble, I looked more to the children for my needs and less to him. That was frustrating to him, I learned later. Together we were not only frustrated but also frustrating to each other. Is it any wonder that things turned upside down? By the way, how's your tea?

JENNY: Warm! I needed something warm. Minnie, I feel all alone in the middle of this mess. That's the main problem. Together AJ and I might possibly be able to get through it, but I'm all alone because he's taking his frustration outside of the home. I try to bring up the subject and his heart runs for cover. He doesn't want to talk. He just gets angry, yells and screams, and that doesn't help matters. Know what I mean? Minnie, did you ever consider ending it all in divorce or some other way?

MINNIE: Of course. There are always options instead of working through your problems. Some couples turn to emotional separation and others to divorce, but those solutions are only temporary. Jenny, true problem solving happens at the spiritual level as people become acquainted with what God wants them to be. This transformation changes a person's character from within their hearts. Unless a marriage can change its spiritual makeup through the changed lives of a husband and wife, the solutions for marital strife are only temporary.

Abraham Lincoln once said, "Marriage doesn't consist of having the right partner, but of being the right partner." The same is true with parenting. Unless parents face their need to become the right parents through spiritual direction and renewal, then their solutions to parenting problems will likewise be only temporary. Jenny, if you leave AJ and get a divorce, you've chosen the path of least resistance. Staying in the marriage, committing your lives to God and applying biblical principles will improve your marriage and your parenting skills. Don't run! Allow God to change your character from the inside out through His Word, and through the counseling of people who love you. Your problems aren't a dead end street but a fork in the road. But you and AJ must decide which fork you're going to take. One fork will lead you down the same path you've been on all these years. This is the non-spiritual path. The other fork is the spiritual path, and God will change your lives if you go down that fork. It's true, child! Does that make sense?

JENNY: I don't know what to think. I do know I've lost my will to try. Looking back over all these years it seems as if we've held this mess together with pure guts and stubborn endurance. I don't think I've got much left. Minnie. I'm sorry for being so negative but I'm getting a horrible headache just thinking about it and I'm so tired. Here it is almost midnight. I'm ready to go to bed, if you don't mind. Thanks for your help.

MINNIE: Good night, my dear. We love you. Jenny, when you put your head down on the pillow, I want you to go to sleep with this thought in mind. It comes from Psalm 107:12-15: "Therefore He humbled their heart with labor; they stumbled and there was none to help. Then they cried out to the Lord in their trouble; He saved them out of their distresses….Let them give thanks to the Lord for His loving kindness, and for His wonders to the sons of men!"

Jenny, God *will* deliver you and AJ from this marital and family nightmare if you'll only turn to Him in faith and repentance. Jesus Christ *will* transform your marriage and your relationships with your children if you'll receive Him into your heart. The Bible tells us when that happens, "old things are passed away and all things become NEW." Did you get that, Jenny? Maybe the NEW is the other fork in the road! Good night.

JENNY: I'll think about that, Minnie. We could use something NEW! Talk to you soon.

MINNIE: I can hear Old Carter snoring. It sounds like a rather large cow groaning while giving birth to a calf. Every once in a while he jumps in his sleep, and just scares me to death. When he does this jumping routine, I think the police just caught up with him in his dreams for some scandalous activity. One time I was sound asleep, and Carter kicked me so hard he knocked me completely out of the bed and onto the floor. When I came to my senses, I couldn't believe what had happened. Apparently, Carter was dreaming. He was out hunting and a rattlesnake tried to bite him in the foot. He kicked to get out of the way, hitting me square in the you-know-where. You think *your* life is hard. Think again, girl! Bye for now, and sleep well.

TO: AJ
FROM: CARTER
SUBJECT: Fishing for the family

You old rascal, it was great to hear from you.

I showed Minnie your last email. We agreed it must have been pretty uncomfortable having the boys tear into you like that. All I can say is they must really love you a bunch to be so honest, but they must really be hurt and angry over this whole situation.

AJ, it may have made you uncomfortable but now you've been put on notice. The boys won't keep taking all your abuse, nor will they ever be that honest again unless you handle the confrontation in the spirit it was given. The Bible says that the wounds of a friend are better than the kisses of an enemy (Proverbs 27:6). Your boys are telling you this because they care about you and want the family to work, not because they hate you. They want their dad plugged into their lives.

AJ, they miss you and need you to be their father, not their slave master! Is there anything wrong with that? What kid wants to go through life with an absentee father? Seems to me that the ball is in your court. You can either continue to pull out of the family, or get plugged back in. Stu's right about one thing: your decision will determine your legacy.

AJ, maybe reconciliation starts with the words "I'm sorry." I guess I should use the same words. AJ, I'm sorry! I forgot that you don't want me counseling you, but sometimes I just can't help myself. Minnie says I have a problem keeping my thoughts to myself. I apologize in advance for overstepping my bounds. I'm trying to respect your wishes, but I'm such a slacker.

I hope the fishing trip with Jenny, Stu and Stacy will be great fun. Turn the weekend into a fantastic memory. Who knows, it might affect your legacy forever! Not bad, big guy! I have another conference about 150 miles from your house, and Minnie and I would love to come see you. That's in a couple of months. What do you say? Minnie can hardly wait to get her hands around your throat for the way you treat me.

Gotta run. The veterinarian is just driving into the barnyard. We're going to worm the horses and vaccinate for the West Nile virus. I just wish I could discover a vaccination for protecting men from the deadly virus of self-centeredness, which makes them such lousy husbands and fathers. You got any ideas? We could make millions of dollars off that vaccination. Just think of it! Then we could go fishing and hunting all the time. HA!

Check your boat for leaks,
Carter

TO: MINNIE
FROM: STACY
SUBJECT: How do you solve a problem like Jenny?

Minnie, thanks for your "heads up" after talking with Jenny through the wonder of instant messaging. I dropped by to see her first thing this morning to check on her. Basically, all was well if discouragement, depression and loss of direction are all well. Really, she was doing OK after a pretty sleepless night.

I followed your suggestion and we went out for a latté at the corner bagel shop. I could tell by her shaking hands and rat-infested hairdo that she was pretty uptight about things. However, coffee must be a miracle drug because she began feeling more upbeat by the time we left. She even apologized for her appearance! It probably felt good to her to know somebody who cared was alongside of her. What do you think?

She was thankful she talked with you, and was willing to start on a list of some alternatives to throwing in the towel, as she put it. When she finished, she had a list of about 20 different short-term options. (Between her marriage problems and the stress of the children, she obviously needed something to give her hope and a reason to keep trying!)

I remember having to do a little homework after Mitch died because I also wanted to throw in the towel. When I was finished, life didn't look like such a disaster after all. Here's what I suggested to Jenny for homework.

I asked her to take inventory in six different areas of her life. She needed to make a list of three positive things and three negative things that were happening in her life for each area. Here's the list of areas:

1. Spiritual Inventory
2. Emotional Inventory
3. Mental Inventory
4. Physical Inventory
5. Marital Inventory
6. Parenting Inventory

Then I asked her to stop being so negative long enough for her to see the positive things that are presently going on in her life. Minnie, actually God is working in her heart if she could only see it. I hope this evaluation will help. I had three general questions for her to answer regarding each of the areas to inventory. The questions went something like this:

1. What is your goal for each area?
2. Write down what has happened during the past five (5) years in each area. Include both positive and negative.
3. What counsel does the Bible give you regarding each area? Read Ephesians 1-6 and pick two verses for each area.

Then I encouraged her to work with me on some short-term objectives for each respective area. The job wasn't complete until she had written down some very specific steps to improve each area. I told her I *wanted* "steps" plural, but would settle for just one step in each area.

And guess what? Jenny agreed to follow through if I would get back with her in a couple of days to make sure she was on task. Simply put, she needed to discover what *God* says about her situation. For her to rely on me or the Parenting Co-op to fix her problems would be too easy. Instead of complaining and finding fault with AJ, she needs to take charge of her own family situation and be more responsible for the outcome.

Minnie, I hope this all sounds good to you. The reason I wanted her to do these things is because it has been so helpful to me to take inventory on a regular basis in my present family. Sometimes, life gets so hectic that we don't stop long enough to think through what's going on. We're all bombarded with the tyranny of the urgent and important matters get sidetracked or ignored. Until Jenny stops long enough to evaluate her marriage and parenting problems in light of what God teaches in His Word, she won't have the slightest direction on how to bring about the necessary changes. Don't you agree? I can speak only of my personal experience, but it sure has helped me. Without regular personal inventories, I'd be stuck and who wants to be stuck?

Well, we're all off fishing this weekend. Stu and I are so looking forward to a break. I understand that we might see you and Carter in a couple of months. Hopefully by then, AJ and Jenny will be doing better.

Thanks, Minnie for being interested in us youngsters. Give Carter a big hug for me.

Stacy

TO: JENNY and THE PARENTING CO-OP
FROM: CARTER
SUBJECT: When the going gets tough,
the tough get going!

I really appreciated Stacy's counseling to Jenny.

It's important to always remember that our thinking controls our emotions. That's precisely why it's so important to monitor our thinking. The Bible reminds us that "...as a man thinks, so is he." When we consistently focus on negative thoughts, we lose control of our emotions like a runaway train. We're left frustrated, angry, tired, lonely, depressed, anxious and headed for serious trouble. We're literally stuck in the middle of a messy situation and can't get out. We all know it takes more energy to think biblically and take action than it does to just stay put and keep moaning and complaining.

So, Stacy's on the right track. Jenny must conserve some energy and spiritually work through the practical inventory in order to get her thoughts under control.

For now it's back to the matter of parenting. Remember the email I sent a few weeks ago about the importance of **knowing your child** in order to be more effective in your parenting? Well at the bottom of this email, you'll find a personality test for children.

I think you'll find that completing the worksheet will help you understand what makes your child tick. That will help you determine what will be the best pathway for teaching and training. Remember, every child will be different but that's OK. Here's the little test:

CHILDREN'S PERSONALITY INVENTORY

Rate your child's temperament in each category using numbers 1 to 4 (4 being most likely, 3 moderately likely, 2 less likely, 1 least likely). For each question, enter a number in each category. Then total the scores in each category and use the graph following to plot the child's strengths and weaknesses.

ANALYTICAL/ CONSCIENTIOUS	AMIABLE	EXPRESSIVE/ RELATIONAL	DRIVEN/ DOMINANT

A. Do you consider your child most...

_____Cautious	_____Pleasant	_____Playful	_____Intense

B. You could see your child becoming...

_____Accountant	_____Counselor	_____Salesperson	_____Boss

C. When your child plays, he/she usually focuses on...

_____Doing things right	_____Getting along	_____Having fun with others	_____Leading & dominating

D. Your child works...

_____Carefully by self	_____Slowly with others	_____Fast-paced with others	_____Fast-paced by self

E. If someone took ten unposed pictures of your child, how would you describe the most frequent expression on his/her face?

_____Serious	_____Warm	_____Expressive	_____Confident

F. Your child's speech is usually most...

_____Thoughtful	_____Congenial	_____Excited	_____Direct

G. In school, your child's teacher would consider him/her most...

_____Careful	_____Steady	_____Talkative	_____Impatient

H. The word that best describes your child is...

_____Concerned	_____Loyal	_____Optimistic	_____Confronting
TOTAL	**TOTAL**	**TOTAL**	**TOTAL**
_____	_____	_____	_____

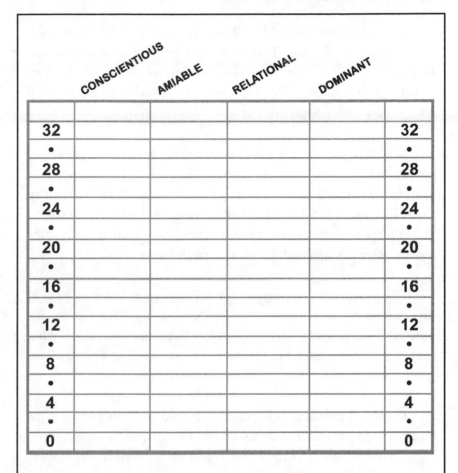

	CONSCIENTIOUS	AMIABLE	RELATIONAL	DOMINANT	
32					**32**
•					•
28					**28**
•					•
24					**24**
•					•
20					**20**
•					•
16					**16**
•					•
12					**12**
•					•
8					**8**
•					•
4					**4**
•					•
0					**0**

ANALYTICAL/CONSCIENTIOUS: detail oriented, perfectionist, quality control, serious, cautious, non-assertive, analytical, data collector, organized, reserved, creative, conscientious

AMIABLE: steady, cooperative, good listener, peacemaker, non-assertive, quiet leader, supportive, gentle, loyal, patient, family oriented, amiable

EXPRESSIVE/RELATIONAL: emotional, talker, persuasive, unorganized, center stage, change oriented, enthusiastic, inspirational, impulsive, fast paced, positive, delightful, relational

DRIVEN/DOMINANT: confident, decisive, change oriented, independent, results oriented, direct, impatient, forceful, competitive, problem solver, adventurous, dominant

Did you notice something about the test? It didn't measure a child's spiritual condition. This is something that is often overlooked in parenting. It's very important to remember that your child, as sweet as he might be, is born a sinner, has a sinful nature and will always be a sinner. Don't forget it!

Now take the test on your children and get some personality testing done on you and your spouse. You'll see the difference in your understanding of other family members. Remember, **healthy families understand each other**. Unless you seek to understand the other person, chances are you'll never bring conflict under control or parent as successfully as you might like.

This brings me to a passage in the Bible. 1 Corinthians 7:32-34 emphasizes the importance of a husband doing what pleases his wife, and a wife doing what pleases her husband. Now that's what makes a good marriage, but you must first understand what is pleasing to your spouse before you can get on with it.

Then in Ephesians 6:4 we're instructed to "not provoke [or exasperate] your children to anger; but bring them up in the discipline and instruction of the Lord." How do we keep from exasperating our children or making them angry unless we understand them? So use the test, get a better understanding of your child, and then go to work on your parenting. Trust me, it will make the process much easier.

By the way, you ought to see Minnie's test! No wonder she's been so hard to live with. My test was basically perfect. I'm actually a dream to live with! Maybe I'm a supernatural angel! She's so lucky to have me for a husband. I think I just heard her choke in the kitchen. I better go see what's going on.

Carter

TO: CARTER
FROM: STU
SUBJECT: A fishing trip gone bad!

Whose idea was it anyway for all of us to go fishing? I know getting more acquainted with AJ and Jenny was part of our plan, but maybe we should've been more careful. What initially sounded like such a great idea really went upside down in a hurry.

Carter, you know what kind of boat AJ has. It's no small potatoes. The boat is actually what I'd call a yacht and must be at least 30 feet long. It has an engine that sounds like a racecar, with plush chairs and couches everywhere. The boat sleeps about six people should anyone be stupid enough to spend the night bobbing around in the water.

Of course, I'm joking because that's precisely what we did on our fishing trip. About 15 miles off the Texas coast, we began fishing and basically were all having a great time. Tanya (our little girl) had caught a rather large fish (38 pounds to be precise). Jenny and Stacy had also caught a fair number of sizable fish and were quick to remind AJ and me of their impressive success. (Can you say "bragging"?) Well, I could care less because deep-sea fishing isn't that high on my priority list, but that wasn't the way AJ felt. I could tell he was getting really upset.

The constant ribbing the gals were dishing out was getting under his skin—and wasn't helping the situation one bit. The more fish *they* caught, the more frustrated *he* got. The more frustrated he got, the angrier his actions became. He started stomping around and….well, you know what angry people do to act out. In fact, it became very apparent to me what Jenny and the children experience at home when AJ loses his cool. Fact of the matter was, I was getting pretty annoyed with AJ's self-pity party as well. After all, they're just FISH!

I honestly tried to manage the situation and even tried indirectly to get the gals to lighten up on the teasing but they'd have no part of it. They had found his soft spot and wanted to rub it in. The nastier AJ got, the hotter I got. How's that for male testosterone overload? Fortunately, our children were below in the galley playing a game and couldn't hear the verbal bantering that was going on deck side.

Carter, I still don't remember exactly what happened. All I know is AJ called the ladies some unmentionable names and told them to shut up. That was all it took. I was on my feet before you could say "Let's be stupid." I told him very directly to knock it off or else. That's when he redirected his anger at me, popped me in the kisser and knocked me backward onto one of the seats.

I snapped. I got back on my feet and popped him right in the nose, which obviously made matters a whole lot worse. Stacy and Jenny were screaming, and the children arrived on deck scared to death just in time to see AJ push me into the yacht's control panel, breaking off the key and bouncing my head off the steering wheel.

Now that I look back, I shouldn't have whacked him with the water ski, but somebody was going to get hurt and I didn't want it to be me. The water ski vibrated as it connected with his fishing hat. Things got pretty quiet on the deck almost instantly. AJ was laying head first down the stairs that lead to the galley below. He was knocked out cold as a cucumber. As Jenny rushed to his side, he gave out a groan, rolled over and sat up on the bottom step with his eyes wide open as if to say, "Where am I and what in the heck happened?" Actually, I think he was resting but by the look in his eyes, he was trying to collect his thoughts that had been dislodged with the water ski.

Stacy and the children had me pinned against the back seat near the motor, wiping the blood off my forehead and telling me I should be ashamed of myself. Anyway, I started to get to my feet when AJ finally got to his feet and continued his descent down the steps into the galley. He was gone about ten minutes and came up the stairs carrying a harpoon gun. Stacy and Jenny started screaming at him. Just as he reached the top step.........Carter, lighten up a bit, I'm just kidding you!!!! He actually came up out of the galley carrying a cold beer and headed straight for the bow of the boat.

Are you enjoying this story? Do you want me to finish or wait until the next email? The story really gets juicy! You know what the moral of the story is? Always stay fit, because you never know when you might need to swing a water ski at somebody. (Please don't tell Stacy I wrote that. She doesn't see the humor in any of this.)

Well, as it worked out, we couldn't get the motor running because the key was busted off too far into the ignition to work. Nobody could hotwire a Soap Box Derby car, let alone this boat, so there we sat in the middle of a million acres of water with nowhere to go. Do you ever wonder why God allows things to happen? Romans 8:28 tells us that all things will be for our good, and that's precisely the end of this story.

After taking care of our wounds, we couldn't get away from each other, so there we sat looking at each other. Yes, we had put in a call for oceanside assistance (kinda like roadside assistance), but help didn't arrive for about six hours. We literally sat there for over an hour without saying a word to each other. Even Jenny and Stacy didn't talk to each other. We could see Jenny quivering with emotion and using tissue after tissue to wipe her tears.

Finally, Stacy relaxed the tourniquet grip on my left arm and went over to Jenny and they sat together holding each other and talking in whisper tones for some time. I was left alone and the kids were sitting around a party tray playing UNO. I kept asking myself the question, "What do I do now as a Christian—especially after making such a big mess out of what was supposed to be a nice fishing trip?" I felt this compelling need to explain my actions, not necessarily to defend them.

"I may have mishandled the situation, but the situation needed handling one way or the other," I told myself. "Nobody calls my wife those awful names and stays on their feet."

Yet I feared that if I waited to talk with AJ until after we returned home, I'd never see him or Jenny ever again. Carter, I wanted to try to at least mend our relationship to some degree before it was too late. However, I didn't want to fuel the fire and have another problem with AJ. Then I thought, "So what if one of us gets thrown overboard. The boat can't go anywhere because it won't run."

As if lightning struck me, I was on my feet and headed for the bow of the boat. Stacy demanded I tell her what I was up to. I assured her that this time I was fighting to save a friendship, not fighting to ruin one. I moved closer to AJ. I asked him if I could say something to him in the way of an explanation, and then promised to return to the rear of the boat the second I finished. He took another sip from his beer can and replied, "OK." Carter, this is in short what I said to him:

"AJ, your friendship means a lot to me and I'm very thankful that God has brought our families together. I'm sorry for what happened. By the way, you have one heck of a punch! I need to apologize for acting the way I did but not for why I did it. I could feel that you were getting angry at the comments and jesting from our wives. It seemed to me that you were taking the fishing much more seriously than they were.

"I was all right until you spoke as you did to Stacy. Calling her those ugly names and telling her to shut up was totally unacceptable. That's when I lost it. If you want to speak to Jenny that way it's your business, and if you want to call your children names then that's your business as well. But I won't allow anyone to talk to Stacy or my children that way or they'll have to deal with me, come what may.

"AJ, Stacy and I want to be friends with you and Jenny. We love you and your children, and would like to be a part of your family in the future. But we can't if you don't understand what I've just been saying. I don't verbally abuse Stacy and the children and I'll be darned if anyone else is going to. I pray that you'll understand what I'm saying so we can continue our friendship and, with that, I'm out of here."

Carter, I promise you, I went right back and sat down with the children and didn't say another word to AJ. I felt tears coming down my cheeks probably because my emotions had peaked. I felt enormous relief saying what I'd said. Technically it was all over, and I couldn't think of anything else to do. I looked over at Stacy expecting to get an angry look. I was joyfully surprised to see her wink at me then whisper, "I love you." Stacy told me later that Jenny said to her, "AJ's needed that sermon for a long time."

There we sat. It was like two dogs at the end of a dogfight, with both dogs being held back by their masters. You could cut the tension with a knife. After about two hours of deadly silence, AJ made his way around the rail and walked over to Jenny and Stacy. I started to get on my feet, but sat there like a bump on a log.

AJ began speaking. "I want to apologize to you both for the way I was acting. I was being childish over the fishing and couldn't control my emotions. As you know, this has been a problem for me over the years and I'm really sorry. Jr. and Tanya, I didn't act properly to your parents and I'm sorry."

Looking directly into Jenny's eyes he said, "Well, I know you're mad at me and rightfully so. I'm sorry to embarrass you in front of your friends. My head hurts so I'm going to lie down." Then AJ turned to go down the stairs into the galley. Before doing so, he thanked me for being his friend and reached out to shake my hand.

And there we sat until help arrived. Jenny asked us (me, Stacy and the kids) to all ride on the rescue boat so AJ and she could be alone on their boat. Jenny thought that was better for everyone, especially since she needed to go home with him alone. Even though AJ put on a good front, she was still afraid of what might happen after getting to shore. Who wouldn't be? When we docked, we immediately gathered up our things, cleaned the fish and headed off to the car.

Carter, I haven't talked with them since. Of course, it's been only three days so we'll see what happens, and let you know if we hear anything.

Stu

TO: AJ and STU
FROM: CARTER
SUBJECT: Boys will be boys!

When I first learned of your fishing adventure, I could only wish I was there to watch. Slapping each other around deck side may not have been the best way to handle your disagreements according to Minnie, but I know "boys will be boys." On the other hand you're both men, and "men should be men." But what does that look like? It probably begins by avoiding abusive speech and insults, as well as learning the skill of defending your wife's honor in other ways besides thumping someone on the old melon with a water ski.

Minnie says you "boys" need to rebuild your friendship pronto. AJ, you acted in a very honorable way by apologizing to everyone. Maybe that's the beginning of becoming a real man. Minnie says, "Men need to act like men, not like a bunch of neighborhood knuckleheads." She often reminds me of this when I'm driving and someone cuts me off, or turns in front of my tractor. I want to take matters into my own hands and bounce someone's head off the front-end loader or slam their knuckles in the tailgate of my truck. This kind of behavior from her husband always makes Minnie pretty unhappy and she wants to burn my hand in the toaster. I'm just kidding, but you get my drift.

When I was much younger, a couple of guys drove by my polished 1949 Ford car and made some obscene gestures to Minnie. I didn't like it a bit, and wasn't about to let that pass without giving someone a headache. I motioned for them to pull over. After popping each other a few times I returned to my car, bloody nose and all, only to find Minnie madder than a wet hen. She reamed me out for the better part of an hour and hasn't forgotten the incident for over 40 years. But frankly, nobody's going to treat my girlfriend like that without getting slapped upside the old noggin!

What does it really mean to be a man, a defender of those you love? Do real men just sit back and let someone degrade their loved ones? Today, the influence of feminist ideology has greatly affected both guys and gals. The very essence of masculinity is being attacked. Everything associated with maleness has been the subject of ridicule and scorn. Parents encourage their boys to behave like little girls and wives seem content to have their husbands be passive, weak and effeminate.

Just look at your television and observe the so-called men. They're depicted as dumb, horny, fat and stupid. These guys aren't men! Guys who have stuck by some of the traditional roles associated with manliness are considered macho or male chauvinist pigs. Feminist Karla Mantilla calls it the "trap of masculinity" in her article entitled "Kids Need 'Fathers' Like Fish Need Bicycles."

In contrast, I like what Dr. Dobson says about the subject. He said the following in one of his newsletters:

> "The bottom line is that many men have lost their compass. Not only do they not know who they are, they're not sure what the culture expects them to be... It is time that men acted like men—being respectful, thoughtful and gentlemanly to women, but reacting with confidence, strength and certainty in manner. Some have 'wimped out,' acting like whipped puppies."

Maybe it's not so bad to get angry and defend your wife and family even if it means popping someone in the nose or parting their hair with a water ski. Men should be men and act like men to defend and protect their families. In my opinion, you wouldn't be a man if someone calls your wife a blankety-blank and you just sit there on your thumbs and do nothing. A real man would confront that situation head on, just like Stu.

Fact of the matter is, Jesus got pretty upset when the religious elite were abusing His Father's house. Shouldn't we? He got hold of a good whip, used strong language, mixed in a healthy dose of anger and threw the whole bunch of them out on the street. Meek and lowly Jesus cracking the whip! I like His style—His manliness. Jesus was outraged at the evils of His day and it would do well for us to follow His example.

Can I vent a minute? Our biblical values, morals and ethics are abused, scoffed at, ignored and degraded every day while passive Christians sit back and watch. What's happened to our men? Why do we sit back and allow a 3% minority of homosexuals shove the gay marriage amendment down our throats and never say one word?

So at what point do you finally **stand** against those who seek to destroy your family? How long will Christians sit back and allow pornographers to degrade our loved ones? Think about it!!

AJ and Stu, you've just literally lived out one of my favorite proverbs from the Bible. It says, "Better are the wounds of a friend than the kisses of an enemy." AJ, I guess it's better for Stu to smack you over the head with a water ski than it is for him to just sit back and do absolutely nothing about your abusiveness.

Now I'm not advocating fist fighting every time you confront abusive behavior, but what I am saying is that abusive behavior needs to be dealt with **somehow by someone**. It could be a loving wife, a man's children or possibly a friend like Stu.

You know something AJ, you should be thankful for Stu. He's a good friend and called your abusiveness into account. Nonetheless,

I admire a guy who will be a man and stand up for his wife and family even if it means wearing a nosebleed.

AJ, I love you but honestly, if you called Minnie those awful names, I'm not too sure we wouldn't have tangled as well. Wouldn't you defend the honor of your own wife and children if another man called her a name or tried to disgrace your children? I want to believe that you would do the same.

But the bigger problem is the need not only to defend our families against those attacks from outside, but also to protect them from the abuses that happen from within. AJ, this is why your children are in another home and Jenny is threatening to leave you. You haven't protected them from your own abusiveness. You yell, demand, cuss and strike out at them. I can't approve of that kind of parenting. The purpose of our Parenting Co-op is to help each parent build strength into their relationships by using healthy parenting techniques, and by throwing overboard parenting practices that are hurtful. **Remember, good parenting starts at that moment when protecting, defending and respecting your family is worth fighting for.**

I don't want you two guys to start feeling sorry for yourselves. I can assure you of my unconditional love for you both, even though I can't totally agree with how you've acted. It's the "hate the sin, love the sinner" scenario. Now get your sorry rear ends out for a cup of coffee, shake hands again and move forward in building a better relationship together and with your families. Apply that masculine energy to working at making your homes better and safer places to live. Your wives and children will be thankful forever.

When's the next fishing trip? I need to catch more fish, but I'd better handle the water ski!

Carter

TO: AJ and JENNY
FROM: GERRY
SUBJECT: Enough is ENOUGH!

I've really hesitated to write this email. Sue and I have prayed every day for guidance because I know this email has the potential of becoming very destructive. I've asked myself, "Would it be better to just let everything ride since it involves my sister-in-law and brother-in-law?" I guess we both have concluded I should go ahead and send it since we love you. We must believe that God will preserve our relationship.

Before I jump in with both feet, I want to make a couple of things indelibly clear. First, Sue and I are far from perfect in our marriage and our parenting. This was one of the main reasons for starting up the Parenting Co-op. We need as much guidance and practical suggestions as the next couple. Secondly, I want to say something to AJ. AJ, Sue and I have always enjoyed being a part of your life and family. We love you for who you are and don't look down upon you at all for not being a Christian. For us, your spiritual journey is a matter that God will handle in His time and He doesn't need us to be judgmental in the meantime. While I understand that you might feel like an outsider, we don't feel that way at all. We want to continue to be a part of your future and for you and Jenny to be a part of ours.

Now that I've said all that, here I go.

It was over two years ago that Sue and I went through a horrific marital mess with a couple that lived up here in Cheyenne. By now you both know of whom I'm speaking. Stacy was married to a man named Mitch, and they had two lovely children. Their marriage was a total wreck, and so were both of them. (You can read about them in the email book I put together sharing their unusual story entitled *OOPS! I Forgot My Wife*. Remember, it was at the bottom of the Christmas goodies Sue sent you last year.)

I'm assuming you both know most of the story by now. The part you *don't* know is what Sue and I learned from their mistakes. I would like to summarize this for you in the form of some very specific statements about abusive family relationships and particularly parenting relationships. Ready?

- We can love abusive people for who they are, but dislike very much what they do to hurt other people.
- Abusive people don't always know they're being abusive. They might have been raised in an abusive home or they just don't understand how their abusive ways hurt others.
- The abuser can't measure abusive behavior. The person who is abused is always the one to measure abusive behavior. If children feel abused by a parent, then chances are the parent is being abusive. The same is true with our spouses.
- Abusive people generally live in a state of denial. For example, an abusive parent might say "I would never hurt my children," or "I don't know what you're talking about." They're deceived.
- Abusive people justify their abusiveness by shifting responsibility to others. For example a mother might say, "I slapped you because you were smarting off." A dad might justify his abusiveness by saying, "If you'd do what I told you to do when I told you to do it, then I wouldn't have to kick you down the stairs."
- Abusive people are manipulative. They manipulate by conditional love, guilt tactics or through emotional outbursts.

- Abusive people are controlling. Abusers want everyone to follow their commands to the letter. No disagreements! No altering the rules. No compromises, period!

- Abusive people are self-focused. They actually personify self-centeredness. Everything is about them, their interests and their needs.

- Abusive people don't allow for individualism. A wife will become a non-person, and children lose their individual identity under the thumb of an abusive husband or father. A child's unique creative ability is lost when a parent is abusive.

- Abusive people hate being exposed. The abuser is afraid others might know. That's *precisely* why abusive people isolate family members from others. They don't want to be discovered. This is why abuse is called a "closet sin." It happens in private.

- Abusive people hate someone confronting their abusiveness. Why is that? Because the abuser is insecure and fears losing control. It's when family members begin addressing abusive behavior that the abuser gets frightened.

- Abusive people don't understand the meaning of a "loving relationship" built on mutual consideration, cooperation, shared goals and individualism.

- Abusive people don't understand the personal needs of those they are abusing. They understand only their own needs. An abusive parent doesn't understand the basic need for a child to feel safe, comfortable, understood, accepted or loved unconditionally as an individual. The same is true with an abusive spouse. They don't really understand the need for their mate to feel a sense of freedom, independence, individuality, unconditional love and acceptance.

- Abusive people have little ability to control their emotions. They lack self-control. Abusers don't know what to do with their frustration, anger and feelings of insecurity so they take it out on their subjects.

- Abusers can be Christians. With abuse there is no religious distinction. Some Christians are very controlling, manipulative and abusive as parents and spouses. The problem is they cover it all over with the cloak of religion and use the Bible as a whipping stick.
- Abuse can be physical, emotional, verbal, sexual and religious in nature but it all needs to STOP in order for our families to be safe, healthy and nurturing.

AJ and Jenny, as you can see, this is a list of observations I've made over the past couple of years about people like Mitch that have abusive tendencies. That being said, I also see some of them in Sue and me. Now granted, abusiveness is a measured problem. Some people have it worse than others. However, if your family is going to do well, abusiveness must be eradicated entirely and God's principles of unconditional love followed exclusively.

After Mitch died, Sue and I have run into other couples with similar problems. We first made this list for our personal benefit so we could catch abusive behavior in our own family before it got a foothold. Since then, we've also given it to other couples so they could measure their family relationships to detect any abusive tendencies or behaviors. Sue and I are sending this list to you without comment, asking you to go over it very carefully to determine if your relationships are safe, secure and free of abusiveness. We are sending a copy of this to Stu and Stacy for their benefit as well.

We love you both and we'll stay in touch.

Gerry

TO: THE PARENTING CO-OP
FROM: CARTER
SUBJECT: A more excellent way (1 Corinthians 12:31)

You'd think a guy 60 years old would realize he's getting too old to be playing softball with a bunch of guys half his age. Well, here I sit in my recliner waiting to go to the doctor.

Last evening I was hit on my right instep with a fast-moving grounder. I managed to finish the game and get through the night, but this morning Minnie is convinced I need to see the doc. Maybe it's because I can barely walk. I told her to just get me some medicinal marijuana (ha!), but she threatened to smack my other foot with the meat tenderizer she was holding. Oh well, we won the game! Isn't that what counts?

I just finished reading the email Gerry wrote the day before yesterday and thought it was so insightful. I also thought it would make a great launching pad for my next email on parenting tips for our co-op group while waiting to see what the doc thinks about my hoof. Gerry's email was a perfect description of many homes, Christian and non-Christian alike. So many homes have abusive elements and border on some very dangerous parental patterns. The problem is that we as parents get entrenched in certain methods of parenting, and can't seem to break our bad habits. That's why I felt this email might be very timely.

Let's first create a hypothetical family model or case study:

Dad's had a very busy day at work and comes home tired, out of touch with the children's needs and ready to mas-

sage the remote after dinner for the evening. Mother is also tired and has had it up to her neck with the children. She's been fighting with the children since daybreak, trying to get them off to school on time. They disagree about everything: clothes, makeup, straightening their rooms and brushing their teeth. (Of course, Dad has been at work during all of this bantering.) After school Mom and the kids argue about friends, phone calls, snacks before dinner, homework and the like. (Of course, Dad is not home yet because his golf game is running late.)

When Dad finally arrives home from his busy day, his brain is fried. He is emotionally and physically exhausted following a terrible day at work. To make matters worse, Elmer Fudd beat him on the golf course. He's greeted at the door by his wife's meltdown. She's physically, emotionally and mentally shot. She blames him for everything that's happened during the day. Add some demanding and disobedient children into the mix, and you have the recipe for abuse.

Regardless of the age of the children, most homes are marked by these rather typical frustrations. It's quite easy to understand why parents begin to scream, get angry, slap, hit, call names and eventually disconnect.

Abuse happens because the parents attempt to get control of the situation using threats and anger instead of patience and understanding. Since they lack parental energy for building a positive family environment, their family life turns into an abusive disaster. Can you all relate?

It's always been troubling for me to ponder the question, "Why do parents who say they love their children do so many abusive things to hurt their children?" The answer has been even more troubling than the question. Parents are self-centered in the first place. They're in love with themselves. Secondly, they don't really understand the true meaning and characteristics of genuine love.

Actually, the word "love" has been tremendously misused in our generation. You can love anything from an automobile to the latest designer jacket. You can love the weather, a particular shovel, the newest restaurant, a favorite pet or even the most sinful movie. So to say that we love our children and yet continue to be abusive isn't really that hard to understand. Self-love has generally replaced **true love** for others.

At the top of this email, I've given you a quote from the book of 1 Corinthians. It simply says, "I'll show you a more excellent way." When the apostle Paul was writing this, he was writing to a church in the city of Corinth. There were many problems within that little church that prompted him to write. Frankly, people were treating each other in very abusive ways sexually, verbally, and legally. This church was even using spiritual gifts as the basis to minimize one another. It was sad indeed!

Well, Paul wanted to show them "a more excellent way" to have a loving church family instead of all the self-centeredness resulting in fighting, confusion, and abuse. That more excellent way was simply in the practice of true biblical love as defined in Chapter 13 of 1 Corinthians.

What Paul does in Chapter 13 is to take love and show its marvelous characteristics. It's like Paul takes a beam of light (love) and passes it through a prism. In doing so, the prism projects all the beautiful colors (characteristics of love) of the rainbow individually. Let me list for you the 15 characteristics of this marvelous word LOVE!

Love:
    Is patient (long suffering)
    Is kind
    Does not envy
    Doesn't brag
    Is not arrogant
    Does not act unbecomingly
    Does not seek its own
    Isn't provoked
    Does not keep track of wrongs
    Doesn't rejoice in evil
    Rejoices with the truth
    Bears all things
    Believes all things
    Hopes all things
    Endures all things

The counsel that worked for the church in Corinth certainly would work in our families, wouldn't it? As you can readily see, this foundation of *love* for any home would radically change it immediately. It would alter the way we discipline, the way we express our disapproval and frustration, and even the way we handle our disappointments and disagreements. It would also affect the way we train and teach our children.

Carefully look through the list. Ask yourself this question: "How would 'true love' change the way my family handles our relationships?"

Every successful family is built upon these 15 time-tested characteristics. How about your family? To Christians, this chapter of the Bible has become so familiar we've forgotten the necessity of applying it to our everyday relationships—**especially family relationships.** The reason Christians are often referred to as hypocrites is because we fail to apply what the Bible teaches to our personal and family life.

So let's get practical following this email. It would be good for each couple to discuss the following questions for not more than 15 minutes in total, lest the men become overwhelmed with discouragement, despair and thoughts of bodily harm. Talk through these:

- What shall we have for dinner? Steak, roast beef or meat loaf?

- What would you like to watch on television tonight? Football, baseball or *60 Minutes*?

- Which part of your spouse's parenting would fall into the category of abuse?

- List three things your spouse did this past week that would be classified as "biblical love." How come?

- Rate your spouse on a scale of 1 to 10 (1 being the low end of the scale) for each of the 15 characteristics of love. Now rate yourself. Exciting!

- One of the characteristics of love is that it "does not seek its own." That means love isn't self-centered. Give you and your spouse a grade of A (excellent) to F (failure) regarding this matter of being self-centered.

Well, now you have the fourth and final principle which completes the necessary foundation for good parenting. Sorry it's so late in coming. Each of them is extremely important, so memorize each one:

1. **Knowing your child**. Each child is different and requires individual attention.

2. **Building healthy relationships with your spouse and children**. Nothing will work if your relationships are not what they should be.

3. **Sovereignty of God in Parenting: Believing** in Jesus Christ, **trusting** in God's divine sovereignty over your children, and **praying** continually and effectively (1 Peter 3:7) for them.

4. **Love biblically in your home**. Live by the 15 characteristics of love found in 1 Corinthians 13. Make them your goal.

Begin thinking of these four principles as the true essence of parenting. Without them in place, all other aspects of parenting fall short of the mark. You may have a great formula for disciplining your children, but if you neither know nor have a relationship with your child, your formula will not stand the test of time. You may have the best environment to ensure the safety of your children from all outside evil forces, but if trusting God isn't on your list of high priorities, disappointment isn't far around the corner. Love must be the way of life in your parenting because anything less will eventually lead to disaster.

Well, it's time for the foot exam. I'll finish this when I get back. I'm off to the doc.

Back again. Did you miss me? I'll finish this before Minnie shoves more pain meds into me. Doc says I have a broken foot. Doc says I gotta wear this cast. Doc says it'll take six weeks to heal. (I say two.) Minnie says she'll put my other leg in a cast if I don't behave.

Guys, I need something I can put over this cast that will double for fishing boots, baseball cleats and cowboy stompers. Any ideas? I'll watch for your emails. Till then, let's remember our families and each other in prayer. OOPS! Minnie's tapping her foot at me. Must be time to take drugs!

Later, gator.
Carter

P.S. Apparently *Life at the Lazy-U* isn't built on love.

TO: AJ
FROM: STU
SUBJECT: Thanks for the cinnamon roll and coffee

Boy, you sure know how to take a high cholesterol coffee break! Thanks so much!

I think it was good for us to get together—especially after our shameful display of male foolishness or as Carter called it, "anger management."

By the way, you and your boys did pretty well last evening on the basketball court. It was great watching you have so much fun together. When Carter emails us about building relationships with our kids, you were a living example of doing that very thing. AJ, I noticed your response when Troy got the personal foul for intentionally body checking his opponent. He got angry and I just about threw him out of the game, but you managed the situation with him so well. You actually came across pretty cool. Congratulations! Apparently water skis have some residual value. (You know I love you, man!)

At your request, I visited with your case manager at Social Services yesterday. She still feels it's in the best interest of the children to leave things as they are for the time being. However, she would be willing to negotiate a couple of visits for you and the kids without supervision. She's very pleased with the progress you and Jenny are making and thought that in another month or so maybe the kids might be able to return home. I was thankful to hear that. Of course, she wants to compare notes with your anger counselor to verify your attendance and progress. (I intentionally *didn't* mention the anger management class we both took on the fishing excursion for fear she might put our wives in a safe house somewhere in Hawaii. Ha!)

AJ, I hope you'll forgive me for this personal note, but I wanted to pass along some very personal tidbits that are bouncing around in my small brain. Now I know this email thing and counseling with Carter has been a no-no for you. I understand your reluctance because there was a time in my life when I felt exactly the same way. My life was a disaster. I didn't need anyone to remind me about what I already knew. I see things very differently now. I want to be brief so here's a quick list of some of my reflections that I hope will encourage you.

1. My problem wasn't that I didn't need help; I was too proud to receive the help I needed.
2. I thought it was more manly to hide my problems instead of discussing them with someone else.
3. I lacked true friendship. I really desired some good, solid and honest friends but I had just surface friendships.
4. Building character wasn't on my to-do list. Having fun was.
5. I always resisted spiritual solutions to life problems. "Real men don't need religion," I thought.
6. Learning a life of self-discipline was blurred by my self-centeredness.
7. My stubbornness and self-will blocked the value of other opinions. I thought I knew it all.

Then by accident, some new companions came into my life. There was Mitch, my friend who died from an aneurysm. There was his wife Stacy and their children (now my wife and children), their friends Gerry and Sue (your brother and sister-in-law) and then there was Carter and Minnie. After I became a Christian, these relationships, along with others from my church, have transformed my life. Together, these special people have helped me lay hold of spiritual realities and many personal and family values I would never ever have found on my own.

This leads me to the Parenting Co-op. AJ, I want to personally invite you to get involved with all of us and learn together about parenting. Basically, we all share the same goal of having good families. We all can benefit from the experiences and insights of each other. It seems a shame all of us should be deprived of your insights because you're such an unwilling, insecure, stubborn, boneheaded SLACKER! (AJ, you know I'm kidding.) But I'm asking you to join us by writing an email that explains some of your latest accomplishments with your family.

You seem to be gaining ground with your kids, and I would like to know how you're doing it. As much as I sometimes hate to admit it, there *is* more to life than fishing and chasing pigs. Join us, won't you?

AJ, I'm thankful that we got the kinks worked out of our friendship so I don't have to whack you over the head with a water ski anymore. Thanks for forgiving this hothead! You might be better at forgiving than I am, though. I don't know if I'll ever forgive you for giving me that bottle of chocolate raisins with the label that read "Take one each night before bed for SLUG'S DISEASE." It was real funny until I discovered that the chocolate raisins were actually deer droppings. Now it's become all-out war!

Hey, how about some pork roast at our house Saturday at about 4:30 in the afternoon? Have I got a surprise for you!

Love to all,
Stu

TO: CARTER
FROM: JENNY
SUBJECT: Hanging on by the skin of my teeth

Hello Carter! I'm sorry about your foot injury. Wouldn't you like to go back and try that catch again?

Life just doesn't work like that, does it? Whether it's broken feet, broken hearts or broken homes, you can't just go back and change the instant replay. You'd better listen to Minnie and follow your doctor's orders or else! It takes time and patience to heal a broken bone. If you're not careful, you'll be back in the cast. Isn't it true that all of us want whatever is broken to heal faster?

I know that's the way I feel about my broken home. Maybe we should put our marriage and family in a cast for about six weeks so I can heal. I just wish someone would wave their magic wand over us and—walah!—all would be well, but like your foot, we must go through the process of healing and follow doctor's orders. Only this time you're the Doc! Now that's pretty scary! Do you have any malpractice insurance?

I'm hanging on by the skin of my teeth to my marriage and family. I know my emotions are all goofed up and that makes me think crazy, but what's the point of all this? I'm married to a man I don't care to be with right now. My children live with someone else that is better for them than their own mother! Why should I even stick around?

Carter, I see you're online and I could switch over to Instant Messaging. I'll send this to you so you know what's going on.

Jenny

JENNY: Carter, it's Jenny. I just sent you an email. Could you open it up, please?

CARTER: Good evening, young lady and yes, I have your email. So you're hanging on by the skin of your teeth. Well, girl, that doesn't sound like a bit of fun. I only hope you don't have false teeth. Tell me something, Jenny. Does AJ know what's going on with you?

JENNY: I believe so. Actually, we've been talking more than ever about the children and us. As you thought, asking each other questions that begin with How? When? Why? Where? have opened up a whole bunch of hurt and a boatload of uncertainty. Yet at the same time, they've helped us understand each other better. But we really don't know where we go from here.

CARTER: Jenny, you and AJ have been on the wrong path for so long that you can't recognize what a good path even looks like. It's understandable that you still feel lost even while you're on a good path. Improving your understanding of each other is a very important piece to fixing the "fam." However, what you learn about each other can be very discouraging. Let me give you an example.

The past five years my mother, who is well into her years, became very difficult to be around. She became very angry, obstinate, controlling and argumentative—not at all like the Mom who raised me. Well, a bout with severe pneumonia put her in Intensive Care. In the process, her medications were evaluated. Many of them were eliminated, and guess what? During her recovery my mother changed back into her old self. When we talk together about her behavior over the past five years, she becomes very embarrassed and ashamed of her actions and wants to apologize to everyone.

My point is this. For the longest time your family members have been angry, distant, agitated, and controlling. Then a serious situation threw you all into Intensive Care. Since then you're all being evaluated, and are evaluating each other. Now you're beginning to understand what you've been like to live with. That's embarrassing and discouraging, because nobody likes to put their dirty laundry on display. Now, like my mother, it's time for you all to apologize, confess and chart a new course for your family life.

JENNY: But Carter, we've been so hurtful to each other. We've all said and done some awful things. How can I ever............

AJ: Sorry to butt in, Carter, but I wanted to say a couple of things. Do you see what Jenny is saying? "**We've** been so hurtful..." and "**We've** all said and done...". Carter, **I'm** the one that has messed up this family, not Jenny. She's been a great wife and mother. I'm the one that's caused all this stuff with Social Services, not Jenny. The children are in the care of Social Services because I can't control my emotions, not because of her performance as a mother. We need to get this straight before anything good can happen between us. Carter, would you just tell her to put all this behind her so we can move forward?

CARTER: Well AJ, it's just not that easy. To begin with, you don't just tell or order people to put things behind them. You can ask them, counsel them, teach them how or pray for them, but you don't tell them or order them. They need conviction from the Holy Spirit, not just a push, shove, or kick in the pants from you. You're learning this principle if you've been reading my emails. People are individuals, not robots. They need understanding and time, especially when they're recovering from personal hurt and despair. AJ, the best thing you can do for Jenny is relax. Try to understand her as a mother and as a wife. Probably asking more questions would be in order. Think PATIENCE!

AJ: I think Jenny would tell you that I'm trying to do better in that department, as would the children. It's actually feeling pretty good to me, too. I'm more in control of not only what I say but also what I do. The anger management people are pleased, but I don't have to live with them.

JENNY: Carter, now I feel guilty. Everybody sees AJ doing better and is glad for his progress. Everyone, that is, except me. I'm having trouble converting into the "positive" mode. Not that I'm not happy for him, but I'm suffering the consequences of the years when he wasn't doing so well. The kids and I are products of the past. None of us can get on the let's-encourage-Dad bandwagon until the broken emotional bones have time to heal.

CARTER: It's so helpful to understand you both better. Men, especially, are what I call "quick-fixers." They want to say goodbye to months and years of problems in just a day or two. They want relationships fixed in seconds and minutes, when it's taken months and years to destroy them. The best advice I can give to you both is to be patient. Don't throw out the baby with the bath water. Some good things are happening; just give each other space and time. You'll begin to feel the difference in your relationships down the road.

MINNIE: I wanted to add just a bit to what Carter is writing. Reconciliation happens in various stages, and one of those stages is "removal." Old hurts, deep resentments and rejection must be dealt with, forgiven and removed. You can't just blow a building apart one day and start rebuilding the next. You first must deal with the debris. Don't get in such a hurry to rebuild that you fail to remove all the debris and set in place a new foundation.

AJ: If it's true that the children will be coming home in the fall, it seems to me Jenny and I had better get busy dealing with debris. Minnie, thanks for that great illustration. It helps me understand what needs to be done.

JENNY: In the meantime, keep the emails coming. When I visit the children it seems like they want to come home, but why? Guess I need to ask more questions to help them with their debris, right? For now, I'll say goodbye as well.

CARTER: Good night, our good friends. Let me close with this reminder. Don't get the cart before the horse. Fixing the family is preceded by fixing your faith. For some, that means accepting Christ as Savior and Lord. For others it means renewing their relationship with Christ. For all it means obedience to the Word of God. There is a spiritual battle raging here—not just family conflict—so don't confuse your priorities. Rather, put on "the whole armor of God."

TO: THE PARENTING CO-OP
FROM: CARTER
SUBJECT: Consistency pays huge dividends
in parenting!

There sure are some advantages to having a broken foot. Minnie waits on me hand and foot for at least the first hour in the morning. Since I can't lift a foot (so to speak), I sit in the recliner most of the time or on the tractor seat as the case might be.

I spent the majority of the day cutting weeds from the tractor seat. Minnie's still trying to get control of me. However, tonight one of my sons and his family dropped in to check on Old Grandpa, take a ride on a couple of horses, enjoy a Popsicle and torment the barn kitties. As the sun disappeared behind the mountain, we started discussing the subject of parenting.

What jump-started our conversation was a terrible auto accident over the weekend that killed some teenagers and an older gentleman about 72. The driver was 16, had his license for a very brief time and was traveling well over the speed limit on slippery roads and in foggy conditions. He lost control of the car and smashed into the oncoming vehicle driven by the older man. The young driver was the only survivor.

We discussed what a parent might do to prevent such an awful thing from happening. Join us in this discussion by discussing it yourselves. Take about a half-hour and make a list of three strategic parenting tips that you might use with your children when they get close to driving age. Do it now, before you read any further.

All right. Have your list handy? Compare it to these suggestions my son and family came up with:

1. Go to hospital Emergency Rooms and see the auto accident people come in on stretchers.
2. Limit the passengers in their car until they have at least six months of driving experience alone. (Many states already have these restrictions.)
3. No cell phones in the car.
4. Make them work to buy a vehicle they can afford, instead of giving them a 300 horsepower car and kicking them out the door for a night of fun.
5. Teach them the importance of defensive driving (use newspaper articles, magazines, the Internet, etc.).
6. Have a family Safe Driver Award each 500 miles, 1,000 miles, and 5,000 miles.

Now those were six real quick ones. There are more, I'm sure. While we were wrapping things up, someone made this observation: "When a child reaches 16 years of age, you can't tell them anything anyway." To which I replied, "That may be true, but you can **train** them at any age if you're consistent." Would you agree?

Let's give a little more time to this subject. As we all know, the secret to good parenting/training is consistency. What you set out to accomplish, you must stick with. Where parents fail is not sticking with a particular training, teaching or disciplining program.

(*Life at the Lazy-U* must lack consistency as well!)

Let's say that your child has a difficult time remembering to put away his Tonka truck. If you speak to him about this today but fail to follow through tomorrow, your child will never sense the importance of putting away Mr. Tonka Truck. Why? Because it's not important enough for you to consistently follow through on. The same would be true in preparing a responsible driver for the highway. Whatever your teaching strategy consists of for your child, consistency will either make it or break it!

Let's add a little footnote to this discussion. As I've already written, consistency needs to be applied to teaching, disciplining or training a child to do what's important. But part of consistency is our modeling correct behavior. In other words, as responsible drivers we shouldn't be exceeding the speed limit, driving recklessly or using our cell phones. Right? Wouldn't it be inconsistent if we left the wheelbarrow out in the back yard alongside the Tonka truck? As they say, "What's good for the goose is good for the gander." We should be consistent with what we teach, train and model. In a nutshell,

1. Teach your child consistently what you want him to learn until he learns it.
2. Train your child consistently what you want him to do until he does it.
3. Train day in and day out until it becomes a habit.
4. Do and live what you're teaching and training. Be consistent yourself! Kids need to know what's good for them is also good for you.
5. Stay at it! Don't stop! Make necessary adjustments! But keep at it! Keep your goal in mind and push forward!

When erecting a building on the four parenting principles we discussed in a previous email, the next important piece of the program is consistency. You perfect your parenting by being consistent. Check it out:

✓ Consistency pays off: If I eat junk food consistently, I gain weight.
✓ Consistency pays off: If I exercise consistently, I'll be in better shape.
✓ Consistency pays off: If my heart beats consistently, that's good.

✓ Consistency pays off: If I read my Bible consistently,
  I grow spiritually.
✓ Consistency pays off: If I obey the law consistently,
  I stay out of jail.
✓ Consistency pays off: **If I parent consistently,
  my children will grow up as responsible
  children.**

Speaking of consistency, I feed my little kittens every night around 8 PM, so I'm out of here. Love to all, and you'll be hearing from me shortly. I guarantee it!

Carter

P.S. Can't you sometimes be inconsistent? That's a good question. One of my daughters consistently gives her children healthy cereal every morning except on vacations. Before vacation, each child picks out whatever "candy cereal" they would like to take along. Is that inconsistent? Actually, I remember something similar when I was raising children. I told the kids that, during vacation, we all needed a break from discipline and training. Not bad, but inconsistent. I call it "planned inconsistency"! What do you think about that?

TO: THE PARENTING CO-OP
FROM: AJ
SUBJECT: The last bull to be rounded up

As you can tell from the subject line, I've been reading the previous emails secretively. Carter wrote about getting all his cattle pointed in the same direction, but occasionally there were some stubborn ones that needed a little encouragement. I guess I've been the stubborn one. Well, you've all been very patient (except Stu, who tried to knock some sense into me with a water ski).

I know Stu's given you his version of what happened but you can't believe everything you read in an email. Did he tell you how hard he cried? No! Did he tell you how much he begged for me not to hit him again? No! Did he tell you what a sissy I was? Hardly! Well then you don't have the whole story. What's strange to me is that we're still friends.

Stu did encourage me to jump on board with the Parenting Co-op, so here I am. He also told me it would be helpful and maybe interesting to all of you if I would send out an email describing what's been happening in my fuzzy brain regarding my family. This is really hard for me. I'm not very good at getting in touch with my thoughts or feelings, but I'll try.

I actually have a very thoughtful and sensitive side to me. It probably seems to you that I'm bullheaded, mean, controlling, insecure, abusive, short-tempered, and hate religion. Well you're almost right. You forgot stubborn, pushy, arrogant, self-centered, self-righteous, self-willed, self-absorbed and that I live in a state of self-denial. Actually, when people take the time to get to know me, they often wish they *wouldn't* have taken so much time to get to know me. I'm really not that likable. I can fish and hunt pretty well, but if someone catches more fish than me I get cranky and turn into a monster.

You all know about that side of me already. Let's get to my thoughtful and sensitive side. Carter was quick to pick up on this side of me shortly after we first met. He was asking a lot of questions about where I grew up, what my dad and mom were like, and my favorite pets. I started talking to him about my dog Smokey. So many great memories shot through my mind and out of my mouth before I could grab onto my tongue. I loved that dog when I was a kid, and it broke my heart when I buried her in Mom's rose garden. We were buddies! It brings tears to my eyes thinking about it again.

Anyway, Carter asked me a very pointed question for which I had no answer. In fact, when I look back, the question hit me square on my thoughtful-sensitive side. That darn Old Carter got within six inches of my face, lowered his voice and very calmly asked, "What has happened to that little boy anyway?"

That Old Carter is sly like a fox isn't he? Initially I just blew off his question by answering, "I guess he went fishing!" But since that very moment, I started trying to get hold of that little guy again. When I found him, something very sad happened. I watched him gradually disappear, like sand out of an hourglass, and slowly turn into a less desirable young man. I don't like that young man near as much as I did the little guy. The little guy was thoughtful and sensitive, caring and innocent, helpful and dependable, humorous and exciting. The young man was just the opposite.

Stopping long enough to wander around in my history has been very revealing to me. I could almost point you to events and days when the little guy started his gradual descent into Mr. Undesirable.

Yes, the divorce of my parents was one of those events. My father's harshness made up many of those days. But that wasn't all of it. I made decisions to take matters into my own hands, to exclude God from my life and resist any and all authority. So over time, the little guy turned into an adult who didn't have time for a little dog. In fact, he was so wrapped up in himself that he wanted nothing to do with dogs, kids, wives or even God.

That was when I started to realize the depth of what I had done to my family. If I had treated my dog Smokey the way I've treated Jenny and the kids, she would have run away and wanted nothing to do with me. So it's not too hard to understand my present situation. During all this reflection, along came another email from Crazy Carter entitled "When does the black dog quit biting?" All I can tell you is that I'm trying to "put some milk down by the creek" for Jenny and the kids.

I've been uncertain, even hostile, about spiritual things. But as I read through all the various emails, I can certainly see that something or Someone is certainly at work here. I'm convinced that what's happening isn't coincidental. Before I push "send" and this email lands in your inbox, I want to say thanks! My family is going to need a lot of help from here on out. It's pretty obvious that I don't have a clue about being a good husband or father, but I'm intent upon learning. I feel I'm now in the proper frame of mind to listen to your counsel and suggestions. Keep up the emails!

AJ

TO: AJ and JENNY
FROM: GERRY and SUE, STU and STACY,
CARTER and MINNIE
SUBJECT: What goes around comes around

AJ and Jenny,

This email has been produced by the Parenting Co-op couples, each one sending a little word of encouragement to your family from theirs. We understand that your children will be coming home in the not-too-distant future. We're all very excited! Let the count-down begin! **CONGRATULATIONS!**

FROM GERRY AND SUE:

- **Gerry:** Glad you finally gave up your stubbornness and joined the email gang. It's exciting to hear that the kids will be returning shortly. You both have much to be thankful for. Think of it this way: you get a second chance to enrich your marriage *and* build a good relationship with your children.
- **Sue:** Jenny and AJ, we love you both so much. I'm excited for what is happening in your lives. The children will sure be anxious to get back home, and I know everything is going to work out for the best. Jenny, stay with your Bible Study group over at Stacy's home and allow yourself time to heal. AJ, your email to the Parenting Co-op was thrilling to read. I can tell that the future will be a lot different than the past for your family. See you all soon.

FROM STU AND STACY:

- **Stu:** Well, you finally did it, you slacker. You just couldn't stand to not be the center of attention. AJ, glad you're on board because we can learn a whole heck of a lot from a dog lover. Jenny, I think the old boy has finally come up with some meaningful insights to the many years of hurt. My prayer for you is that you'll be receptive of the "milk" God's offering. AJ, don't worry about finding God, because He specializes in knowing where His kids are. He'll find you when it's His time to find you!

- **Stacy:** AJ, I'm still mad about the deer dung chocolate raisins, but if you'll help us become better parents by sharing with us by email then maybe, just maybe, I'll forgive you. I want to remind you both how God radically changed my life. The danger is not giving credit to God for what has happened and is happening. You see, God uses the past to prepare us for what He wants to do in the future. What you see as evil today is really good, because God promises to use it to build His life into yours. Through the teachings of Jesus Christ we are told that we "can have life and have it more abundantly." I'm so anxious to see the kids home and excited for you all to be together. God Bless!

FROM MINNIE AND CARTER:

- **Minnie:** Well, dear friends, these will be challenging days in preparation for your young ones to return home. Preparation will take several forms. Clean house, extra groceries, and more gas in the cars to say nothing about the increased need for determination, perseverance, patience, and joyfulness. Don't forget to sharpen your sense of humor, and maximize your willingness to listen. It wouldn't hurt to pray about all this either. Remember God wants to change more than where the children are living. Did you get that? That's the difference between a HOUSE (four walls and a roof where people live together) and a HOME (four walls and a roof where people LOVE together). Carter and I will sure be praying for the transition.

- **Carter:** Darn that Minnie! She always steals what I was going to say. Ticks me off! I'm exhausted just thinking about the children coming home. I think I'll go get a cold drink, some peanuts, sit in my recliner and massage the remote.

- **Minnie:** Carter, get out of that chair and write something to AJ and Jenny. They need to hear something important and encouraging.

- **Carter:** Do you want to go fishing?

TO: CARTER
FROM: GERRY and SUE
SUBJECT: Children + Chores = Nightmares

You can tell by the subject line that there's trouble brewing up here in windy Wyoming. Clayton (he's nine now) and Jessica (she's six) will be the first children in Wyoming to either end up on STRIKE from all chores or dangling by their belt loops from coat hooks in the basement. We've about had it!! Every time we ask, demand, threaten or plead for them to clean up their rooms, take out the trash, and rearrange their shoes after finding the mate or picking up after Spice (our little Poodle), it's total warfare. Sue goes ballistic and threatens to count to 5...then 10...then 15...and nothing happens. Did you get that? *Nothing happens!*

183

We're not so sure where to go from here, except maybe to a Holiday Inn after dropping the children off at the all-night bowling alley in town, or at our pastor's home (whichever is closest, fastest and safest).

Trust me, this is no slight problem. Sue's getting back spasms from picking up after them. I'm getting tired of tripping all over trucks, dolls and underwear on the way to their beds for our nightly prayer time. By the time we say "Amen," I'm usually angry with the mess that's staring me straight in the face. Toys everywhere and piled to the ceiling. I feel like such a hypocrite.

Sue's even started complaining that I should pick up my own socks and underwear and put them in the clothes hamper. Imagine that! Now doesn't that take the cake? Why does she think I married her anyway? (Carter, lighten up you old guy. I'm just teasing you a bit. I *do* pick up my socks and underwear, but that doesn't change the mess in the children's rooms.)

I just found Clayton's new baseball glove out in the driveway. IN THE RAIN NO LESS!!! How about 50 lashes with a cat-o'-nine-tails? (For your information, Carter, that's a whip. What do you think?) You know I'm just blowing smoke because I'd never ever do such a thing, but kids and chores just don't seem to get along very well. I talk with other parents that have similar problems, so it's not just something we wrestle with. Is there something we're missing? We don't want to discipline all the time, but it seems like that's all we do.

Could you give us a few practical suggestions about getting the CHORES DONE? PLEASE?

Gerry and Sue

TO: THE PARENTING CO-OP
FROM: CARTER
SUBJECT: Where there's a will, there's a way!

First things first: *aren't children wonderful?* By the time they're off on their own, their parents have gray hair, bite their fingernails and their nerves are shot. They're on pain medicine for back spasms, anti-depressants and Alka-Seltzer for stomach problems. Further-more, they can't find half their tools, the carpets are worn out, the furniture looks like it's been salvaged from a third world country and the cars are a disaster with enough food under the seats to feed the average family for two weeks. Aren't children *great?*

In spite of it all, yes, they're truly GREAT! None of us would trade them for anything in the world except... never mind. (I was thinking about a new chain saw.)

Gerry and Sue, you've raised questions that people have been asking for centuries:
- "How can I get these darn kids to do some work around the house?"
- "What should I do to encourage some responsibility in my children?"
- "Should I beat the tar out of them?"
- "Shall I do nothing, let everything go and save the problem for their spouses to deal with?"
- "At what point in time do my children do their chores with-out me riding them?"

Since every situation in every family is different, I'd like to pack-age all this into one general theme: HOW DO I TRAIN MY CHIL-

DREN? And the answer to that question will have to wait until I finish dinner. Minnie's waiting.

I'm back! There's nothing like a tri-tip steak, slightly rare, with a sweet potato chaser. My! My! It makes all the cares of this world step aside for dessert, which was a small slice of cherry pie with a tiny little bit of vanilla ice cream on the side because I'm dieting. Now where were we?

Oh yes, back to this matter of training the youngsters. You might want to go back to the email I wrote about the city-slackers under the title "Training parents vs. digging postholes." That email discussed the importance of training as a general principle. This email will deal more with some of the specifics in training the untrainable.

So it's easier to remember, I'm going to give you some suggestions in the form of several statements. I'll use boxes before each statement so you can check off those that you're messing up. Here we go…

❑ Define the goal in simple terms. For example, "Little Albert needs to put his toys away each evening before bedtime."

❑ Communicate the goal to Little Albert in terms he can understand.

❑ Explain why you feel this is important.

❑ Be sure to have Little Albert tell you what you just said.

❑ Do a walkthrough with him, explaining your expectations.

❑ Put his toys away with him for the first few times.

❑ Have Little Albert pick a couple nights a week that you will do it for him if he's tired and doesn't feel like doing it. That teaches servanthood to Little Albert. Remember, serving children isn't an exclusion of the Galatians 5:13 passage where it says, "Through love, serve one another." Then you can utilize his help the next time you wash the dirtmobile. That will make him feel important, not just a slave. He'll see the advantages of teamwork.

❑ Explain to little Albert the accountability or discipline piece. He can choose life in prison or a malted milk, depending on how effectively the job is done. We'll discuss discipline in a later email. But you must have some way to follow through when the job isn't getting done and Little Albert pitches a fit. Incidentally, Little Albert should participate in the discussion about what the discipline will be should Little Albert forget to pick up his trucks. He'll have some good discipline ideas! This keeps the responsibility directly on Little Albert's shoulders.

❑ Throughout the day, teach Little Albert the value of putting things away. Remind him that come evening, he'll have less to do. Maybe by evening his room will already be picked up. Perhaps suggest to Little Albert that putting a few things away before his nap would reduce the amount of work come evening.

❑ Don't be too hard on Little Albert, because he can see Dad's garage and Mother's bathroom countertop.

❑ Commit to not nagging Little Albert all day about his room. Live with the disaster until it's time for bed, and then see to it that Little Albert stays on task until the room is cleaned. Be willing to find another time to clean up, since Little Albert might be too tired at night for anything except snoozing.

❑ After a week or so, do an evaluation marked with kindness and encouragement. Little Albert should recommit to the task at hand for at least another week. By now, you should begin to see improvement in Little Albert's room.

❑ In a very short time Little Albert will be trained. You'll be careful to tell Little Albert how proud you are of him and compliment his progress. Assure him that from now on he's on his own to keep his room respectable—not perfect, but respectable. You'll just be his coach from now on and remind him occasionally of the need to keep up his part of the bargain.

Here's how Minnie solved the shoes-all-over-the-house syndrome. Before bed, she would collect all the shoes in the house that weren't in their proper place (including mine). She put them in a barrel down by the barn. Talk about solving a housekeeping problem in nano-seconds! I hated walking in the snow to get my boots, and so did the children. No discussion. End of problem.

The main thing to keep in mind is an intentional, concentrated, strategic, determined, flexible, consistent and loving approach to getting the chores done. Don't overload Little Albert with a hundred tasks at once. Rather, work together on building his confidence and self-worth through tackling a single aspect of his training so Little Albert does one chore well.

Make adjustments as the need arises. Adjust your expectations! Be careful! Make sure your expectations don't exceed Little Albert's self-control, attention span, concentration or ability. Make sure he's ready for the assignment. I've counseled some families that drive their kids crazy (almost literally) with making the bed perfectly. No wrinkles, pillow fluffed, spread eight inches from the floor on both sides and stuffed animals all facing the same direction. It's weird, but parents don't realize that a five-year-old could care less about wrinkles save for those on Grandpa's face.

Now understand a couple of things. I realize that households get pretty hectic. Dads and moms get frustrated with constantly having to direct or redirect the children. Nagging is often the discipline of choice. Parents fail to understand the value of methodically training their child to do one thing at a time and doing it well rather than overloading their child's circuits with constant nagging over everything. You might need to let some things go as you concentrate on a few. Got that? OK!

You see, this is the same problem I have when Minnie wants me to do the dishes, take out the trash, pick up my socks, empty out the vacuum, hang some pictures and mop the kitchen floor all at the same time right in the middle of Monday Night Football and without a break for some peanuts and soda.

Parents really need to prioritize what should be trained first and what should wait for another time. Maybe learning to keep their rooms clean should follow teaching them how to sit and read a story. Maybe it's more important for them to learn how to get dressed on their own. Try to be effective in one or two of these areas before starting on another. It's important to not tackle everything at once!

You can use the same technique with older children, too. I don't know if keeping their room clean is a high priority for teenagers (or should be for their parents), but what I do know is you must have a consistent plan for training a teenager to be home on time, to get out of bed without parental nagging, to keep their room respectable, to do their part in keeping the general living area clean, to control their temptation to be disrespectful to their parents and to manage their self-centeredness.

Hey Gerry, you dabble in different sports. How frustrating would it be for you if I took you to Windy Park and started you in a training program to improve your golf game, baseball skills, throwing a Frisbee, fly fishing and kicking a soccer ball all at the same time? Our children must feel the same frustration when their parents bark at them about a whole bunch of chores, none of which they're very good at or interested in.

In all of this, children are still children. Don't expect adult behavior from them, or you'll just end up a frustrated adult yourself. Let me give you a little practical suggestion about getting the chores done. Say, for example, that taking out the trash is a weekly chore for one of your children. Now like children of all shapes and sizes, they don't like taking out the trash. They forget, rebel, ignore and resist the assignment. Consequently, Dad and Mom are nagging, yelling, counting to ten and getting more frustrated by the minute.

What's the solution to this battle of the wills? Try this: take the trash and put it in the child's bed without saying a word. Do you think he'll get the message? What do you think he'll do with the trash? Will he take it out to the dump container or will he put it in his closet or under his bed? Either way it's a win-win for Mom and Dad. See how easy it is to arrive at a clear understanding about the trash? Think CREATIVITY!

Hope all of this is helpful. Remember—be more **intentional** with your training as a parent.

Carter

(I just got a kick out of this *Life at the Lazy-U*. It reminded me that parents need to be on the same page when training.)

TO: CARTER and THE PARENTING CO-OP
FROM: AJ and JENNY
SUBJECT: Teens without a mission

Carter, Jenny and I wanted to write this email together so we could both express our fear and anger independently. As you know, our whole family is in "intensive care." Yes, on some levels we're doing better but on others the saga continues.

We're gradually getting back on better footing in our marriage as well as with the children, but the whole situation is still quite tenuous. We continue to meet with Social Services. I'm completing my anger management commitment. Everyone's counsel has been very beneficial. Playing basketball with the boys has improved our relationship. And get this: Troy has been going to a youth program at Stu and Stacy's church. He really seems to be getting plugged into his new friendships. Speaking of church, Stu and Stacy have got us involved in a small group from their church that goes bowling each Thursday evening. We have really enjoyed doing something together that we both like to do.

On another front, Tyler (age 12) and Carrie (almost 17/going on 20) are not doing well at all. In fact, they're sometimes downright nasty to both of us. So when they get home, Tyler will sit on the couch and do nothing. Carrie will be off with her friends or that "nut case" of a guy she calls her boyfriend. We want you to understand something, Carter. We won't be able to put a stop to anything, or both of them will have a tizzy and it'll turn into a power struggle just like before. We'll not be able to get those two kids to do anything around the house. Such activity will produce nothing but a huge explosion and some serious brain damage for Mom and Dad.

We read your last email with great interest and wished we would have practiced those principles a long time ago. Now our children are older and more rebellious than ever. Getting a three-, six- or nine-year-old to do some chores is a lot different than getting a teenager to do some chores. Physically they're bigger, mentally they're sharper, verbally mouthier and emotionally their wheels are coming off. It's really too late, isn't it? How can a change in their dispositions happen now when they don't even respect us?

Carter, I'm (AJ) doing better with my tendency to be a controlling type person but I know exactly what will happen when one of the children says "No, I won't!" or "Stick it!" Talk like that will bring out the worst in me, I guarantee it. Nuts with anger management; it'll go right out the window. I've already seen it in our family conferences with Social Services. Keeping a lid on my anger will be one heck of an assignment.

You've told me about needing to be the leader of my family. Well, I think I lack leadership ability. What should I be doing in preparation for tackling these teenagers that drive us crazy and push us to our emotional limits?

Carter, it's Jenny. I find it very defeating to have the children show me so little respect. They talk terribly to me. It's like I'm a non-person. They scream whenever they want. In Tyler's case, he won't talk unless he wants to. He just ignores me when I speak. I can't stand the rejection and hurt. That's a lot of the reason why I feel leaving is the best option.

Now the writing is on the wall. When the children come home and they start acting like monsters, *then* AJ and I will start disagreeing about how to handle them and *then* we'll start taking out our frustrations on each other and the kids. *Then* we'll be right back in the same mess as before. Where do we go from here?

In our case, this isn't about getting a few chores done. It's about survival. I know as sure as I'm sitting at this keyboard that if I ask Carrie to pick up her room, everything will break loose. She won't do it. I'll threaten to stake her foot to the ground for a month, she'll smart off and run to her room and slam the door.

Then what do I do? Just let her rule the roost with her nasty attitude? I'll need something pretty strong to quiet my nerves or a big piece of lumber to quiet hers.

For all of you in the Parenting Co-op, you'd better follow the suggestions from Carter's last email about systematically, lovingly and consistently working with your children or you can expect these types of problems in your own home when your kids get into their teens. Don't get too busy and fail to follow through. Don't ignore attitudes and dispositions until it's too late. Don't forget to build good relationships with the children. Don't be slackers like us. Isn't that what Carter would say?

Carter, I think the ball's in your court. Can't wait to hear from you.

AJ and Jenny

TO: AJ and JENNY and PARENTING CO-OP
FROM: CARTER
SUBJECT: My home or OUR home?

After reading your email, I couldn't help but reflect on an event in the life of one of my children. As it happened, one of my sons who had reached the ripe old age of eight became disillusioned about living in our home.

He cited many reasons why **he** was unhappy as an explanation for **his** unacceptable behavior. Most things weren't going **his** way. **He** was making life miserable for everyone in the household. In other words, **he** wanted to live in **our** home as if it was really just **his** home. Keeping up **his** part of the bargain was out of the question for **him**. **He** thought **he** could talk to his mother any way **he** wanted, eat whenever **he** wanted, play as long as **he** wanted, and ignore all of **his** responsibilities whenever **he** wanted and be sour grapes to other family members.

Do you see a bad pattern developing? So did I. You see, **his** life was nose-diving right into Self-Centeredness. Well, God and I had a discussion one morning about this matter with his Mother (Minnie), and we decided that our son should check out the neighborhood for alternate living situations since **he** was unwilling to be part of **OUR** home.

At the ranch, houses aren't stacked on top of one another like they are in the concrete jungle. That presented quite the dilemma for our little lad. Around noon that day, I put his sleeping bag and some clothes in a sack out on the front porch and watched this little adventurer begin his long journey. It would need to be a place that was more willing to tolerate his self-centeredness than we were.

When the little guy walked out the front door, we had an understanding that he couldn't just walk back in as if nothing had happened. He would have to knock on the door and ask if he could live with us. He would then have to answer some questions starting with, "Are you going to be part of **OUR** home which includes a loving attitude, working together on responsibilities, and showing respect for others?" I assured him that he was more than welcome to live with us provided he agreed to do **his** part in **our** home.

One thing his mother and I knew for sure was that darkness would be our ally. It was approaching evening when there was a slight knock on the front door. I could hardly hold back my tears as I looked into the eyes of this little Prodigal Son who just showed up on my porch. He asked if he could come in. I asked him the questions we had agreed upon before he left. He agreed to change his attitude and be part of our team.

Well, there's nothing like a party at the old ranch. Minnie broke out the mixer and fixed malted milks for everyone. We sat around the table, thankful for each other and glad to have our son back in **our home** with all his limbs still attached.

When I laid my head on the pillow that night, I thought of Luke 15:24 which expressed my heart. It says, "For this my son was dead, and is alive again; he was lost, and is found. And they began to be merry." (KJV) Now this method may not work in your neighborhood, and it may not work for your child. But *something* needs to happen when foolishness gets bound up in the heart of your child (Proverbs 22:15).

AJ and Jenny, the integrity of your family must be protected. Self-centeredness can tear a family to shreds. When a child's self-centeredness comes home to roost through disrespect and disobedience, you have to ask that child the tough question: *Do you want to be a part of this family?*

Now I don't want to be too harsh, but not naïve either. You must have a plan.

Let me give you a checklist of some pretty important principles you should be discussing with the children **prior to their return**:

1. Make sure your family has INTEGRITY. This means that your family is a protected place, not an abusive place. Your family unit has character, morals, principals and disciplines. It's a place of respect, reverence, compromise, cooperation and communication for each of the family members. It stands for something. Value your family and tell the children that there's been a change in definition. Don't let harm come from either outside **or inside**. That doesn't mean living in a "Christian bubble" where children are incarcerated for fear of the world. It simply means that from now on, your home is a place that has the respect of everyone in it.

2. See your family life as TEAMWORK. Families that do well together operate as a team, instead of individuals who merely live together under the same roof. Remember you're not flat mates, but family. Generally, a family that's having trouble is suffering from an overdose of self-centered behavior. Isn't that why your family is in such a mess? Remember, it's **OUR** family. AJ and Jenny, this will be an important distinction for your children to understand before they walk back through the front door.

3. Discuss the spiritual aspect of your family. Troy is already learning about spiritual things at his new youth group. You should be in a position of encouraging him in that regard.

Start slowly, but possibly once or twice a week you could read a chapter out of a book that has spiritual content. Stu and Stacy could direct you to a good Christian bookstore or you could ask some of your bowling friends what works for their family reading. AJ, I think this would be a good assignment for you to undertake.

Perhaps, around the supper table, you could discuss the top two headlines in the daily newspaper. That both develops our reasoning abilities and also trains everyone to live in the tension of disagreement without blowing a fuse. This will tell your children that from now on, there are new purposes and goals for your family. They need to accept the new definition before moving back home.

4. A family life shouldn't be an intermission from what's really important. That's backwards. Family is what's important. Thus a home should be a place where everyone gets comfort and guidance, but not the place where everyone lets out his or her nasty behavior after a difficult day. Rather, a home is a place where we grow and mature in love, patience, kindness, and self-control. It's really a training facility of sorts. Everyone doesn't just come home, fall on the floor and expect the mother to do everything for them. It's everyone pulling together for the common good.

5. In order to protect the INTEGRITY of the family, you need exit points. There are various forms of exiting, from missing dessert to missing a family party or a baseball game. What if someone thinks the whole household revolves around him? What if one of the team members doesn't want to share the load? What if one of the team doesn't respond to correction? What then? Well, then there should be some exit strategy.

This is true especially with teenagers. Younger children generally aren't quite so rebellious or cantankerous and will respond to thoughtful discipline. Teenagers are a different story. They can make your life downright miserable. I know of parents that have taken their rebellious teens to the police department for conversation with an officer when they get uncontrollable. Others go to juvenile delinquency counselors or foster home workers to discuss alternative living arrangements. Some take them to the church pastor or youth leaders. It's amazing what a teenager decides when Dad and Mom put their foot down and ask a very important question: "Where do you want to live?" followed with the comment, "You can't live in our home without being a team member and without respecting the integrity of our family." Period!

So in order to protect the integrity of the family and other team members from abuse, the wayward person might decide or be asked to leave the family for a period of time. Knowing that anyone can leave the family at any time creates a responsible environment for everyone. (This goes for you too, Dad and Mom. You get abusive, out you go!!!)

6. Forgiveness is a family value. Everyone gets a "new beginning," no matter what. A new beginning might look different because of additional boundaries, but forgiveness is forgiveness nonetheless. That goes for a dad and mom who haven't done so well as parents, too. Children need to learn forgiveness as well.

7. Sometimes families need to reconstruct the way they do family. This happens through careful communication, patience and lots of family meetings. It's difficult for everyone to make changes, but persistence pays huge dividends.

Stay with the changes you feel are necessary. Keep talking them through with the children. Remember it's TEAM-WORK, not just a parent dogmatically setting his or her own agenda.

8. **Finally, it's decision time.** Everyone needs to make a decision about the family. Do they want to be a part of the family? Will they see themselves as part of the team? Will they strive to make **OUR** home a positive experience for everyone? AJ, Jenny, Troy, Carrie and Tyler need to seriously make that decision.

Now let me give you just a couple practical suggestions leading up to the children's return. You can do these while the children are still out of the home. For that matter, the families in the Parenting Co-op can also apply these suggestions:

1. Do something different at home. Move the furniture around, re-carpet the entryway, or buy a different picture for the wall. Give them visual reinforcement that your home is not the same place anymore.
2. Get new drinking glasses to symbolize the importance of eating supper together. Each night for a month, toast your new team. Give your family the place of honor.
4. Make a list of things you feel you could do better as a parent. **Be vulnerable**.
5. Have the children make a similar list. Share the lists with each other. **Be reflective.**
6. Have each child list a couple of items Dad and Mom could work on to improve their parenting. **Be open to criticism.**
7. Schedule a day and time for consistent Family Teamwork Meetings. **Be determined.**

8. Find some fun activities you can attend together. Movies, plays, outdoor concerts, sporting events, maybe even camping. **Be adventurous**.

9. Now you add one. **Be creative.**

AJ and Jenny, my list is by no means exhaustive. Nor does it fit into every family situation. Each family is truly unique, after all. I hope my suggestions will simply prime the pump and you'll come up with tons of better suggestions. Keep me informed as to how it's going.

Remember to stay in the saddle, even though things get bumpy!

Carter

Does this *Life at the Lazy-U* speak of teamwork?

TO: CARTER and THE PARENTING CO-OP
FROM: STU
SUBJECT: Once upon a time, there was a little girl...

Our friends AJ and Jenny asked me to write an email to you (and copy everyone else) about a new development down here in the wastelands of Texas.

As if enough wasn't enough, I got a call from AJ the day before yesterday that sent me recoiling smack dab into my recliner. I said to Stacy, "If some people don't have bad luck, they don't have any luck at all!" Here AJ and Jenny are making strides toward putting their family back together, and all of a sudden CRASH!—another obstacle hits them right in the middle of their road to renewal.

Remember in the early stages of the Parenting Co-op when some heated comments were made about Carrie and some guy-friend at a party? Jenny refers to him as the local "nut case." Apparently the nut case and Carrie got too friendly, and Carrie is pregnant.

It appears that AJ and Jenny knew nothing at all about this until just this past week when they all had a meeting with their family social worker. Carrie's announcement hit the table like a nuclear warhead. It seems that others knew about it long before AJ and Jenny.

AJ responded by chewing out everyone in the meeting. "What in the hell is going on here?" he demanded. "Why hasn't anyone told us before now? What do you mean my daughter is pregnant? Why is it that her parents are the last to find out anyway?"

"Now settle down, AJ," the counselor suggested.

"Settle down! Are you crazy? My daughter is pregnant, living in another home and I'm the last person in the world to be told about her condition and you want me to settle down?" AJ retorted. "I want to get my hands on the young man that got her pregnant! After that, I'll settle down."

You can imagine how the meeting concluded. Dead silence! Everyone was mad at everyone else. I guess there'll be another meeting Thursday afternoon.

I knew nothing about this. Did any of you? Anyway, AJ and Jenny are in a state of disbelief, trying as they might to make a decision about where to go from here. According to Jenny (if her dates are right), Carrie will have the baby sometime in the fall around Thanksgiving.

That is, if she doesn't abort the baby. I've been talking to AJ and Jenny about the baby's right to life and frankly, they seem to agree. Carrie, on the other hand, doesn't want to be bothered with a baby at her age. I don't know what she'll actually do. The father of the child has vanished out of the picture, so he won't be a part of the decision-making. I guess that's good in some respects.

As it stands right this second, AJ, Jenny and Carrie are trying to get back on their emotional feet so they can think more clearly. Adoption has been presented as a very possible option. So has keeping the baby. These seem to be strong options to her having an abortion.

I saw an interesting bumper sticker the other day that said, "Only people who haven't been aborted vote for abortion". I thought it noteworthy that if the parents of everyone who supports abortion had aborted *their* children, we wouldn't have the problems we have today with the murder of millions of babies. Right? I've often wondered how many who support abortions have killed their own babies. Or do they think abortion is just for other people? Do people who support abortion tell their daughters to kill their grandbabies?

Back to Carrie and her baby. Carter, AJ wanted me to ask you what your thoughts are at this point. I really think there are a couple items on the table. Of course, the baby is the main item, but what about the living conditions for this new little family? Then of course, there are the questions about finances, and insurance, and…well, we all know that picture, being parents ourselves.

Carter, it's these kinds of bumps in the road that give Stacy and me so much concern for our children. I don't know how many times we've reread your email on the sovereignty of God. Trusting God in parenting is a wonderful assurance for Stacy and me. I can tell you one thing; it sure has improved our prayer life!

AJ and Jenny are facing huge issues. It'd be one thing if their family was healthy, but with their problems? Please get back to them as soon as you can.

Stu

TO: AJ, JENNY and CARRIE
FROM: CARTER
SUBJECT: Walking through a minefield

I hope it doesn't offend you, but congratulations to all of you from Minnie and me. Every time we hear of a new life in the making, we get pretty excited. I know it means some tough decisions for you, but it's a new life anyway. It's your baby and grandbaby.

Carrie, what's going on in your womb is nothing short of a miracle. Start right now thinking about this new baby as a wonderful gift from God. You'll quickly find that abortion is not an option. This little person has the right to live out his/her entire life, not just the first few weeks or months in your womb prior to being killed.

I'd like for all of you to get out the Bible and read from Psalm 139 about the creation of this new life. You'll learn how God has already done so many wonderful things for this new baby. This baby has already received personality, gifts, talents and good looks. It's all been set in motion. The baby's days are already numbered. Doesn't that excite you? I would beg you, please, don't let anyone talk you into killing this little life. On the contrary, do everything you possibly can to ensure his/her future by making decisions that will bring hope and blessing to the child.

Many years ago, I gave a lecture at a local public high school about parenting teenagers. It was a very unusual setting for a cowboy, I might add, but I think they actually liked me! After my lecture, about 100 teenagers started asking questions as fast as I could fire back answers. One right after another! These young people weren't attacking me. They were on a valuable learning curve about serious life issues. I'll never forget the question one teenage girl, about 16 years old, asked me. She said, "Mr. Carter, what would you do if your daughter came home and told you she was pregnant?" I responded, "Before or after I stoned her?" The class went nuts with laughter.

When I finally got control of the classroom again, I answered her original question. I can remember as clearly as if it was yesterday: "I would love her as I have always loved her, and we'd work together on a solution." You could hear a pin drop. I asked the girl what her parents might do in a case like that. She said, "They'd disown me!" Then all sorts of parental punishments were verbalized throughout the classroom.

Now let me ask you a question: *"What should parents do when the 'unthinkable' does happen?"* My answer is, "We just keep loving them, and work together on a God-honoring solution."

AJ and Jenny, Carrie needs to feel your love right now, not your judgment. Yes, something has happened that will impact her and your family for years to come. But that's still no reason to be abusive and unkind to each other. Blame casting, screaming and yelling will only escalate the situation. So everyone take a deep breath and relax so you can think clearly.

Over the next couple of months some important decisions will need to be made concerning Carrie, the baby and living arrangements. Over many years of counseling I've helped lots of couples through similar decisions, but eventually each family needs to make their own. Let me give you a list of some objective considerations, knowing that probably you're more subjective than objective in your thinking right now:

1. Start at the very beginning by being open and honest in communication. State how you feel or what you think clearly

and in a loving way. Don't be demanding or pushy. Try to understand the other person.

2. End the discussion about abortion as an option as soon as possible. Be gentle with Carrie and help her understand why abortion is wrong. Explain that even though the father won't share in the responsibility of the child, she must still do what is right for the baby. Abortion is a very self-centered thing for a parent to do. The baby will thank you for not accepting abortion as the solution.

3. Discuss possible living arrangements for Carrie during the pregnancy. There are facilities that will help her, counsel her and support her until the baby is born. There are also other relatives or friends that might allow Carrie to live with them. Certainly, Carrie can continue to live at home with the family but privacy often becomes an issue for an expectant mother. With Troy and Tyler still at home, it might just be a little crowded for everyone.

4. Choosing to raise the baby is a difficult decision for any family. I've prayed and wept with many families as they've tried to make this decision. Everyone must be patient during this process, because one day you'll feel one way and the next day you'll feel just the opposite. Take your time!

5. Keep in mind what the best long-term solution for the baby might be. A sentimental decision to raise the baby isn't necessarily the best decision. Keeping the baby might put enormous strain on an already stressful situation. With the children just returning home from Social Services, it might be very difficult to handle all the emotional baggage that will arrive with them. Then compound the situation with a pregnant young lady and a little baby later on, and you might have the recipe for disaster.

6. Putting the baby up for adoption is another choice that will take a lot of thought. I've seen many young ladies give up their babies for adoption and years later marry and then raise a family. I've also seen young girls keep their new-borns and do a fairly good job of raising them—but more often than not, the grandparents become the primary parents. AJ and Jenny, you need to take this into account should Carrie decide to keep the baby.

We have several couples in our church that would love to adopt a baby. In fact, a couple of years ago a young lady Minnie knew gave her baby to a very fine Christian couple that I knew from another church. This couple has adopted additional children, and loves all of them like their very own. This has been very positive for everyone involved (especially the baby!).

As you all know from your family life, stability is very important to a child growing up. This child who will be entering the world is entitled to as much stability as possible even if that means adoption. Frankly, Carrie needs additional time to work through the issues that have been troubling her.

Two wrongs don't make a right. In other words, if the pregnancy is the first "wrong," be careful not to make another wrong decision thinking that it will make everything right. It doesn't work that way.

Here are a couple of pointers Minnie and I've found helpful when we've faced hard times with our children. First, I think it's important to be realistic. These tough times affect every parent, so there's little reason to be casting blame or succumbing to self-pity. Remember this too, in time, will pass. Secondly, listen to the counsel of friends and family. You can't follow everyone's advice, but you need to collect as much information as possible.

There's nothing like knowing Christ during the time of trouble. In Hebrews 13: 5 and 8 we're reminded that "He [Jesus Christ] will never desert us nor forsake us," then that "Jesus Christ is the same yesterday and today and forever." Isn't that terrific? God will take this present situation and use it in the future for His marvelous plan in your life.

How good is that? The baby's even excited!

I want you all to know we love you. We'll be praying for you and the decisions necessary in the future. AJ and Jenny, this is the perfect time to check in with God and seek His advice in the matter. Don't be discouraged, because we're in this together.

Love to all,
Carter

TO: GERRY and SUE
FROM: CARTER
SUBJECT: Bear one another's burdens: Galatians 6:2

Parents must model important values for their children. How else will children ever learn what's right or wrong, essential or non-essential, true or false? It is my strong conviction that unless parents demonstrate their core family values by lifestyle, it will be nearly impossible for their children to learn those values for themselves. Let me list some examples:

A. Parents should obey traffic laws
   if they want their child to be a responsible driver.
B. Parents should be reading books
   if they want their child to be a good student.
C. Parents should control their tempers
   if they want their child to be self-controlled.
D. Parents should be growing in their spiritual lives
   if they want their child to have an interest
   in spiritual things.
E. Parents should be respectful of their spouse
   if they want their child to be respectful.
F. Parents should show concern for others
   if they want their child to be caring and merciful.
G. Parents should serve others
   if they want their child to be willing to help.

You get the idea. Those of us who are Christian parents should be doers of the Word and not just hearers of the Word. In other words, all of us are called to put our faith into action. Too often, however, the Christian community is found sitting on their proverbial thumbs, getting fat on what the preacher is *preaching* instead of *doing* what God is commanding us to do.

When our children observe us not carrying out what the Bible teaches, what must they think? Surely they must conclude that living the Christian life is not very important after Sunday services.

It is my observation that the families that do well have modeled their core values at home. Minnie and I have been very concerned about families for many, many years. I didn't just counsel with people at my office. Sometimes they were temporarily residing in our home, and my children were a part of the helping process. I can remember having a heroin addict withdraw from his addiction right in the back bedroom of our home. My children were eyewitnesses to this tragic situation. My son actually touched the track marks in this addict's arms and legs.

My children to this day are friends with alcoholics and others who have lived in our home during their healing process. They know that their Dad and Mom are serious about helping people because they experienced us helping people. Now, they're helping others as well. They've taken our biblical family values into their own homes and families.

Gerry and Sue, I've said all this to ask you about the possibility of helping AJ and Jenny with Carrie. Without any pressure from me, I'd like for you to consider taking Carrie into your home until she has the baby. Sue, I know this would be an inconvenience but I thought it might be helpful to this young mother-to-be. It seems like a better idea than her moving into a pregnancy center of some sort. Your experiences will be very valuable to her and she'll be able to learn from you. It might help her in dealing with her fears and uncertainties.

I don't know whether AJ and Jenny would be in favor of this, but early indications from Carrie before this all happened were that she didn't want to return home anyway. Maybe this is the Lord leading her into a healthier living situation. What do you think? If you're uncomfortable with this, it's perfectly fine. Frankly, you might not even have the room to spare. Just pray about this. OK?

If this doesn't work for you, I wonder if Stu and Stacy might be interested in having Troy come live with them and have Carrie stay at home with AJ, Jenny and Tyler? God is at work, and I can feel it! So put on your spurs—it's going to be an interesting ride!

Let me close this email with one final thought. When it comes down to parents modeling important core family values, the age of your children doesn't make any difference. Every parent in our little co-op should be aware of the need to put family values into action, and not just preach them.

I'll be thinking about you. Give my love to your children.

Carter

TO: CARTER
FROM: JENNY
SUBJECT: Riding on a slippery banana peel

Carter, I'm sure you know what it's like to stand on a patch of ice, ski on a slippery slope or gracefully make your way down the stairs after stepping on a banana peel. Well, that's what it's like around our house. All of us feel like our footing is pretty tenuous.

AJ's barely able to keep his wheels on, and my wheels are falling off. Every time I turn around, something else is falling apart. As if the children's coming home wasn't enough for me to deal with, Carrie ends up pregnant and AJ and I are discussing the possibility of a controlled separation to buy our marriage some time. Stu and Stacy think it might be helpful for me to regain some emotional strength. Frankly, I'm not doing so well. I learned a lot about controlled separation from the *OOPS! I Forgot My Wife* book. I think it might help.

So what's next? Well, I'll tell you!! You know the young man who is the father of my grandchild, who was supposedly out of the picture, out of town and never to be heard from again? Apparently we're not that lucky. He's back in the picture again. I'm told my daughter is with him somewhere between here and South Dakota, where his grandmother lives. Apparently, they got together last week and decided to elope. That's right: *elope*! Can you believe that? Can you feel my blood boiling? An 18-year-old guy and my little daughter, who's going on 17, have apparently eloped!

We've notified the police about her disappearance. We're sitting on pins and needles, waiting to hear of their whereabouts. She's too young to be doing this! Furthermore, we don't know who this guy is. As far as we know he might be kidnapping her. We'll keep you informed but for the time being, please be praying for them and us because AJ and I aren't handling this very well. AJ would like to get his hands around one young man's throat and squeeze—slowly squeeze!

Carter, I have such a nasty attitude about everything. I blame AJ for all of these problems. I know you warned us to not cast blame, but it's too hard not to. He just hasn't been there for us through the years. Now it's all coming back to haunt us. I often wonder what life would've been like had we worked together on our marriage and our parenting, instead of me doing both. Now I'm too tired and resentful to work on either. In some respects, I wish it were me that was on the way to South Dakota instead of Carrie. She's free and I'm stuck. Now *that's* a pathetic thing for a mother to conclude.

I want God to just swoop down and solve these problems but nothing, and I mean nothing, has changed one tiny bit. It's just more of the same. Well, that's not altogether true. It seems to me that AJ is really trying to change. He's become much more patient with me. He seems interested in finding solutions instead of casting blame toward me and anyone else he can think of. Ever since he's been meeting with Stu and the anger management folks, his disposition has changed. You might say that God is working on him, but I'm not there yet.

In the meantime, I'm checking on bus tickets to I-Don't-Care-Where. But now that I think about it, Anywhere is pretty unrealistic when the only option is Nowhere. I'm just stuck!

Jenny

TO: AJ and JENNY
FROM: GERRY and SUE
SUBJECT: Speaking of "slippery"

Whoa! Every time I check my email there's something else going on in Texas. AJ and Jenny, we're both constantly thinking of you. Our prayers are that Carrie will be found, and that both of you will really use these events to build strength into your relationships.

While I was talking with a buddy over at the bank yesterday, I remembered a passage in the Bible that got Sue and me through a lot when the waters of our marriage got pretty murky. Read these verses from Psalm 66:8-12 very carefully:

"Bless our God, O peoples, and sound His praise abroad, Who keeps us in life, and does not allow our feet to **slip**. For You have tried us, O God: You have refined us as silver is refined. You have brought us into the net; You have laid an oppressive burden upon our loins. You have made men ride over our heads; we went through fire and through water; **yet You have brought us out into a place of abundance.**"

AJ and Jenny, these verses should remind us that God does not allow our feet to slip—even on a banana peel. In spite of various trials, He will bring us into a place of blessing and abundance. Psalm 37:23 says, "The steps of a man are established by the Lord." Psalm 147:3-6 says God "heals the broken-hearted...binds up their wounds...counts the number of stars...great is our Lord and abundant in strength...the Lord supports the afflicted and brings down the wicked to the ground." When you trust in the Lord with all your heart and lean not on your own understanding, God will do great things in your life. When you acknowledge Him in all your ways He *will* actually direct your paths.

You know something? God is taking a trip to South Dakota at this very moment and He is right there with Carrie. Whatever happens along the way God will use in your life, and will bring you into a place of abundance.

We understand that this has been very difficult for both of you. I'm sending by snail mail a couple of books on growing through hardship. Hope you'll be encouraged by them!

Love you both,
Gerry and Sue

TO: CARTER
FROM: STU and STACY
SUBJECT: Expect the UNEXPECTED. That's faith!

Carter, I'll first get you up to date on a few items. Then Stacy and I will present our series of questions about discipline, OK?

Let me begin by reiterating what Jenny has already emailed you about. She's struggling, and Stacy and I were at a loss as to what to do. She really seems to be in a fight or flight mode. We feel for her. It actually wouldn't surprise us to wake up one morning and learn that she has split the scene. Maybe she realizes that's not an option and puts up a good front for Social Services. Having the children back home could be the make or break part of the whole equation.

AJ seems to be doing pretty good. We're actually a bit surprised. (Oh, we of little faith!) He still plays basketball each week with the boys. He's also getting together with Stu and a few other men for some good fathering interaction. While there's no real interest in spiritual parenting, he seems interested in becoming a better father. I know the situation with Carrie disturbs him a lot. He feels responsible for her actions.

AJ told me yesterday he felt that their marriage wasn't going to improve very quickly, if at all. He realizes Jenny doesn't want to live with him anymore. Everyone knows she's doing so just to stay on the good side of Social Services and protect the kids.

But here's the shocker in this whole scenario. Troy, their oldest son, has accepted Christ as his personal Savior. He's been attending a mid-week Bible study at our youth leader's home. This is exciting to those of us in the Christian family, but AJ wasn't the least bit impressed. He just said "You did what? Oh, never mind!"

To which Jenny responded, "God hasn't helped us, so maybe He'll help you."

But I can assure you their remarks didn't discourage Troy in the slightest. He finished the announcement with a quote from the Bible that says, "God is our refuge and strength; a very present help in trouble." (Psalm 46:1, KJV) And with that he left the room.

When I talked to Troy about this afterwards, he was very excited because he wants to be a good son (unlike before) and help his parents work through their difficulties while witnessing to them about Christ. Even before all this happened, Troy and I had been discussing his living with us after his graduation to give his parents a break for the summer. Stacy and I wanted to help by creating another alternative living situation after Social Services finishes their part. We thought Troy could live with us during the week, and then go home on the weekend or vise versa. Maybe their family relationships would improve in the short term without so much confusion and tension as before.

Carter, you should have been there when I asked AJ and Jenny what their thoughts were on that subject. All heck broke loose!

"Now you're trying to take my son from me with all your religion!" AJ blurted.

"Troy is the only one who can hold us together," cried Jenny.

"No he isn't!" demanded AJ.

"Whoa! Wait a minute," pleaded Stacy.

"We thought this would help you get back on your feet as a family," I argued.

Jenny emphatically added, "Nobody's moving out! If anyone is moving out, it's going to be me."

Troy responded, "Whose life are we talking about anyway?"

"MINE!" Jenny screamed at the top of her voice.

Of course, you get the gist of the conversation. It went over like a lead balloon. But you'll never guess how it ended up.

That's right, *Jenny* is moving in with Stacy and me for two or three months in hopes of getting some emotional rest, renewed direction and personal counsel. Since Jenny has been doing so poorly, a "controlled time of separation" seemed in her best interest. There were only three conditions. (Carter, you'll like this arrangement.)

1. Jenny must agree to move back into their house around the middle of November, at the very latest. No questions asked! AJ and the two boys will stay in the house until then. Until something develops with Carrie, the three guys are on their own. I bet they'll lose some weight; what do you bet?

2. Secondly, AJ, Jenny and the boys all agree to spend Tuesday evening each week doing something together besides fighting. Nice, very nice!

3. Thirdly, I asked that each person be involved in one small group at our church. It actually surprised me because everyone agreed. Jenny wanted to go to a ladies support group for abused wives, Troy goes to a college-age group, Tyler will go to a small group of middle school guys and gals and AJ will join a small "fishermen's" group that's studying a

book on being a godly man. Is that perfect or what? I couldn't believe it and told myself once again, "Oh, me of little faith!"

So there you have the summary of events. I'm sorry it took so long, but there were lots of details to report. All I can tell you is that it's heating up in Texas, and it isn't the weather.

Stu

P.S. OOPS! I forgot something. Stacy and I wanted to ask you about the subject of disciplining the children. We have a hard time agreeing on the approach and method of discipline. Maybe you could start by hitting just some of the high points and we'll discuss the practical side of it a little later. In the meantime, I'll keep the children locked up in the root cellar!

TO: THE PARENTING CO-OP
FROM: CARTER
SUBJECT: When the going gets tough, the tough—
DISCIPLINE!

I've gotten to the age where things get pretty complicated pretty fast. These days, questions like "Where's my Alka-Seltzer?" or "Have you seen my cordless drill?" or "Where did you hang my jeans?" flat out confound me. Sometimes it all seems so complicated I just don't try anymore.

Not long ago, my tractor got sick. I couldn't for the life of me understand why the poor thing wouldn't run. After all, I turned on the key. It all seemed so complicated until the tractor doctor replaced a small 75-cent fuse in the stupid thing. Then it started like a top. What was so complicated seemed rather simple afterwards. (You can tell I'm not too talented when it comes to fixing things, right?)

The discipline of children seems rather complicated as well until someone shows you the tricks of the trade. Then it seems pretty simple.

Let's look at it another way. A jigsaw puzzle of chocolate chip cookies with about 1,000 pieces is complicated. It takes about three weeks for me to just figure out the border. Frankly, the puzzles my grandchildren build are more to my liking and a lot less complicated. They have 15 pieces about the size of a can of corn and picture a barn and farm animals. That's right down my alley. It's not complicated at all.

Here's the deal. If I can break down the puzzle of discipline into a few puzzle pieces, will you try it? Will you go to work on improving your discipline technique if it's not too complicated? Well, will you?

I want to cover this subject in at least two emails so it doesn't overload your brain cells. This email is about some general principles of discipline. The next email will cover more of the practical aspects of discipline. I'll remember not to get too complicated. To start with, here are some important puzzle pieces on this matter of discipline.

When I was a young parent (about the time the light bulb was invented), I ran across a book entitled *Know Your Child.* This little book really helped me understand this concept of discipline. The author, Dr. Joe Temple, taught me that in the Bible there are three Hebrew words that are translated by our English word "correction." These words suggest a progression toward maturity in discipline.

Two of the words speak of a type of discipline that any parent can do whether they're a Christian or non-Christian. This type of discipline may result in obedience, but that's all. It results in compliance with rules and regulations and nothing more. The third word translated "correction" is associated with God as well as man. In fact, it describes the way God disciplines His children. Of course, the secret to good parenting is to discipline our earthly children like God disciplines his spiritual children. Right?

Having said that, I want you to notice the first word for "correction" in Proverbs 22:15: "Foolishness is bound in the heart of a child; but the rod of correction shall drive it far from him." (KJV) This word correction is a translation of the Hebrew word *mosayraw,* used in reference to corporal punishment. *Corporal punishment* speaks of spanking or beating a child with a rod without the slightest hint of love, understanding, interest or compassion. This word communicates obedience through sheer force because the parent is bigger, older or stronger.

Many parents use this kind of discipline with their children and secure a certain level of obedience using nothing but muscle and brutality and I might add abuse. The problem with this type of discipline is that the child will often remain unchanged on the inside, while still complying with parental demands on the outside. The child's volitional obedience goes untouched. Obedience is secured strictly out of fear. When a child is constantly under the threat of corporal punishment, with no effort from the parents to train positively or to initiate goals and aspirations, it's no wonder that they rebel the moment their parents aren't looking or they're out with their friends.

Now, let's look at the second Hebrew word for "correction" as found in Proverbs 29:17: "Correct thy son, and he shall give thee rest; yea, he shall give delight unto thy soul." (KJV) Here, the Hebrew word *yawsar* is translated into the English word correct. *Yawsar* includes the idea of correction with the *tongue* as well as the rod. You can see it's a little better than the previous word. At least the parent is taking a little time to yell at the child before beating him with the rod. I've seen this type of correction many times, haven't you? A father or mother yells at their child, then pops them one across the rear end. The negative part of this word for correction is "tongue lashing" a child. Often a parent might call the child names or blurt out unloving and abusive words. Another use of the word might be simply nagging the child instead of using loving, strategic and thoughtful explanation.

Let me illustrate. A dad or mom tells their child to pick up a toy, then tells them again, then yells at their other child to wash his face, then reminds the child again to pick up the toy, then answers a phone call, then screams at the child again to pick up the toy, then counts to 5, then goes to the bathroom to cool off, then threatens them with a trip to the wood shed, then, then, then…. This word for correction describes a type of discipline that includes using power and force physically and using a tongue lashing or constant nagging in the process.

What's really interesting here is the word "delight" in the last part of the verse. It has the idea of "not being bothered." So when you mix force with tongue lashing, you'll probably not be bothered as much. But have you disciplined your child very effectively?

The third Hebrew word translated "correction" is the word *yawkahh*. This is the word the Holy Spirit chose to describe the type of discipline the Lord God uses with His children. It isn't related exclusively to God. It also has a direct connection with human parenting, as in Proverbs 3:11-12: "My son, despise not the chastening of the Lord; neither be weary of His correction: For whom the Lord loves He corrects; even as a father the son in whom he delights." The words "correction" and "corrects" are this word *yawkahh*. Why should we not be weary when God corrects us? Because we know that "whom the Lord loves He corrects."

So it should be with parents. It's out of our great love, compassion, concern and understanding for our children that we discipline them—not out of frustration, anger and impatience. Yes, loving discipline might take the form of a spanking or verbal correction, but it is done in a different manner. Unlike the previous verse, the word "delight" in the last part of verse 12 suggests the parent's admiration and satisfaction.

So here's the crux of the whole matter: *discipline is a loving act of the parent on the behalf of their child but there is a* **SPIRIT** *in which the discipline is administered that will either make or break the child.* Did you get that? It's very important! Do you see it, my friends? **Two parents can give the exact same discipline, but in a dif-**

ferent spirit. Both parents may use a form of corporal punishment or a verbal rebuke. One parent's child may dislike their parent, be angry and rebel. Another parent's child will feel love, understanding and compassion from their parent following the same discipline procedure.

Why? Isn't it because the one parent disciplined with a God-given attitude of love, understanding, and compassion toward their child whereas the other parent had a self-righteous, self-absorbed and possibly abusive attitude toward their child? I think so.

In summary, I want you to focus on the correct attitude of proper discipline. What is your attitude when you discipline? Is it considerate and compassionate or is it angry, insensitive, abusive and destructive for the child? Is your intention to train the child or do you simply want the child to quit bothering you? Maybe it's time for you to think about God's loving discipline.

Well, there you have it. I've given you three pieces that form the border of our puzzle on discipline. Next, I'll throw in several other pieces that will finish the job. See, it's not that complicated, is it? If as parents you've been guilty of not parenting in the proper spirit, then down with your pants and out with the old pine paddle.

Love to all,
Carter

P.S. AJ and Jenny, we sure are concerned about Carrie. Please keep us posted. I'm also informed that your living situation is changing in the near future. Jenny, I know the time away will be restful and spiritually refreshing. Stacy has some great tips on marriage restoration, and how to benefit from a controlled separation. So be sure to read the emails that surrounded her marriage problems in the book Gerry put together called, *OOPS! I Forgot My Wife*.

TO: THE PARENTING CO-OP
FROM: AJ
SUBJECT: Hindsight is 20/20

They say that hindsight is 20/20. It sure has proven to be true in my case.

For three days now, I've been trying to recover from Carter's email about those three main puzzle pieces. It reminds me of a time when Jenny and I lived in a little house on the outskirts of El Paso.

Our house was small, but livable. The driveway was congested with broken down cars, but doable. One morning I got into my big old pickup that had a box on the back for hauling stuff. I used my door mirrors to back out of the driveway. I didn't move but a few feet and I heard a crash. I had just put out the trash the night before, so I figured I'd hit the trash barrel. So I did what any non-thinking, lazy man would do: pulled forward and moved over about two feet to miss the barrel. I tried backing out again, and—you guessed it—crash! again.

Finally, I thought it might be better to move the stupid trash barrel myself. I got out of the mudmobile ready to throw aside the object that was impeding my exit. To my chagrin, I wasn't banging into my trash barrel after all. I was beating up the front of Jenny's little Volkswagen Bug. That tiny little car was hiding behind my big truck! The first time I hit it on the right fender. The second time I clobbered the left front fender with my massive trailer hitch. *What's $3,000 damage anyway?* All that said, I'd do it a lot differently today given another chance. Hindsight is always 20/20.

Following this episode, Jenny bought me a nifty little present as a reminder. It's a brass horse with a pair of glasses balanced on its tail covering its rear end. The caption at the bottom reads, "20/20 Hindsight."

And now Carter's email seems to strike me again with enormous regret over my whole family situation. In hindsight, I sure would do things differently. Do you all remember how this whole situation began? Go back in your emails to the very beginning, when I knocked around the kids and Jenny. Everything that Carter has put in his emails about negative discipline, I was busy doing. Corporal punishment was my strong suit. I wouldn't take the time to be understanding, compassionate or loving. I just lashed out at everyone when things didn't go the way I wanted.

I understand now that the only reason the kids obeyed me even part of the time was because they knew there'd be heck to pay if they didn't hop to it, right that second. I can clearly remember being verbally hateful. I thought yelling, cursing and threatening was the pathway to family tranquility. Yeah, right! I called Carrie stupid and referred to her friends as imbeciles. I told Tyler he was a sissy for playing the piano. All the while, I shouted at everyone to stop crying and bellyaching and grow up. What a lousy parenting style! Jenny would try to help me see what I was doing to the children, but just like other insensitive men I couldn't have cared less. "To hell with them!" I would shout. "These kids are going to obey or I'll knock the tar out of 'em!"

Does it really surprise you that my daughter is with her boyfriend, and I don't know where they are? Does it shock you that my young son is scared to death of me? Does this help you understand why Troy tells me, "I never ever want to become a man like you"? It shouldn't even surprise you that my wife needs to live somewhere else. I've murdered her emotionally.

Maybe what you all could learn from my mistakes is that because hindsight brings light, it also exposes the ugliness of dark behavior. Hindsight can instruct and teach about the future but it also reveals devastation, pain and suffering from the past.

You've all given such helpful advice to me. Now I'm going to give you a little advice of my own: *don't take what Carter has written with a grain of salt.* He's right! Many dads and moms discipline in very hurtful ways. They do tremendous damage to their children in the process.

As parents, we must maximize understanding, compassion and love while we minimize force, muscle and verbal attacks. I must confess that I know little about God's type of discipline, but I'm trying to put the puzzle together. I can hardly wait for Carter's next email about discipline. I need more puzzle pieces!

So long for now,
AJ

TO: THE PARENTING CO-OP
FROM: CARTER
SUBJECT: Here are the missing puzzle pieces

Yesterday, I was out looking for a missing cow and calf. For some reason the grass must have looked greener on the other side of the fence. The calf probably jumped through the fence and was off to the neighbor's for lunch. Mama didn't approve, but the calf couldn't have cared less and wandered quite a distance away. Mama wasn't about to let her calf get too far off, so she took matters into her own hands (or hoofs as the case might be). She tore down another section of fence and was off to the races as well. After all, who doesn't like eating out once in a while?

Like other mothers, this cow didn't allow herself and her calf to impose on the neighbors very long. After lunch, she just got her calf by her side and headed toward town. Maybe they wanted to go to the local feed store. All I know is I had a devil of a time finding them.

After getting them back into the pasture, I headed back to the ranch. Strangely enough, I began thinking about discipline and the need for better fences. After much pondering, I concluded that children especially need systematic discipline and strong fences because they too think the grass is greener on the other side of the fence.

All that said, since I just spent about two hours in the saddle, let me explain it this way. A saddle has many different parts, and yet we simply call it a "saddle." A saddle is made up of a rawhide tree, a yoke, a biscuit, two fenders, two stirrups and a seat. Nonetheless, we still call it just a "saddle" because…. I don't know why, we just do!

Discipline is like that in a way. There are several parts to discipline, but we're only familiar with the word "discipline." Today, let's look at the parts that make up the word discipline. These represent the missing puzzle pieces I promised to send your way.

I'm going to stick with the saddle illustration. The goal in every horse riding experience is to GET ON, STAY ON, HOLD ON, LEAN ON and REST ON. Then, you can enjoy your ride. Fair enough? The first step is to throw the saddle onto the horse's back, and then tighten the saddle down using the cinch. Correct? A loose saddle will never work (unless you want to ride upside down).

After you get the saddle securely in place, you use the various saddle parts to help you enjoy your horseback ride. Understanding the purpose of these saddle parts will help you arrive at your destination in one piece. Here's how they work:

- ✓ Stirrups – help you GET ON. Left foot in the left stirrup; then swing right leg over horse's rump. If all goes well, you should be in the saddle facing forward. How'd you do?
- ✓ Fenders – help you STAY ON. They hold the stirrups and your legs against the horse while you squeeze tight with your knees.
- ✓ Biscuit or the "horn" – helps you HOLD ON. This is always the last thing you remember holding onto before you hit the ground.
- ✓ Yoke – gives you something to LEAN ON. A good yoke hits you high in your front inner thigh. You lean against the yoke when you put on the brakes.
- ✓ Seat – gives your buns something to REST ON. Nothing like a good seat when you're headed back to the barn.

Disciplining children has some similarities, and I figure the best way to explain it is by using the same five objectives as I did for riding a horse: GET ON, STAY ON, HOLD ON, LEAN ON and REST ON. After all, like horseback riding, discipline can be a bit scary, at times pretty bumpy, even uncomfortable (especially if you're out of practice) but downright fun when done right. So here we go with some good old-fashioned, time-tested principles for disciplining children:

✓ **TO GET ON:** Initiating a healthy discipline program is always the first step. Proverbs 3:12 encourages fathers to discipline their children. While I feel that the father should shoulder the majority of the discipline, it is a team effort between the father and the mother. Parents must decide to GET ON a systematic and strategic discipline program consistent with the attitude and actions of a loving God. In other words, you must stop ineffective discipline methods and GET ON an effective program.

✓ **TO STAY ON:** Staying on a discipline program is the most difficult thing in parenting. Here's where it gets bumpy. Your child will not respect your word, or respond to your discipline, unless you STAY ON consistently. Being inconsistent in the discipline of your children is one of the major reasons children rebel. You must agree as parents that together you will be consistent in following through with discipline. Parents are told in Ephesians 6:4 to "...not provoke [or exasperate] their children to anger but bring them up in the instruction and discipline of the Lord." One of the most destructive things to a child is the lack of persistent discipline. Your "parenting ride" will have its share of bucking and pitching a fit, but parents must commit to STAY ON, regardless of how difficult it gets.

✓ **TO HOLD ON:** Every discipline program has its ups and downs, and sometimes more downs than ups. Occasionally children get obstinate, kick up their heels, and flat out refuse to follow your lead. You might feel like jumping ship. Nonetheless, parents must HOLD ON by using discussion and reasoning with their children. Be careful about arguing, demanding and bullying. Children should be allowed to discuss, disagree and be a part of the decision about training and discipline. Parents, on the other hand, must be prepared to reason through with the child why a certain discipline is being applied. This interaction is very time consuming and can be threatening, so HOLD ON. Since every child is different, parents must carefully listen to their children's disagreements and explain the reasons for their discipline. Don't let go! Hold on!

✓ **TO LEAN ON:** Many times I've heard a parent say, "My child just won't respond to our discipline." Well, here's what you can LEAN ON when the brakes are on and no discipline seems to be working. God loves your children, so prayer is extremely important in the discipline of children. God is able to touch the heart of a child, whereas parents are unable to do so. Our children need to be influenced by God's Spirit through the prayers of their parents. As parents, we can LEAN ON God and trust that He will hear our prayers and answer according to His divine plan and purposes for our children. Remember, God wants you to lean on Him when the going gets tough.

✓ **TO REST ON:** When the day is done, the sun is setting and the kids are in bed, what do you REST ON? As a parent of grown children, I rest in the fact that *God is working in the lives of my children to accomplish His purpose in their lives.* If my children make poor choices, God knows. If my children behave in an unacceptable fashion, then God can change their hearts. If they say something that brings disgrace, then God can forgive. I REST ON these principles. As parents of young children you, too, should REST ON the fact that God has an interest in your kids. He loves them and has a particular plan in mind for them. Sit back and enjoy the ride! God is in total control of everything!

Have you ever been to a rodeo? Those horses and bulls are trained to buck. They also possess a rather nasty disposition. Consequently, they just want to buck off whoever tries to ride them.

Maybe your training is counter-productive when it comes to your children. Are they always trying to buck you off? Maybe you should consider these five objectives of parenting. If you're disciplining incorrectly, then maybe that explains why your child wants to buck you off all the time. Is that why your child is so ornery? Do you frustrate them, make them angry or spur them all the time instead of properly training them? Most bull riders end up face first in the dirt—and so do a lot of parents.

You know, as I finish up these parts to our puzzle I'm still missing one piece. How could that happen? Anyway, I'll need to throw another email your way in a couple of days. It just dawned on me: *how could you ride a horse without a bridle?* We'll need to PRESS ON with the next email.

Anyway, enough for now. Tighten your cinch!

Carter

TO: AJ and JENNY
FROM: CARTER
SUBJECT: Look what God found!

After returning to the ranch from a day of working fence, I realized that I'd lost my gold watch. Minnie was having a tizzy fit and I couldn't believe that I was so stupid. I have one watch I wear while working at the ranch (a ten-buck waterproof Timex), and another very expensive fancy gold watch (a $53 waterproof, shock-resistant Timex) I wear when trying to impress clients, bus drivers, brand inspectors and bankers.

Being absent minded, I wore my fancy watch while repairing the fence where my cows got out. My lovely watch must have been separated from my wrist when I was fighting with the barbed wire, and it disappeared into the oak brush. I was sick! You know the feeling, don't you? I needed to tell Minnie—and that was scary!

After supper, I tried to mentally retrace my steps in an attempt to pinpoint the exact spot where my watch might be hiding. It was like locating a needle in a 450-acre haystack. However, I did re-member one spot where the oak brush, broken fence and my arm had a wrestling match. It was one of those frustrating situations that cause you to think thoughts and mumble words that aren't in the dictionary, resulting in the loss of your Christian testimony.

Well, I decided to jump on the four-wheeler and head down to our summer pasture to look for the missing piece of jewelry. Along the way I confessed all my sins, hoping that God would show favor to me and lead me to the watch. I drove right to the spot where I had previously lost my testimony and carefully walked into the patch of oak brush. There, sitting on the top of an oak leaf glistening in the sun, was my watch. What an exciting moment! You know the feeling when your eye spots something and your mind registers that it's just what you've been looking for? Your emotions leap for joy, as if you just had a spiritual experience of some kind.

AJ and Jenny, I know I told you this on the phone, but that's exactly what it was like when I saw Carrie walking up the road to our house just before noon. The lost had been found! There's a brief moment when you can't believe your eyes. You're convinced you're either hallucinating or high on Alka-Seltzer. Up the dirt road came this pregnant ragamuffin with nothing but the clothes on her back and a black trash bag. As I began walking toward her, several questions rolled around in my mind like BBs in a boxcar. *Did the car break down? Where is her boyfriend, the father of her baby? How and why did she end up here? Do AJ and Jenny know about this?*

The closer I got to her, the more my questions were already being answered. She was crying. Her countenance spoke of shame, hurt, loneliness and despair. She had a pretty substantial bruise under her right eye that was accentuated by the swelling in her cheek. My heart nearly fell out of my chest. All I could really say was, "Welcome home, my dear." We hugged each other. I could tell she was tired and frightened. Then I put my arm around her and, together, we walked through the barnyard and up to the house.

By the time we got on the porch, Carrie's crying had turned into the sobbing of a person who had just been rescued. Immediately, Minnie picked up on the situation and assured Carrie that she was safe with us. In an instant, the kettle was on and fresh zucchini bread was sitting on the table. Minnie was washing Carrie's face with a warm washcloth, and I just sat there like a bump on a log in total disbelief.

Minnie broke the ice by asking how she ended up at the ranch instead of South Dakota. Carrie just began dumping everything. I don't think I closed my mouth for over 30 minutes. I was stunned with what had been going on.

AJ and Jenny, we spent the better part of the day just pulling together some of the loose ends of Carrie's story. I'll give you some of the details now and we'll talk again over the phone this evening. For obvious reasons, we took Carrie to the doctor. We were concerned about the baby and her overall physical condition. The doctor concluded that the baby is doing just fine, and so is Carrie. However, her cheekbone was pretty bruised where her boyfriend Butch (short for Bonehead) hit her. Before returning home, Minnie and I stopped by the store to get some personal items for Carrie and some more clothes.

Right now, we're back at the ranch and Carrie is sound asleep on the sofa after a very long day. AJ and Jenny, everything is going very well. I just thank God she is safe and away from her crazy boyfriend.

For now, I'll simply recap some of the details because I don't want to forget them. You never know when you might need a detail in the future. So here I go.

After leaving Texas, the two lovebirds just drifted from one spot to another. He had some money, at least enough for gas, food and lodging and a tent they camped in occasionally. Running out of money was the least of their concerns until they actually ran out of money. Apparently, their pocketbook was pretty empty while passing through the Denver area. So they decided to stay in Denver for a while and replenish their money supply. They both did some part-time work, but from what I gather they pretty much lived on the streets. They rented an occasional motel room to shower and rest. However, their relationship was growing more and more strained.

Butch was getting angrier and physically abusive to Carrie because she wanted to return to Texas, find an apartment, have the baby and live happily ever after. He would have no part of that.

On the streets of downtown Denver, Carrie met another young lady, Vanessa, who is involved in a street ministry that works with runaway teens. They talked a lot about Carrie's bad relationship with Butch, and about their failed plans and dreams. Well, this gal planted a seed in Carrie's mind that eventually led to an escape plan for her. At first Vanessa told her she needed to straighten out her life spiritually, and that God had a plan for her. Vanessa then confronted Carrie in no uncertain terms, saying, "Girl, you're God's kid and He don't like it when someone is boxing His kids around. So get out of your abusive relationship with Butch NOW!"

The thought of leaving Butch was terrifying to Carrie. She knew their stay at the motel was coming to an end because their money was in short supply. It would be even harder to escape after they were back on the streets, or running to another town.

A couple days later Butch walked in while Carrie was pulling some of her things together so she could leave. He got so angry he hit the wall with his fist. Then he hit Carrie for good measure. He locked Carrie in a closet until she promised to never leave him. But all of that didn't change her resolve. As sly as a fox, she hid some of her things behind the motel in a trash sack. She knew that when opportunity knocked, she needed to be ready.

It was that same night she got up to go to the bathroom and silently escaped out the bathroom window into the alley. She was desperate, determined and free. Grabbing the plastic bag, she ran down the alley as fast as she could go. She darted in and out of yards to stay hidden and avoided barking dogs that might have alerted Butch to her whereabouts.

Carrie doesn't know exactly what route she took, but after a few miles she ended up spending the night behind a dumpster somewhere on Santa Fe Drive. She was really in a heck of a mess. She had no money, a trash sack of personal articles, the clothes on her back, no friends, no faith and no future. The one thing she knew for sure was that Texas was south of Colorado, and she was going south.

Here's the exciting part of the story. She had managed to get a ride with an air conditioning service man that had a repair job near Castle Rock, Colorado. When he let her out at the Pancake House in Castle Rock, it dawned on her that Minnie and I live in the area. Carrie told us that she remembered the first time we met in Texas, and the fun time we all had laughing about my fishing and pig hunting experience. Butch and Carrie had discussed contacting us when they passed through town. Of course, when they arrived in Denver he refused to let Carrie call us without her promise to ask us for some money. She never did.

Anyway, when Carrie looked us up in the Castle Rock phone book, there we were. She told Minnie that this was the first moment she felt any sign of hope for a long time. "Help is nearby," she thought to herself. A kind lady was glad to let Carrie use her cell phone, but when she called our number both Minnie and I were outside and didn't hear the phone ring.

Carrie's journey continued, only now for different reasons. She wasn't running *away from* someone as much as she was running *toward* someone. One of the locals at the post office gave her specific directions to the ranch. She hit the highway with her thumb in the air. The guy that gave her a ride dropped her off on the highway right in front of our gate. Before she got out he said, "Where's the weasel that popped you in the face?"

"I left him last night and I've been on the run ever since," Carrie said.

"Well girl, your man is a scumbag and you'd do well to never let him back into your life again," he concluded.

Well, AJ and Jenny, there you have it. I'm so thankful that, once again, God has chosen to intervene in the process of healing your family. Carrie will be safe with us. We'll care for her as one of our own children until we can make arrangements for her to return to Texas. Please allow us a little time to evaluate her emotional needs before making any decisions. Feel free to call or send her an email anytime.

Love to all,
Carter

TO: CARRIE
FROM: DAD
SUBJECT: It's time for a new beginning

Mom and I returned home safely after our visit to Colorado. We drove all night. Both of us couldn't wait to see you, and to see for ourselves that you were all right. Actually, the drive wasn't that bad. The anticipation of seeing you made the drive out go pretty fast, and the relief we felt being with you made the return trip go fast as well. Two days didn't seem long enough to be together, but we really needed to get back for the boys. I hope you understand.

Don't Carter and Minnie have a beautiful place to live? It's wide-open spaces but, unlike Texas, it's green. What a difference! But like I told Carter, "We have cactus and you don't."

You see Carrie, Carter's convinced that's the reason you and I have such a difficult relationship: **I'm a "cactus."** You want to get close to me but every time you try, you get pricked. Don't you agree? That guy is sure crazy, but I'm so glad you'll be staying with them for the next couple of months.

As you know, Mom and I aren't doing very well in our marriage. But we're working on it. Mom's staying with Stu and Stacy, and that's been helpful to both of us. We've both needed the space away from each other to gain a clearer perspective about what's really important. Plus, living with the boys in her absence has forced me to discover how self-centered I'd become. She had to do everything and I just went my own selfish way. Basically, she took care of you kids and asked very little in return. She gladly provided a terrific place for all of us to live but I just took advantage of her. I can understand why she got her belly full of it all. As I told you yesterday, no one should be blaming her for taking a break. She deserves a break after all she's been through.

But Carrie, if we are going to rescue our family, each of us must be making changes in the way we think and treat each other. I'm trying desperately to not shrug off my responsibility for allowing all this to happen, but I was only concerned about myself. I believed the lie that making money and paying the bills was the only thing a husband and father needed to do. Loving my wife and providing guidance, healthy discipline and training for my children wasn't that important because I believed those items could be covered by Mom.

Somehow, Carrie, we all need to begin trusting each other. I understand why you don't feel safe with me, especially after the way I've treated you. I guess I'm asking for another chance. When I replay in my mind the events leading up to Butch hitting you in the face, my anger burns a hole in my gut. In fact, I get so angry that I'm scared of what I could do to him.

However, when I'm thinking clearly, I see myself in fits of rage hurting you in the same way—and I'm ashamed of myself. I'm really no better than Butch when it comes to my behavior. As I wipe the tears from my eyes, I want you to know how sorry I am. The tragedy of it all is that this lesson is learned much too late in your case. I've missed the best years of your growing up. Now you're a young lady soon to be a mother. I really want to be a part of your future, but I don't expect you to immediately trust me. I just want an opportunity to earn your trust over time.

What do you think about this idea? Mom is staying with Stu and Stacy until sometime in November. Once she gets home, we would like to plan a family reunion. However, our family has gotten bigger since it fell apart. We want to invite Gerry and Sue, Stu and Stacy, and Carter and Minnie to join us for a big Texas party. What do you think? If you want to wait until after the baby is born, we'll reschedule the event. Just think of it! We'll have a reunion with our new family, and those who loved us enough to help pull us together. Let us know what you think.

Well, my dear daughter, I'll sign off for now but not in my heart. I'll always be by your side loving you and believing in you. Together we'll conquer the world. What do you say?

All my love,
Dad

P.S. Glad you all celebrated your birthday in style—I can't believe our little girl is 17! I only wish we could have been there with you. Hope you enjoy our gift! Try to keep Carter out of trouble. Be sure he gets proper medication, and tell him and Minnie thanks for their hospitality. We'll talk soon, and never forget you can call collect any time.

TO: THE PARENTING CO-OP
FROM: CARTER
SUBJECT: Nose rings, twitches and bridles

You all know I've worked with cattle and horses for many more years than I care to admit. Throughout those years, I've learned some pretty valuable lessons.

One of them is not to ride a horse bareback without a bridle. My brother tried that one time many years ago and lived to regret it. He mounted the back of a big gray gelding that I owned, and decided to ride him off a hill down to the barn. The mounting went very well, but the dismounting was disappointing. As soon as my brother felt hair on his Wrangler jeans, the horse headed for the barn as if he was running the 50-yard dash. All I could hear was "Whoa! Whoa! Whoa!" When I turned around to see what all the whoa-ing was about, my brother was in the midst of making a crash landing. Out from the dust I saw him emerge: rubbing every part of his body, speaking unintelligible words, and at the same time holding a cowboy hat that looked as if it was run over by an 18-wheeler.

Generally we learn lessons from a hospital bed or something like that. But it's always better if you learn lessons while you're still able to walk, run and spit. So I've learned the value of nose rings, twitches and bridles. All these wonderful livestock accessories keep you from getting killed by an animal that's one or two thousand pounds bigger than you. A nose ring on a 2,000-pound bull, for example, is a very helpful item—especially when you want him to get off your foot. A stern jerk on that nose ring will alert him right away of your unhappiness. In contrast, yelling at the top of your lungs generally doesn't do anything except make him step on your other foot.

I've also learned the value of a twitch. Now a twitch is an interesting device that speaks directly to a horse's imagination. Let's say you want to put shoes on your favorite mare, but every time you lift her hind leg she gets an attitude and prefers to be left alone. This is where the twitch comes in handy. It's kinda like putting a clothespin on the nose of one of your children when they won't let you tie their shoes. The clothespin redirects their attention to another part of their anatomy and before they know it, their shoes are on and tied. The same thing holds true with the old mare. The pain in her nose redirects her "brainwaves" to her nose instead of her feet, and she behaves back on her rear end where I'm working.

Make no mistake about it, I'm not advocating the use of nose rings, twitches, bridles or clothespins for children. However, I've seen something pretty similar to that. The other day at the shopping mall I saw a woman who had her child in a harness tethered to the end of a gizmo similar to what you use to walk a dog. When the child got in trouble with his mom, all she needed to do was reel him in and whack him.

I thought to myself, "What is this world coming to?" Children on leashes? You gotta be kidding! How degrading is that for that little boy? Maybe his Big Mama needs a nose ring! Anyway, what I *am* advocating is that there's a time in a youngster's life when they need some external assistance to redirect their attention. Remember Proverbs 29:15? The rod was an external device used by a parent to capture the attention of a child.

If you haven't figured it out yet, this is the final piece in our discipline puzzle. Let's go back to Proverbs 22:6 which says, "Train up a child in the way he should go: and when he is old he will not depart from it." (KJV) The word "train" is translated from the Hebrew word *kawnak* and it means "narrow" or "restrict." This verse calls for parents to restrict or influence the behavior of their children.

Minnie and I placed restrictions on our children, and I'm sure you do on yours. For example, when our children were little we never let them play with explosive devices, dynamite or hand grenades. Do you get my drift? We had reasonable restrictions throughout their years with us. Some things were OK at 15 years old that were unacceptable at age five. My daughters were allowed to do certain things that my sons were restricted from doing—like wearing dresses and makeup. Restrictions can be applied to anything from attitudes to behavior to friends—really, any other reasonable thing that concerns a parent. However, a parent must be very smart when choosing these battle lines for fear of becoming extremely legalistic over every little thing.

Remember, parenting is about relationships. Being overly restrictive or controlling is threatening to your relationships with your children. Be careful and remember that the Bible is a good guide for areas where restriction is necessary. But please, please don't become another legalistic parent (aka Control Freak) with a whole library of rules and regulations. Remember, you're training your child to someday be independent. So cut them some slack!!

The question is often asked, "What do I do when my child refuses to obey?" Children have a way of doing this, don't they? Since we don't use nose rings, twitches or bridles, what works to encourage a child's obedience? There are many books available on the subject of child discipline, and I'd venture a hunch that you've all read some of them. Here's my two cents on the subject.

To me, discipline is an extremely significant event for parent and child. Great care should be given in establishing an effective method in order to avoid revisiting the same disobedience over and over again. Allow me to list some important considerations through a Top Dozen list:

1. Ideally, discipline starts when your child is young. The old saying, "It's hard to teach an old dog new tricks" applies here. With children, it's better to nip disobedience in the bud (or on the rear end as the case may be). However, if you're just starting to apply solid principles of discipline to older children, do stay with it. It will take more time, but you'll still like the outcome.

2. Discipline should fit the child that is being disciplined. You ought not to spank a 16-year-old, nor should you have a curfew for a three-year-old. Some emotional children need a different type discipline than other children. Ephesians 6:4 warns us to not provoke our children to anger. So fit your discipline to each child **individually.** Remember you must **KNOW your child before you discipline**.

3. If you discipline when you're angry, then the child is in danger of being overly disciplined. If you're angry take a break, have a soda, and quiet down. Only then should you patiently discipline your child. Yelling at a child just gives you a headache. Get some control of yourself first. Agreed?

4. Explain to the child why they're being disciplined. Have the child repeat the reason(s) back to you. This way you'll know the child understands. It makes no difference about their age. Every child deserves an explanation of why the sky is falling.

5. After the discipline, explain your expectations about future behavior. Just a hint: if the child goes right back to their disobedience, find out what isn't working. *Don't* just go

through the same discipline drill again. Up the ante! Change the method! Alter the consequence! Got it? Your discipline must be effective, or you're wasting your time and your child's bottom.

6. As with nose rings, twitches and bridles there are *many* options for helping children become responsible, obedient family citizens. Some use time outs, others natural and logical consequences, others spanking, others loss of rewards and the list goes on and on. Whatever methods you use, remember discipline isn't for the purpose of irritating your child but for the purpose of helping the child REMEMBER NEVER TO DO IT AGAIN. Therefore, find something that will get the child's attention so he'll remember and administer it effectively in love. Remember, whacking a child that's tethered to a dog leash through 3 ½ inches of urine-filled diapers isn't going to do anything but irritate a cowboy, namely me.

7. Discipline should also fit the crime. Be reasonable as a parent. A child shouldn't have to mow the grass, rake all the leaves in the neighborhood and sweep the driveway because he won't share his Tonka truck with Jimmy. Be creative. Come up with discipline that surprises your child. My children were shocked when I took them out for a malt for their discipline.

8. Consistency stands out as one of the most important strategies in discipline. Why? It just does, that's why! We send a bad message to our children when we're inconsistent. Inconsistency says, "It's OK to do whatever evil you're doing as long as you do it before I get to ten," or, "You can be a nasty punk as long as you're good when the preacher's here," or "You can be a terror just as long as Dad and Mom aren't frustrated and tired." *What's wrong today is just as wrong*

tomorrow and the next day.

9. Good discipline is always underscored with hope and be-lief in the child. *Never* call your child names. Even though a child does something stupid, it doesn't make him or her stupid. The clever parent will give their child confidence that he can overcome such behavior. After I administered discipline, I wanted my children to know I loved them and believed in them. Positive affirmation and giving clear di-rection after discipline (I'm talking anywhere from five min-utes to five days) are very important.

10. In the Bible, the apostle Paul speaks of putting off bad behavior and putting on good behavior in its place. Remem-ber, training a child toward good behavior is an essential part of disciplining a child for bad behavior. Give the child something good as an alternative to bad behavior. Share with him your clear expectations—and be a good example yourself! Good parenting isn't "Do as I say," but "Do as I do."

11. I believe in the value of discipline reminders. For example, Jimmy sticks a knife in Daddy's ATV tire. Shame on him! After the initial discipline, consisting of chewing enough gum to plug the leak, Dad walks Jimmy out to the ATV later that night to show him all the gum attached to the ATV tire. Since Jimmy's mouth is swollen from chewing 13 packs of bubble gum, it's safe for Daddy to ask Jimmy if he wants to poke another hole in Daddy's tire. Jimmy will mumble "No!" and Daddy agrees. Now the next day Daddy might repeat the drill. He might even do the same thing the following month. My point is this: don't end the training with the initial discipline. Keep training until Jimmy has completely learned his lesson, or you've run out of gum.

12. I believe in repetitive discipline for the same behavior. Let

me explain. Let's say that Little Albert and Sassy Sara conflict with Mother over using crayons on the living room
walls. They refuse to discontinue such outrageous behavior, and the time for discipline has arrived. For the sake of
discussion, let's say the best discipline is to have them wash
their artwork off the walls. It might be a good thing to consider having them wash part of the walls today, part tomorrow morning, part tomorrow evening after school and finish the next day. The conclusion is the same: the children
washed the walls. However, I'll bet you a nickel that the
repetitive discipline method will make a bigger dent in their
crayon box.

Now smarter people than I have better and longer lists. But
since I'm doing an email instead of a book, 12 tips will have to do.
I hope you'll find them helpful. If all else fails, nose rings, twitches
and bridles (including leashes) are still available at the local feed
store. Just kidding!!

In the meantime, it's everyone out to the malt shop for a party
because you're all doing a great job as parents. Just stay with it!

Love you all,
Carter

P.S. Aren't you all thrilled about Carrie? Isn't it wonderful what
God has accomplished in her life? Everyone has certainly
had an important part in the success of our Parenting Co-
op. To God be the glory, great things He has done! Amen?

Life at the Lazy-U is definitely **not** do-as-I-do!

TO: AJ and JENNY
FROM: CARTER
SUBJECT: Vengeance is whose?

Well, this morning we had a very interesting time here at the old El Rancho. I tried to reach you by phone, but got only your answering machine. Thus this email—and you'd better sit down and get a cold drink before reading it.

I was wrapping up some chores down at the barn and up the drive came this old clunker-looking thing that barely qualified as an automobile. I could tell the driver wasn't sure where in the heck he was as he turned into the barnyard. When I walked over to greet him, he asked in a demanding voice, "Is Carrie here?"

I immediately realized that this was Carrie's old flame carrying a pretty big chip on his shoulder. Well, I can be as slow as the seven-year itch, but not when it comes to somebody looking for trouble. I knew right away this was *not* going to be a pleasant morning.

"Well," I said, "the answer to your question depends a lot on who you are and what you want."

"None of your business!" was his immediate response.

"Then I guess she doesn't live here," I concluded and started walking up to the house from the barn.

Here's where it got a little interesting: I got right in front of his old jalopy and walked right up the middle of the road so he couldn't beat me to the house. By the time I got to the top of the porch, I could tell he was right on my heels.

Now I need to tell you something that nobody knows except Minnie and me. Since I counsel with all kinds of goofballs and occasionally get into some very dangerous situations, we have a little code word that will alert either of us that there is a significant problem and we'll probably need the police, an ambulance or a mortician before it's over. It's a word like "Honey" or "Sweetheart," but we never call each other by this special word unless a nasty situation is brewing. Looking back, we've needed to use "the word" only one other time while we were dealing with a mad alcoholic.

Well, I walked over to the front door and hollered for Minnie. I called her by our code word and asked her to get some iced tea. Minnie acted in a split second, locked the door and called the sheriff's department. I turned around, faced Mr. Bonehead head-on and asked him a very important question: "Do you need help getting back into your clunker?"

"Until I talk to Carrie I'm not going anywhere," he retorted.

"Is that a fact?" I shot back with my nose about two inches from his. "Well, young man, you aren't going to talk to her. So you might as well get back into your car and leave now, or we can spend some time sitting here on the porch getting to know each other better. We'll have a glass of iced tea, and when you get tired of visiting with me, you can leave. Either way, you aren't going to talk to Carrie."

Bonehead started yelling for Carrie to come outside. He tried to push past me to get to the front door. Well, *that* wasn't going to happen. I moved over in front of him again. I reminded him that he was on private property, and if he moved one step closer to my house and my family, there'd be a price to pay. You see, he was standing with his back to the stairs. That proved to be rather convenient. He let out a volley of descriptive terms about my mother and other family members, mostly with words of four letters.

Like a nice little boy, he turned around and started down the stairs. He stopped about halfway down the stairs, turned and looked me right in the eyes. I could feel his anger burning under his black t-shirt while I prayed he'd just keep going down the stairs and into his car.

"You get the hell out of here, Butch," shouted a voice from behind me. "I never want to see your ugly face ever again." There stood Carrie, just outside the front door yelling at Mr. Bonehead.

Things had actually been pretty well under control until that moment. Now they were getting more complicated. Minnie managed to drag Carrie back into the house. That left me on the porch, and Butch halfway down the stairs leading to his old jalopy. His blood pressure had to be at an all-time high, because his face was as red as a cherry.

When you mix youthful stupidity and an oversized ego with anger, you get foolish behavior—and that's exactly what happened. Butch started back up the stairs and tried once again to shove me out of his way. Now I must confess I don't like to be shoved, period, let alone out of the way. Before I could think of something nice to say like a Bible verse, I planted my size 9 1/2 Justin work boot directly between his legs with the authority of an NFL field goal kicker. Only another man can understand why he winced with enormous pain.

Now I normally don't advocate violence but honestly, he wasn't going after Carrie during my watch and under my roof. Not if I could help it. Furthermore, I needed to protect him from Minnie because she can't stand it when men hit women and children. She was probably just inside the door with a shotgun in one hand and a rolling pin in the other. Anyway, when I pulled my boot out of his groin, he rolled back down the stairs and landed on the cement headfirst. He looked a bit like a poached egg lying there—yellow and pale.

I chop wood for my fireplace at the bottom of those stairs and keep my axe right there stuck in the chopping block. I hustled down the stairs about as fast as Butch could roll down them. My adrenalin was pumping and I was getting madder by the second. All I could see was Carrie's bruised cheek and the black eye this bully gave her a couple days before. I pulled the axe out of the chopping block and informed him that he'd better get into his car before I cracked his head wide open like a coconut.

Before he managed to get his aching groin to his car, Mr. Sheriff drove up. Before you could say "jackrabbit," Butch was handcuffed and sitting in the rear seat of the patrol car. His face color was no longer red like a cherry, but rather green like a cucumber.

When the officer ran his name through the computer, we discovered Mr. Butch was a suspect in a robbery in downtown Denver last week. How's that for a surprise? Carrie wondered where the money for the motel had come from. He apparently told her he'd borrowed it from a friend. Well, maybe he's going to make some new male friends in the Colorado State Gated Community for Criminals. That sounds like a great idea to me! Doesn't it to you?

I must confess that I was pretty shaky by the time it was all over, but I feel God was protecting us from a very bad incident. Butch is a very angry, unstable, and extremely dangerous individual when he doesn't get his way. I'm thankful that God was with us, and that the sheriff came when he did. I shudder to think what might have happened if Butch would have come at me again while I was holding the hatchet. (Can you say, "Crack"?)

Well, what's done is done. We're off to bigger and better things. Call us this evening and we'll go over everything with you then. I just want to assure you that we're all doing fine. We went out for a hamburger and a malted milk to celebrate Carrie's deliverance from a horrible relationship, and God's protecting love for all of us. We'll all go to church this weekend and have some time for reflection and relaxation.

AJ and Jenny, we love you both and anxiously await your call tonight.

Carter

P.S. God says, "Vengeance is Mine; I will repay." It sure was satisfying to see some of it first hand.

TO: THE PARENTING CO-OP
FROM: CARTER
SUBJECT: Black Cats and Friday the 13th

What do black cats and Friday the 13th have in common? Superstition, that's what! Well, I guess the deck is stacked against me today because it's Friday the 13th and a black cat just ran in front of my truck on the way to the barn. Oh well, I'm not a very superstitious person anyway, so black cats and Friday the 13th don't bother me.

After the events yesterday with Carrie's boyfriend Butch, today seems like a pretty lucky Friday the 13th, black cats and all. Frankly, I prefer to see God's hand in all of these events. Last night Carrie, Minnie and I sat down and went over step by step all that could have gone wrong but didn't, and all that went right that shouldn't have. That discussion resulted in many prayers of thanksgiving to God, Who had protected all of us. Carrie was able to see how God was using all of this to bring her family back together. Even the email AJ sent was so unlike him. She couldn't believe the changes in his attitude, behavior and even disposition. It's exciting, isn't it?

Well, this morning around the breakfast table we were talking about Friday the 13th. Carrie was telling us about Butch's family life. We decided to compile a list of 13 (seemed appropriate for the day) reasons why parents fail the parenting test. When you know someone like Butch, it's impossible to not stop and ask yourself the question "What went on in his home?" We'll never know for sure but our list might shine a little light on the subject. At best, it could be a rudder to keep your families on course.

So here we go with our list of 13 REASONS WHY PARENTS FAIL:

1. Some parents don't apply biblical principles or take personal holiness and spiritual disciplines seriously. This makes a child doubt God and His Word.

   This *Life at the Lazy-U* says it all!

2. Moms and dads don't understand their personal self-centeredness and its effect on their children. Their self-interest comes first; they're selfish. This teaches self-interest, not servanthood.

3. Occasionally they can't or won't control their anger; they lack self-control. This builds fear in a child.

4. Often parents become lazy in their parenting; they lack both creativity and implementation. This communicates indifference to children.

5. They become fearful because their God is too small, so they're overprotective. This diminishes a child's faith.

6. They're too busy with other things and stressed out, resulting in the loss of focus and loss of energy. This minimizes a child's importance through neglect.

7. Parents can become reactive instead of proactive; they're heavy on discipline, light on training. Training communicates a desire to invest in their child.

8. Parents can become unwilling to learn about good parenting; too often they parent by the seat of their pants. Men especially need to grow their parenting skills. Learning new skills lets children know their parents are growing.

9. It's far too easy to ignore the individuality, self-worth and significance of their children. Children need to know they're made special by God; they're not simply a Mom or Dad Look-alike.

10. They don't respect the rights of their children. This teaches abusive behavior to children.

11. Some parents are dogmatic, legalistic and controlling; they become dictators. This encourages rebellion in a child for lack of approval.

12. Sometimes dads and moms are emotionally needy, and exhibit an unhealthy emotional dependency. This cripples a child for emotional success in life outside of family.

13. Too often parents have marital strife, resulting in poor role modeling and a loss of security for their children. A child will learn you don't have to "walk your talk."

It's one thing to be superstitious. It's quite another to deal with reality. There's not one thing superstitious about this list. It's not like this list is a black cat that runs in front of your car and *maybe* something bad will happen. This list represents a series of frightening realities almost guaranteed to shipwreck your parenting!

Parents who constantly and consistently fall prey to these 13 Negative Parental Patterns will produce nothing but a bunch of Butch Clones. But let me soften this blow just a bit. We all fall prey to these 13 parental failures to some degree. The difference is that successful parents are aware when they do these hurtful things. They ask forgiveness, repent of their unacceptable behavior and move forward with healthy parenting skills. *Now that little difference is one heck of a big difference when it involves successful parenting.*

Don't ever get the idea that Minnie and I were perfect parents. We weren't! Many times we, too, could be convicted of any of these 13 failures. However, we tried every day to eradicate or at least minimize each of them, one by one, from our lives through Christ who strengthened us. None of us will ever be perfect parents, but good parents strive to be better parents every day of the week. Remember, parenting is an 18-year-long education with another 45 years of advanced studies. So don't get discouraged. Press on! It pays great dividends.

I'm anxious to hear from you about this email. In the meantime, watch out for black cats.

Carter

P.S. Minnie wanted me to tell you that her 1957 Hoover vacuum just blew a gasket, puffed out some smoke and died. Maybe there *is* something superstitious about Friday the 13th and black cats after all.

TO: CARTER
FROM: GERRY and SUE
SUBJECT: The villains are among us

Hey, Carter! Sounds like it got pretty exciting around the ranch last week. Wow! Sue and I were so thankful that it turned out the way it did. Butch is certainly an angry, impulsive and demanding young man. No wonder Carrie wanted out. His abuse must have crippled her emotions. Can you imagine what it must be like living with a man who is unable to control his emotions? Poor girl! I just hope and pray that she'll be able to see how foolish it was to run off on a lark with somebody she barely knew anything about. We're concerned about the baby and hope she'll do the right thing when the baby is born.

Your email about the events at the ranch formed a great illustration about our home life. Butch was insisting to get into your house. He wanted to drag off Carrie, for whom you were responsible. Your resistance and eventual removal of Butch from your property was both significant and necessary. You were very determined and took aggressive action to protect those under your care. I'm impressed, and I admire your courage, strength and assertiveness.

Some people might be offended by your self-defense tactics, but not me. At times there isn't a nonviolent solution to some situations. We wondered what would have been the next step if you allowed Butch to pass you on the steps and get hold of Carrie. What would have happened then? What if he was going to take her against her will? What if she resisted, then what? In any event, Carter, thanks for handling the matter and protecting Carrie.

When it comes to our families, dads and moms have become very lax about protecting their children from "the villains," haven't they? There are so many "Butches" or villains out in the world that are constantly trying to take our children from us. The problem is we invite them right into our living rooms. We don't get angry about their insistence to take our children; we just sit back and allow it to happen. What's wrong with parents today? Where is our anger about the villains, anyway? Not only that, but why don't we teach and train our children to confront the villains rather than train them to be passive, non-confrontational and to run and hide behind "religious bushes?"

Carter, what Sue and I have been discussing is how should we prepare our children to make good decisions about the villains? They're everywhere. The villains can be anything from the TV to the computer, from angry and evil friends to religious charlatans, from distorted values of what is right and wrong to relativism and postmodern thinking. They distort, twist and redefine our family values and spiritual commitments.

Sue and I were wondering if you wouldn't send us another email about how to control the villains. We know they're there, and so do you. Do you have any advice for us?

Before I sign off, I want to tell you a story about the local villains in our neighborhood. The other night at supper, I was talking with the children about an article I'd read in our local newspaper. It was presenting some different views about who Jesus Christ is. Well, I thought this would be nice discussion fodder for our family time around the table. We were shocked at what we heard.

My oldest son Clayton, who is ten, let us know that he didn't even believe in Jesus at all. "None of the neighbor kids do, either," he informed us. Then Clayton went on to tell us that he hated Sunday school. I was dumbfounded. He's never expressed any of this to us before until I brought up the subject. Now what? There are villains in my neighborhood as well!

Sue and I are concerned, but we don't want to become paranoid parents who operate in fear of the villains. Building higher fences, circling the wagons, moving into an exclusive Christian neighborhood, breathing only Christian air and drinking only holy water from the church—well, that's never been our style. As a Christian family, Sue and I believe God put us into the world for a purpose.

We want to be a part of carrying out the Great Commission of Matthew 28. We don't want to hide from the villains in our Christianized bunker, but would rather courageously reach lost people with the redeeming message of Christ's love. **And we want our children to come alongside of us in this mission.** We want to offensively take the battle to the lost, not defensively just build edifices to keep us Christians in and the unbelievers out. We've chosen to raise our children in a public environment because we want them to learn how to defeat the villains, not run from them.

We'll be looking forward to hearing from you. Give our love to Minnie and all your children and grandchildren.

Gerry and Sue

TO: GERRY and SUE
and THE PARENTING CO-OP
FROM: CARTER
SUBJECT: What's best: a good offense
or good defense?

Well, Gerry, I can see by the nature of your question that you intend to destroy me and hurt my questionable reputation among my Christian friends. Frying my brain today wasn't on my agenda.

Your question provokes so many responses that I'm not sure there's enough time and energy to answer it properly. Villains do exist. We'd be fools to deny it. A walk around any neighborhood will convince you if you have doubts. I'll do my best to effectively deal with your concerns; just remember that every family is different and so are their circumstances.

You've heard it said that the best offense is a strong defense. That works in football more often than not. But maybe in this case, I think the best defense is a strong offense. You've read my earlier emails about being *proactive* and not *reactive* parents. This is where that thinking is going to really strike home, so read carefully!

The best defense against the villains is a strong offense against the villains. And here, I'm not equating people with villains. Unsaved people aren't villains. Neither are homosexuals, alcoholics, drug users or preachers. We're commanded to love people and seek to serve them. The real villains are concepts, philosophies and evil thoughts that lead to unbiblical actions. One more time: *people aren't villains!* What people **think** and **believe** are the true "villains."

Notice what it says in Ephesians 6:12: "For our struggle is not against flesh and blood, but against the rulers, against the powers, against the world forces of this darkness, against the spiritual forces of wickedness in the heavenly places." As parents we should be protecting our children from wicked philosophies and false teaching, not from people. And yet, because of our fear of lost people, the Christian community is pulling more and more into itself. We circle the wagons and build higher and bigger fences. Hiding behind the sturdy walls of our religious edifices that protect and defend us, occasionally we lob bombs over the fence to establish our offense.

We've begun to think that the best offense is a good defense. What has happened to New Testament Christianity? In the Book of Acts, those men and women came out from their protected houses and their assemblies to confront head-on the villains of their day. Paul the Apostle continually argued against the philosophies of his day. No namby-pamby Christians there! Many were martyred, others beaten, some stoned and others ostracized from their homes and families. As I read stories of families that are really serious about raising their children in the heathen societies that are filled with villains, something very interesting emerges. The reality of the villains (cultic philosophies and secular values and morals) determines the urgency for, and the significance of, proactive parenting.

For example, when a missionary family experiences demonic activity in their backyard, it seems to add weight and a sense of urgency to their teaching and training. When a mother is beaten by someone from a religious cult for sharing Christ in a Bible study, it adds a certain reality to her teaching and training the children about villains. When a family packs up their car and heads for a two-week mission in the inner city, there is a seriousness of purpose that the children will experience as it relates to the neighborhood villains. A child that experiences a life of poverty on foreign soil connects deep in their innermost soul with the meaning of "love your neighbor." A child who hears of the struggles of a Christian man who's been courageously fighting villains all his life has a deep appreciation for commitment, faith, courage and steadfastness.

Take a look at this passage of Scripture that is rather long, but necessary for you to read before we go on. It is a passage that transformed my parenting like none other. It is a passage of offense, not defense. It's not a passage of "run and hide" but rather a passage of "take it to 'em!" Read it very carefully.

Deuteronomy 6:1-15: Now this is the **commandment**, the statutes and the judgments which the Lord your God has commanded me to teach you, that you might **do them** in the land **where you are going over to possess it**, so that **you and your son and your grandson might fear the Lord** your God, to keep all His statutes and His commandments, which I command you, all the days of your life, and that your days may be prolonged. "O Israel, you should listen and be careful to do it, that it may be well with you and that you may multiply greatly, just as the Lord, the God of your fathers, has promised you, in a land flowing with milk and honey. Hear, O Israel! The Lord is our God, The Lord is one! And you shall **love the Lord your God with all your heart and with all your soul and with all your might**. And these words, which I am commanding you today, shall be **on your heart**; and you shall **teach them diligently** to your sons and shall **talk of them** when you sit in your house and when you walk by the way and when you lie down and when you rise up. And you shall bind them as a **sign on your hand** and they shall be as **frontals on your forehead**. And you shall write them **on the doorposts of your house** and on your gates. Then it shall come about when the Lord your God brings you into the land which

He swore to your fathers, Abraham, Isaac and Jacob, to give you, great and splendid cities which you did not build, and houses full of all good things which you did not fill, and hewn cisterns which you did not dig, vineyards and olive trees which you did not plant, and you shall eat and be satisfied, **then watch yourself, lest you forget the Lord** who brought you from the land of Egypt, out of the house of slavery. You shall fear only the Lord your God; and **you shall worship Him**, and swear by His name. **You shall not follow other gods**, any of the gods of the people who surround you, for the Lord your God in the midst of you is a jealous God; otherwise the anger of the Lord your God will be kindled against you, and He will wipe you off the face of the earth."

Your brain cells are going to need a bit of refreshment after reading all that Scripture. Mine do. How about a cold drink and a handful of peanuts?

All right, we're ready to go again! God had delivered the Children of Israel from the land of Egypt. He was going to bring them into the Land of Promise. God's great mission for His people intersected with His commands to instruct the children. Part of God's purposes would be fulfilled through the generations of the family. In other words, the children would need to "catch the vision" of what God was doing in their midst so that they would not only *carry on* the mission, but also *pass it on* to the next generation—and so on, and so on.

So the parents were instructed to teach these things before and during their mission to possess the land. Teaching and Mission joined hands. In every conceivable posture and in every conceivable way, they were to teach their youngsters. When lying down or rising up, the parents needed to use every possible opportunity to warn their children against the villains. Let the villains know they cannot overcome you. Put God's Word regarding your mission on your hand or on your doorposts. Let the villains see your determination by worshipping God alone. Don't get caught up in following the villains or inviting them into your home by satellite, Internet or cable TV. OOPS! I jumped ahead about 3,000 years, but you get my drift.

Today, families need mission. So many go to church, insist that their children go to Sunday school and religiously attend weekly prayer meetings. Yet they lack real God-given family mission. Children today receive so much instruction with little or no mission.

I often laugh at the comments about Obese America. In other words, too many fries and not enough exercise! The same is true with Christianity as a whole, and families in particular. We are *overweight* on the classroom and *underweight* on mission. When I look at families that have raised good children, I see parents who have mixed mission with information.

Gerry and Sue, get a mission. Get *involved* in the Great Commission. Take your children down to an inner city soup kitchen, to a mission in Mexico, to a foreign mission in Indonesia. Don't just sit there and expect your Sunday school teachers and other youth leaders to fight the villains for you. Get to work. The Land of Promise is just ahead. There are victories to win and villains who need to be dealt a heavy blow.

Here's the deal, Gerry. A lot of parents want to have their cake and eat it too. In other words, they want their children to be good, villain-fighting kids but they aren't good, villain-fighting parents. They want their kids to stay away from the villains but, frankly, the villain of non-commitment is already victimizing them. I challenge you, Gerry, to *get those children involved in your mission.* If you don't have one, then find one. If you don't have any ideas, then get hold of someone who has scars from fighting the villains either at home or abroad. Be proactive! Take your Christianity to the streets and your children will follow!

Everyone talks about great family life as if it's a god in and of itself. We are warned that God is a jealous God. He doesn't want us worshipping any other God than Him, and that includes the worship of the family. Remember that the family in the Deuteronomy passage was the means to a greater end. Is it possible that in trying desperately to have good families we've forgotten God's divine mission, which is to advance His name among the nations and slay a few villains along the way? Wanting to raise good children is a good goal, but *not* the only goal!

There's a promise from God Himself. He will bring us blessings—houses that we didn't build, wells of water that we didn't dig and trees we didn't plant—if we follow this instruction. I wonder if God will give us great children and wonderful families if we take on HIS MISSION?

Well, my slacker friend, I have exhausted all my limited intelligence on this email and I'm ready for some steak and taters. Minnie is calling from downstairs and wants me to fire up the old barbecue.

See you later Slugger!
Carter

CARRIE: Dad, are you online yet? I hope you got my phone message telling you I'd be waiting online at 10:30 PM. Hello?

DAD: So I'm a little late. I'm such a loser. Can I ask for a little slack? How's the sweetest girl in Colorado? Are you enjoying the weather?

CARRIE: It's been a bit cooler in the evenings as we approach fall, but most of the days are still pretty warm. Carter says that it's likely to stay this way for another six weeks or so before the frost hits the pumpkin or as he says, "Until my nose starts dripping." Colorado sure is different than Texas. There aren't near as many Texans and a whole lot more cars that run.

DAD: That might be so, but we have a whole lot more rattlesnakes and armadillos plus we get a lot more sunstroke. Since it's so hot and dry, my skin wrinkles up and I look like a 200-pound raisin. After all, we get to be a lot closer to that line around the earth called "the equalizer" or something like that.

CARRIE: It's "equator," Dad, not "equalizer." Well, I wanted to tell you I miss being in Texas even though I tease you about it. Not only that, I miss being at home with you and Mom. I'm sorry that things aren't going so well between you. You must be at a total loss as to where to find your socks. And what about your eggs and bacon in the morning? Are you sick of microwave oatmeal yet, or have you resorted to a bowl of Trix?

DAD: Colorado must also have a way of turning kids into comedians! Nothing's funny about this situation down here, except that I had trouble learning how to operate the washer and dryer. I needed to call your mother over at Stacy's to get the operating instructions.

Actually, Stacy told me she had a name for a husband who can't run the dishwasher, the washer and dryer, do ironing, change diapers and at the same time survive on oatmeal and peanuts. She calls a person like that a "Carter look-alike" and warned your mom to be on the lookout, or "AJ would end up just like Carter." We all had quite a laugh at Old Carter's expense.

CARRIE: Well, we have a lot of laughs here as well. Carter and Minnie are quite the pair. Carter's always threatening to leave Minnie until Minnie gets this beautiful smile on her face and says, "Please don't leave. Your return in ten minutes will be too painful." Or Carter gives her a hug and reminds her that it's the only hug she'll ever get from a "real man," so she'd better enjoy it. To which Minnie replies with a smidgen of a laugh mixed with a slight cough. Carter will say, "The average man would have left you years ago." Minnie responds, "I always knew you were below average." Then we all laugh.

Dad, what happened to us? We're all angry most of the time. There's no teasing that says "I love you," nor any showing of affection with hugs or pats on the back. I can't remember any bantering back and forth to show we really liked each other. We never had any celebrations, even going out for burgers and malts like Minnie and Carter do, because we didn't enjoy being together. All anyone did was sleep and eat in the house.

Dad, you looked at me—but did you ever really see me? Did you ever hear a word I was saying, or try to understand what I was feeling? Since I've been here, the three of us have truly connected. We play games, go for walks together to the mailbox and you name it. We actually do things together. It sounds strange, doesn't it? I'm so thankful I can be here at least for the time being, but I'm afraid to come home for fear of what might happen. I want to see our family happy. It would be so reassuring to see you and Mom laugh together and hug each other. Doing some things as a family would be so nice for a change. What do you think?

DAD: No question about it, Carrie, our family has sure missed the boat. I'm learning to take the responsibility for this mess, but even that's difficult when you don't know how it all happened. Stu's been helping me understand how our dysfunctional family environment has hurt all of us. Looking back, I've made huge mistakes that I fear have long-term consequences. My marriage is struggling, and my children are having difficulty handling all the negative effects of my self-centered parenting.

Just look at you. You ran off with a horrible young man that was just like your father. How could you fall for a loser like Butch? The father of your child is an angry, self-centered young man. I assume he's in jail now. Then look at Tyler, another angry young man who can't control his temper. He runs off at the mouth at your mother all the time. Half the time he's mad at the world and won't listen to anything from anybody. The other half, he's just mad at nothing. He's almost failing out of his classes at school. Troy, being older, lived through a lot of the early fighting episodes and negative attitudes between your mother and me. He's also experienced a lot of despondency and depression as a result.

I don't know if you're aware of it or not, but he's apparently become a Christian (whatever that means). Carrie, the college group at the church has helped Troy a lot. It seems that he's more involved and happier since he started going to church. I've been doing some personal investigation of Bible stuff in a small group of guys that combines fishing for fish and fishing for, I think, me! Most of the guys are pretty nice fellows, and I think their pastor will give a Snickers candy bar to the first guy to squeeze a confession of faith in Jesus Christ out of me. (Maybe they get a gold lapel pin or a can of mixed nuts for each convert.)

All joking aside, I'm learning a lot about the Bible and how to be a better husband and father. I hope I'll be able to put some of it into practice.

CARRIE: There's no question about it, our family's a real mess. Here I am in Colorado—pregnant, alone and lacking any direction for the future. I know aborting my baby is out of the question. Minnie has made that very clear. I couldn't live with myself if I killed my own baby.

Minnie says that there are other options that might be hard at first, but easier to accept later on emotionally. Adoption is the way I'm leaning today. It changes almost every time I see a little baby or think about the future. But actually I'm pretty young to be a single mother, don't you think, Dad?

What makes adoption difficult is that Butch will need to sign off on the adoption papers. What if he wants to keep the baby? Or what if his parents want to help raise the baby? Then what? I can't let that happen.

DAD: Thanks for asking! See, our family is getting better already! Carrie, I just don't want us to make any more foolish mistakes as we try to put everything back together. Six months ago, I was behaving like a very self-centered, self-serving and self-absorbed turkey. I would have said abortion was the thing to do, but not now. I'm trying to think about what's best for the others involved, including the baby. The baby has rights, too. The right to live, the right to think, the right to make decisions—and I think the baby would choose to live. Don't you?

I'd like for you to consider raising the child yourself and hopefully, Mother and I together will be there to help. I mean that, Carrie. We'll be there for you. On the other hand, we also understand that a new beginning might be what's best for you. Adoption will allow you to start afresh with new friends, new convictions and renewed hope. Maybe that's the direction to take.

CARRIE: Dad, I don't want to put all the blame on your shoulders but I just have to get some things off my chest. It hurt me so bad when you wouldn't approve of me. All your put-downs about my weight, my looks, even my laugh crushed me. It made me hate you. I told myself that you weren't telling the truth, but the way you described me felt very real. I never felt that you cared about my struggles at school and with my friends. You just had pat answers to everything. You never went to the trouble to really find out how I felt. Just to have you listen and care would have made all the difference to me. But you couldn't, maybe wouldn't, care about anybody but yourself. No wonder Mom got fed up.

Dad, I know you're trying to be a better father but you need to know how I really feel. Maybe then you won't fall back into the same habits later. I understand now that nobody will ever really take your place, Dad, but Butch was my attempt to find someone who would care and listen even if sometimes he boxed me around. It might sound funny to you, but sometimes I miss him because he was the only man who seemed to care for me.

DAD: I'm sorry for what I've done to you, Carrie. You're my only daughter and I love you with all my heart. I'm beginning to realize that I haven't expressed my love for you very well. In fact, it's very difficult to express love for others when you're so consumed with yourself. I've been such a knucklehead. Please forgive me and allow me to love you once again. I'm not even asking you to trust me now, but to give me the opportunity to rebuild your trust over time. I promise to do a better job. Together, I believe we can salvage the next 17 years.

CARRIE: I need to go because Minnie needs some help pulling Carter's boots off. I'm just kidding! Actually, this pregnant lady needs some rest. One more closing thought.

Carter always uses animals to illustrate a point. It made a lot of sense to me when he said, "Carrie, you remind me of a beautiful young filly who's 'feeling her oats' galloping across the pasture with her mane blowing in the wind. That's where you are in life, girl—frisky but angry and stubborn. Somewhere in the process you've fallen into the hands of mean trainers who've broken your spirit and given you a pretty foul disposition."

But Dad, get this. He added, "Carrie, don't allow what has happened to get in your way of trusting the new people who enter your life. Don't keep kicking and biting, but rather learn to trust. Say goodbye to bitterness and strife and listen to the advice and counsel of people who are your new trainers. Follow the counsel from the Bible. You're going to be just fine, so relax. You're safe now so have another bucket of oats—I mean bowl of oatmeal. And never lose that sparkle in your eyes."

Dad, I'll try to trust you again. I really think I can now. Gotta go! Say Hi to Troy and Tyler, and give a great big hug to Mom. Love you all.

DAD: Thanks for being willing to try again. Mother said she enjoyed talking with you last night. The boys are doing fine. I guess we're all on a rather large learning curve. Goodnight, Sweetheart.

TO: CARTER and MINNIE
FROM: JENNY
SUBJECT: This is what you call a "mother"
of a problem

Minnie, thanks for pushing me forward in my relationship with AJ and the kids. My typical approach to handling family problems was to withdraw, disconnect and offer excuses. Now with Sue, Stacy and you as friends, I seem to have better coping skills.

You've enabled me to regain my personal confidence. That, in and of itself, has given me the desire to confront our family issues head-on instead of hiding from them. Our family life has been horrible, but knowing the "how, when, why and where" to fix it has eluded all of us. Now I feel we're all getting our bearings.

Both AJ and I want to stay with the conditions of our controlled separation but are looking forward to getting back together sometime mid-November. Even during our separation AJ, the boys and I are getting together to discuss what our home should be like in the future. All of us want to be respected as individuals, and to agree to disagree if necessary. AJ wants to get more involved with all three kids. I want to feel free to speak my mind without having AJ or the children jump down my throat. Is that even realistic?

We realize that there needs to be teamwork, and at the same time some boundaries, both in and out of the home. I've often wondered why families don't sit down and discuss what's going on inside. One thing for certain, *we* sure didn't and look what we ended up with! Then it occurred to me why families don't have positive communication. They yell, scream, fight, get angry, insult each other, push their own agenda and jump to conclusions. Is it any wonder? Healthy family communication should be just as selfless as the other parts of family life.

This is what I think about good communication these days. If each of the parties wanting to communicate will think of the other people first, then communication will be a snap. But everyone must be of the same mind, or there'll be difficulties. In other words, our selfless concern for one another should spill over into the way we communicate.

One of the social workers is a Christian. She told me the Bible says to "speak the truth in love." There you have it! We should all speak the truth, or share our opinions, in a loving way. In the past, we shared our opinions, all right, but in an angry, hateful and indifferent manner.

I have just a couple of additional observations about the whole mess. When AJ and I started parenting, we were simply holding it together by the skin of our teeth. His parents, by his own admission, didn't know what they were doing and neither did mine. I'm reasonably sure both sets of our parents parented in the best way they knew how. Yet they, too, lacked the skills for good parenting.

I don't believe I ever saw a book on parenting in my father's hand. My mother simply did what nearly all women do: she covered for my dad's indifference and abuse. She told us after an abusive scolding, "Daddy meant well," or "Remember that Daddy is doing what he thinks is best for you children." She even told me one time not to make Daddy angry, or "you know what will happen." No wonder I have difficulty confronting anyone about anything.

Here's the way I see it now. Every parent needs to be "policed" by the other parent (or by a close friend if they happen to be a single parent). Even the children make pretty good policemen for uncovering parental abuses. Unacceptable parenting (whether it's excessive spanking, physical, verbal, emotional abuse or simply parental indifference) needs to be confronted and dealt with immediately. An accountability partner would help.

You see, I let everything go because I was afraid of AJ and didn't want to disappoint the children or turn them against me. I see now that was a terrible mistake, and my children have paid the price. In good families, it seems to me that both the mother and father should be willing to submit their parenting style to the scrutiny of someone else. That is, of course, if the parents choose to be healthy and successful parents.

Someone certainly needed to confront our parenting but AJ wouldn't listen to anyone and I was afraid to say a word, as were the children. We were frozen in place. Given the same situation now, I'd be on the phone to Stu or Carter or somebody for counseling no matter what AJ thought.

Don't think for a minute that I've thought all of this up on my own. I'm not that well informed, but I am a pretty good student of Stacy. I've read back through all the emails in *Oops! I Forgot My Wife* and realized how self-centeredness strangles good marriages and makes for terrible parents. When AJ and I get back together, there'll be accountability for both of us. I guarantee it!

Minnie, thanks for empowering me to come out of the closet and confront my situation head-on. My becoming a biblical "husband helper," as it says in Genesis 2, builds hope into our future. I'm praying that God will change AJ's heart and allow him to hear without getting angry, to feel enough to care and to lead without becoming a dictator. I think AJ is really doing some deep soul searching. I believe that God is patiently "hunting him down."

Don't you get the feeling we're on the right track?

Love you all,
Jenny

> P.S. My conversations with Carrie have been like none other. I can't believe how mature she sounds over the phone. I get the feeling that she's very lonely and uncomfortable as the baby gets bigger in her tummy. I'm glad she enjoys her work down at the Quik Stop store in town. At least she has some spending money. Thanks for all you're doing!

FROM: MR. CARTER
TO: THE **CHILDREN**
OF THE PARENTING CO-OP
SUBJECT: Children of the 21st Century

Some of you young guys and gals can read this email. The others will need an adult to help you. Either way, this email is just for you YOUNG PEOPLE.

To start things off, I want all of you to find your parents and ask them for $5 in cash. Tell them Mr. Carter wants you to go out and buy something you really like. It could be a piece of hot apple pie, or a Hot Wheels car, or a dry diaper as the case might be. Be sure and tell them that Old Carter will pay them back as soon as the snow flies at our great upcoming reunion.

One other thing: tell them that you love them and thank them for all the things they do for you like putting a roof over your head, keeping the toilet flushed and buying floss for your teeth. It's also pretty nice having new underwear every now and then. Also remind them that every time you run out of bubble gum and peanuts, you feel unloved. See what they say!

By the way, when was the last time you jumped into Dad's lap and asked for a raise in your allowance? Doesn't hurt to try, you know!

You all know that Mr. Carter is an old cattleman who lives out in the "boonies" with Minnie and Blu, our dog. Our children are all grown up and live in different houses with their own families. So Minnie and I live here all alone, but we still love children a lot.

That might be why we have Blu. She's kind of like a kid. When she was a young puppy, I had to spank her for wetting on the floor and tearing apart my cowboy boots with her sharp teeth. She was such a rascal, she even chewed some leather off my saddle! Now that makes any cowboy pretty upset, so I'd let her know I wasn't very happy with her.

After all these years, though, Blu has become a wonderful cow dog. In the winter, she brings the cattle into the corral every morning. Then she goes everywhere with me. If the bull isn't going where I want him to go, she'll bite him on the back of his rear heels and off he'll go.

It took a long time to train Blu. Do you know why? She needed to learn to obey because I was her master, and what I said was the way it was going to be. The most important lesson Blu needed to learn was to obey. Did you get that? If Blu doesn't obey me, she wouldn't be any good on the ranch at all. Since I'm nice to Blu and pet her and compliment her on her work, she respects my voice and doesn't bite me or wet on my jeans.

I'm writing you this email to let you know how important it is that you learn to obey your parents. The Bible makes this very clear. In the book of Ephesians, children are told to "obey your parents in the Lord, for this is right" and it doesn't make one bit of difference how old you are. Obeying your parents is the right thing to do. Disobedience is the wrong thing to do. If your parents tell you to do something like take out the trash and you disobey and refuse to do it, then God doesn't like that. He wants you to learn obedience.

That's precisely why God tells your parents to discipline you when you don't obey. If your parents don't understand how important discipline is, then you'll gradually become undisciplined and self-willed. But you ask, "Mr. Carter, what if I don't want to obey?"

Well, my answer is, "That doesn't really make any difference because God tells you to obey your parents whether you want to or not."

Understand what I'm saying, my young friends. Your parents are like shepherds for your family. Do you know what a shepherd is? It's a person who cares for a flock of sheep. A shepherd feeds the sheep, protects them and uses his crook to correct them. *Every* family needs shepherds, and yours is no different. Your dads and moms are learning new skills so that they will be even better shepherds. You'll help your family a lot by obeying your parents.

There's one other Bible verse I want to tell you about. Do you remember what the Ten Commandments are all about? They are God's laws for all people for all time. One of those commandments is specifically for children. It says, "Honor your father and mother, that your days may be prolonged in the land." (Exodus 20:12) Not only is a child to *obey* their parents, but they are to *honor* them as well.

Now what does that mean? It means that a child is to respect Dad and Mom, and to hold them in high esteem. Do you know that honoring your parents is one of the main things that makes the world run smoothly? Children aren't only to show respect and reverence for their parents, they are also to honor their parents' authority over them.

When the children of Israel went into the Land of Promise, there wasn't to be any juvenile delinquency or there would be serious punishment. You might be tempted to think that since your parents aren't perfect parents, you don't have to respect them. That's wrong thinking that'll get you into a boatload of trouble with God. Even though your parents make mistakes, you're still to respect and reverence them. You got it? Great! The reason for honoring your parents is "that your days may be long upon the land." Sounds to me like your choice is to honor your parents, or settle for shorter days.

Kids, this is what will make God happy with you. Do what your parents ask you to do. Do it when they ask you to do it, and be nice to them while you're doing it. That's fair, isn't it?

Thanks for paying attention to what I've written. You're wonderful children. Go out into the kitchen and have some potato chips now, but don't spoil your dinner, OK?

Mr. Carter

> P.S. Hey, parents! It's one thing for children **to be told** to "obey and honor their parents." It's quite another for parents to **give the kind of servant leadership (not dictatorship) that will inspire their children to respect and honor them at home.** If you tell your child to stop kicking the dog or stop talking back, then it's your job to follow through until that child obeys. Talk with the child, pray with the child, explain to the child, discipline the child and see to it that the child obeys, honors you and respects your authority when it's all over. That's a huge assignment, Dad and Mom. Your children are depending on you.

TO: CARTER
FROM: GERRY and SUE
SUBJECT: Hip-huggers, piercings, tattoos
and what's next

Gerry and I are already beginning to see a problem on the horizon. It's becoming a regular part of our conversations around the table. "Well, Jimmy has an earring. So can I?" our ten-year-old Clayton will ask. Our inquisitive daughter follows with, "Yeah, why can't he?" Stacy's been getting similar questions from her six-year-old Tanya. Questions like, "Can't I wear this top that shows my tummy?" and "What's wrong with tattoos?" I can't believe what comes out of the mouth of a six-year-old.

When we asked Jenny and AJ about what to expect with regard to earrings, tattoos and the like, they both said simultaneously, "You haven't seen anything yet."

They say that an ounce of prevention is worth a pound of cure, so I thought the subject would be worthwhile for our Parenting Co-op. To get you up to the 21st century, Carter, here's a list of items that come up for discussion all the time with families at our church as well as in the neighborhood:

- What about earrings for boys?
- How many earrings for girls and boys?
- Should I let my daughter wear spaghetti strap clothing?
- Should my son be allowed to wear those ugly low-crotch baggy pants that are about four sizes to big?
- Should my girls wear the low cut—and I mean *low* cut— pants?
- What about shirts, tank tops and blouses that are so short that it exposes about 10 inches of tummy skin?

- What about hair color and styles? Purple and green are in!
- How do you deal with computer games and videos?
- What about cell phones for kids?

Of course, Carter, the list isn't exhaustive because movies, tattoos, curfews and a host of other issues also become points of controversy. Our concern is being able to walk together as a family through these pressing issues without hurting our relationships.

Now Jenny has warned all of us about the dangers of coming down too hard. Apparently that's pretty easy to do. Where she and AJ failed was in being too disconnected from the children. Carrie would go out of the house dressed in tight shorts and a tiny tank top, and Jenny would say nothing. Jenny told us she was afraid that fighting over anything and everything would become the greater enemy, so she gave in to keep the peace. AJ, on the other hand, would get demanding and abusive—but eventually he ignored what the children were doing because he couldn't have cared less. Sometimes if AJ caught Carrie going out looking like that he'd yell at her and make her go change, but even that didn't last.

Carter, I'm not asking for specific answers to every point of contention. But what's your advice about how to confront things like peer pressure, contemporary clothing and the everyone-else-is-doing-it syndrome? All of this affects the way our children want to dress and act.

Thanks for being there Carter. Just having someone to bounce ideas off is very important to parents.

Love you and Minnie,
Gerry and Sue

TO: GERRY and SUE and PARENTING CO-OP
FROM: CARTER
SUBJECT: Cowboy boots, Stetson hats and
Wrangler jeans

Times have really changed, haven't they? Now it's navel rings, purple hair and tattoos. When I was a kid, it was about long hair, loud music (the Beatles), shirts hanging out and white tennis shoes. What it was is no longer, and what it is will give way to what it will be. Then it will return to what it used to be, and the cycle continues. As Solomon says in the book of Ecclesiastes, there's nothing new under the sun.

My parents didn't agree with the modern styles of the 50's and 60's. I didn't agree with the styles of the 80's and 90's. Parents today struggle with the current trends of the 21st century. Nothing's changed; only time.

Wait a second. That's not totally true. There has been a decline in some major areas of our society, like marital commitment, moral values and personal purity. As a society, we're becoming more lenient. The "villain" of sexual permissiveness is altering our views on clothing. Attractiveness is measured by jewelry instead of character. The amount of exposed skin determines popularity. What a shame! Truth of the matter is, our present state of things isn't working out very well, is it?

Just today, I met with two families who struggle with these troubling changes. One father thought that the battle is an incremental battle that deals with extent and inches. The other father said, "Unless there are principles to which we adhere, parents will be overwhelmed by the pressure to conform." There were some other factors they shared with me that might be worth noting:

1. Some parents lack personal commitment to sound moral judgments. They often don't take the time to think through difficult issues. That complicates matters.

2. Some parents, themselves, occasionally regress into unacceptable behavior and dress. Poor role models don't have a lot to say.

3. Some parents don't encourage greatness in their children. They're satisfied if their children look like all the other kids.

4. Some parents are overly committed to their children's popularity and status. Those parents argue that there's a price for popularity. Is compromising family values too pricey?

5. Some parents don't handle their own peer pressure very well. They want to "keep up with the Joneses" too.

Those are just the opinions of a couple of committed dads and moms. Regardless if you agree or disagree with them, the major point of it all is that **parents must take personal responsibility** to lead, protect and educate their children against failing moral trends that affect everything from how they dress, to how they recreate and what they think.

Wherever you come down on issues of dress, curfew, hairstyle, piercings and the like, the following suggestions might just serve as a rudder to guide you and your children through these complicated minefields. Feel free to disagree!

1. To be successful, you must purposefully communicate with your child regarding these issues. It's not wrong because you didn't do it when you were young and it's not wrong because you wouldn't do it today yourself. Use a lot of questions that begin with "How?" "When?" "Why?" and "Where?"

2. It's OK to set clearly defined guidelines (length of dress, shortness of blouse, size of trousers, and bodily damage

through piercing or branding) but **be prepared to explain them** without using "I told you so, that's why." For example, "No piercing until you're age 12, because we feel you're too young." Or, "I protect your body until you're 17, and after that you're on your own."

3. Be guided by principles of Scripture. For example, 1 Peter 3:1-7 says to seek godly character over external dress. Train your children to be people of the heart. Introduce your children to true greatness through biographies of men and women who are godly examples of biblical character. Greatness isn't measured by how much skin is showing or the color of your hair. Those external issues may ring true on Planet Earth, but not in heaven.

4. You need to trust your children to make decisions at some point. Parents must start **training their children's freedom** while they are yet at home (before college freedom sets in). Appropriate compromises with your children are in order. At age 17 your children should be prepared to make many of their own decisions, including items of dress and holes in their body. If you haven't trained their values by then, you're probably out of luck anyway.

5. Be informed about what's going on in your child's world mentally and emotionally. Then you can gently apply your principles to areas of real need. Be equipped with knowledge (use books, daily paper and magazines) about your child's culture. Be prepared to respond to your child's peer pressure intelligently—not just with power, laws and rules.

6. Don't be critical but be observant of what's being worn that is both good and bad. Help your child to blend good taste with current fashion. Spend money where you can agree.

7. When it comes to these issues, learn the place of balance. It shouldn't always be your way. Remember relationships are destroyed over these issues. Try to find ways to agree. Part

of good Christian living is submitting one to another (Ephesians 5), even to your children.

8. Don't focus on what others are or aren't doing. Do what works for *your* family values. Teach your children that every family has the right to make their own decisions about these things. Don't spoil your uniqueness by doing what everyone else is doing. And don't put down your child's friends, either.

9. Work to understand how your child feels when they're not as trendy as their friends. When the boys chase girls that are scantily dressed, it gets pretty lonely for a young girl that is modestly dressed. Help them to handle those kinds of feelings. Teach your children to be successful and at the same time be different. Teach them to think and reason independently and biblically. These are the consequences of godly living.

10. After things have been discussed and agreed upon, write them down together and table further discussions for a stated period of time so the same issues aren't constantly coming up and stressing the family.

11. Don't wait for lightning to strike (through unwanted pregnancy, drug overdose or lust addiction) before taking action to teach and lead.

In conclusion, patience and understanding mixed with solid principles and good communication will get you through the minefields. Suppose one of my sons came home with purple hair sticking straight in the air, baggy pants dragging the ground, an earring in his right ear and one in his tongue and a tattoo on his right buttocks. I'd tell him I love him and invite him down to the barn for a "coming out" party. You see, he'd be coming out of the house to sleep in the barn until he understood that purple hair belonged on monkeys, baggy pants on infants, earrings on women and tattoos on cattle. But then again, I'm pretty old-fashioned so maybe I'd better just love him anyway.

Minnie has been so patient with me over the years. You see, our problems are just the opposite of yours. She's tried to get me to dress more fashionably. Some of the clothes I wear are more 1900's than 21ˢᵗ Century. She understands how important my Justin work boots are to me. But she doesn't like me wearing my boots with my swimming trunks when we go to the beach. She thinks I look stupid with my boots on, my glow-in-the-dark-legs and cowboy hat. Since I like Justin boots, she contacted the Justin Boot Company and bought me a pair of Justin sandals with the Justin boot logo right on the side of them. Then she bought me a John Deere ball cap. Anyway, now we both are happy at the beach and I look foxy!

You see? Understanding, creativity and patience works even with stubborn cowboys. I'm out of here! Love to all.

Carter

Life at the Lazy-U provides a good visual!

TO: AJ and JENNY
FROM: CARTER
SUBJECT: Have you ever been shocked?

Electric fence is always very interesting to work with. You know what electric fence is, don't you? Electric fence holds cattle and horses in a pen or pasture, and just about everything else out—including grandchildren and mothers-in-law.

One strand of smooth wire attached to fence posts with insulators is all you need to get an electric fence up and running. Of course, wire and fence posts are of no use unless one end of the wire is properly attached to a charger and plugged into an electrical receptacle. Once that's done, a current of electricity passes through the wire and should anything touch the wire—KA-BOOM! It gets shocked.

Here's the problem. It's possible that some weeds or sticks could brush up against the wire, which shorts out the electricity. When that happens, the electric fence is worthless. The cattle get out, and the grandkids and other varmints get in. So it becomes very important to test the fence occasionally to see if it's working properly. Now that's pretty shocking! (Sorry. I couldn't resist.)

Really, the only way old ranchers test electric fence is to touch it. When you feel that surge of electricity shoot through your body and heat up your spurs, then you know the fence will hold cattle. Incidentally, that's why old ranchers are missing so many fillings in their teeth.

Well, I might be an old rancher but I've learned how to check electric fence without personally touching it. Here's how I do it. I invite some visitors out for lunch after Sunday morning church service. City-slackers always like an afternoon out in the country, especially when they have little "fence testers" (aka children) running around. After one of Minnie's killer Sunday dinners, it's time to go outside and play. I always plan an afternoon softball game out near the pasture where the electric fence is located. Inevitably some slugger will knock the ball over the fence for a home run and the outfielder will need to go retrieve the ball.

Here's where softball can get real exciting. If the person chasing the ball is real small, they can go under the fence without touching it. Generally, a bigger human can step over the fence without touching it and escape the moment of ecstasy when a jolt of electricity ties knots in your baseball cleats. However, inevitably one of the mothers will go out to assist her child in finding the softball in the midst of hay, weeds and manure. Mothers don't go under fences very well, nor do they go over fences very gracefully. They push the fence down with their bare hand and BANG! She'll momentarily lose concentration as the electrical shock rearranges her Sunday-go-to-meeting hairstyle and melts the tiny hearts on her earrings. For a few brief minutes she jumps around like a rattlesnake has her by the leg, then slowly collects her composure as if nothing happened.

It's a thrilling moment for me. At that instant I know the fence is in top running condition, my cattle will stay in and other varmints (especially wild mothers) will stay out. After a sip of iced tea, Mom has nearly forgotten the whole ordeal. Of course, she's still a bit cross-eyed and the hair on her arms is standing straight out like the hair on a bear rug. That's what I call killing two birds with one stone—getting the fence checked *and* having some healthy exercise after a high cholesterol lunch.

You've heard of vengeance, haven't you? God always seems to get even with me. Just yesterday, I got the shock of my life. By the time I fell into the recliner, my head was still spinning and I was pretty cross-eyed to boot. I looked across the living room at Minnie and she was still rubbing her eyes and massaging her temples. Bolts of lightning can be very shocking.

AJ and Jenny, this bolt of lightning has to do with your daughter Carrie. I should give you an update on how things are going in Colorado before hitting you with that same bolt of lightning. Carrie has been a wonderful houseguest. She's always willing to help Minnie with household chores and keeps her room spotless (for the most part). Apparently she's had pretty good parents some of the time, and this should be an encouragement to you.

Her job down the valley at the Quik Stop provides her with some additional money for personal extras and isn't too taxing on her physically. Her pregnancy is going well. She got a good report at the doctor's just last Monday. She's put on about 25 pounds.

Our counseling times seem to be very helpful to her and she is growing personally and spiritually. She goes to church with us faithfully without the least bit of complaining, and hangs out with some of her new church friends. She says she received Christ as her personal Savior and really wants to grow and mature as a Christian woman. All of this has been very encouraging to Minnie and me. Isn't it something how God is gradually infiltrating your entire family with His Spirit? Truly, His presence will help heal all the problems within your marriage and with your children. Keep believing! The Bible tells us that God replaces darkness with light, error with truth, lies with truth telling, thievery with hard work and unrighteous behavior with righteousness.

Now get this. Carrie is pretty active in the youth group at church. They're involved in a street ministry in downtown Denver. You remember the new friend she made when living on Colfax. The one who told her to get out of her bad relationship? Well, her name is Vanessa, and she's also a Christian. They've become pretty good friends, and Vanessa is discipling Carrie. Anyway, it's so exciting for Minnie and me to see Carrie blossom. You can be very proud of her. This daughter of yours is doing great!

Now that we've covered all that, you'd better sit down for Part Two of this email. It wouldn't hurt if you'd tie your slippers to the recliner. Get some nuts and a soft drink, because your daughter is in love. No, I'm not kidding! I really don't know how to tell you this, but she has a new guy friend that comes into the Quik Stop where she works. He's been coming by for the past several weeks and they've gotten pretty friendly. He works a night shift at a factory in Denver that makes furniture, so he's free during the day to come see her.

When this relationship first began (and it did so very slowly), I told Carrie that we were her parental representatives and thought it only fair to her Dad and Mom that we meet him before they go on any dates. She wasn't ready for that counsel, and rightfully so. Probably afraid of what I might say. She thought I'd ask him "Young man, do you shave your legs?" Or, "Are you housebroken?" Or, "Do you fish and hunt?"

As luck would have it, he apparently wasn't very eager to meet me either for fear of having to answer those same questions. Apparently, Carrie told him I was pretty blunt. I wondered why *she* needed to be so blunt?

Anyway, we kept getting updates from Carrie about her new flame. She tells us he's a very nice young man, and doesn't seem to mind her pregnancy. He, too, has recently begun attending the street ministry and seems especially interested in the coffeehouse, which passes out soft drinks in exchange for an opportunity to witness to street kids about Christ. We had already discussed with Carrie that it was unacceptable for her to get involved with any guy who isn't a believer in Christ. She's not real sure at this point about his spiritual commitment.

We've discussed everything from premarital sex to abusive relationships. Carrie seems committed to purity and to healthy relationship building, especially after the nightmare relationship with Butch. Each night we sit around the table discussing their conversations. We try to help her become discerning about the evil motives of men in general. AJ and Jenny, we're really trying to guide Carrie as you would.

Well, the time finally came for us to all get together. Carrie asked if she could invite her friend over for one of "Carter's famous barbecues" which starts the second Carter nearly blows himself up while lighting the 1965 grill.

"He has Saturdays off work. He'd like to meet with you and Minnie," Carrie commented. "Please Carter, don't be too hard on him because he's scared right out of his skin to meet you." Then she added, "I told him you were a softy at heart and that Minnie loves everybody so there was nothing to be afraid of. I said you two were reasonable people unless someone doesn't treat me nice. Then you both get pretty cantankerous."

So the meeting was set for last Saturday at 6 PM. Oh that Minnie! She's really something! She fixed one heck of a dinner, fit for a king. I started cooking some steak after I put out a grill fire. Sure enough, right on time, our guests arrived. Up the road came a vehicle that resembled something like a car that was inbred with a bus. The blue smoke coming from the exhaust pipe confirmed in my mind that the car would probably never leave the ranch running. When the car stopped running in front of our house, smoke belched out from under the hood with the slight smell of Prestone and oil mixed. Out of the driver's door climbed…. I mean out from under a rock climbed…. OH, NO!

Butch got out of the car. He went around to the other side of the car and opened the door for Carrie. Carrie put her hand in his. I could read her lips as she whispered, "It's going to be fine, so just relax."

"Fine, my foot!" I thought to myself. "What the heck is going on?"

Get this, AJ and Jenny: *standing in my driveway was the same guy we just about hospitalized not two or three months ago.* That's right! Butch, the monster, was back again. In my driveway, no less.

I couldn't believe my eyeballs. I heard a glass break in the kitchen. When I rounded the corner, Minnie's mouth was open wide enough to park a Volkswagen in it. We stared at each other in total disbelief. You talk about getting shocked by a bolt of lightning! We were dumbfounded. By the time we pulled ourselves together and took three shots of whiskey (I'm just kidding), we were standing at the front door. I could only imagine how nerve-wracking this was for Carrie and Butch, as well.

Then to my surprise, Carrie introduced us to Darren Allen Schuster from Denver, Colorado. Have you ever had your tongue go on vacation and simply slide backwards down your throat? Well, it happened to me. I was speechless. Thankfully, Minnie had the presence of mind to invite both of them in. If she hadn't, they'd probably still be standing on the porch as I write this.

Not really knowing what to say I asked Darren, "Do you shave your legs?"

That broke the ice a bit, and we all laughed together. Darren jumped right to the point. He cleared up all the questions that must have been written in plain sight across our foreheads. His real name is Darren. His "tough guy" name was always Butch from the time he was a young boy. His father called him Butch because he wanted a tough son. He told us how sorry he was for his awful behavior, and the terrible way he had treated Carrie. He actually was thankful for all that had happened because it was through those events that he had come to understand his anger and his nasty mean streak.

Carrie told us that Darren had not been involved in the burglary as originally thought, and that the real burglar was a guy that worked with him. So Darren didn't have any court appearances or jail time. Instead, he's been living downtown, has a small studio apartment and works at a furniture shop staining wood.

When he finally got his act partially together, Darren started calling Carrie's cell phone to apologize for his actions. Initially, she refused to even talk to him. But he continued to leave her messages, asking for one final opportunity to talk together about their child. He told her how sorry he was for the way he'd acted, but still wanted to talk to her face to face.

Eventually she gave in and they met at a little restaurant in town. After some initial small talk, she told him that abortion was not an option and that she was considering adoption instead. She asked him if he would sign off in the event the baby was put up for adoption. He didn't think he could answer that question without some serious thought. "Carrie, could we meet again on Thursday? That gives me a couple of days to think," he replied. That was the beginning of their new relationship.

Carrie also apologized for not telling us sooner about Darren, but naturally she was concerned whether we'd act, react or overreact. I guess that's fair enough. We no doubt would have opposed any contact with old Butch given past circumstances. All I can think is, "God works in mysterious ways His wonders to perform."

Our evening together was fantastic. Our initial impression is that Darren is *not* the same young man that forced his way up my porch steps. One thing for sure, he seems to love Carrie. He has stepped out of who he was into the person he wants to be: the father of Carrie's baby, and a loving husband to Carrie.

But Carrie isn't the same rebellious young lady she was before, either. I saw them exchange looks that cheered my heart and put my concerns somewhat to rest. She really does love the guy. I can see it in her eyes.

All that in mind, I do see one big problem: while Darren is involved in the street ministry, I'm not totally convinced he's become a follower of Jesus Christ. He talks about spiritual things, but possibly lacks a personal relationship with Jesus Christ.

As you both know, I couldn't put my blessing on their dating, let alone their marriage, unless Darren was a Christian. The Bible is very clear on this: a Christian (Carrie) shouldn't marry an unbeliever (Darren). 2 Corinthians 6:14 calls that situation an "unequal yoke."

AJ and Jenny, I don't want to be naïve but I really think they're on the way to the altar regardless of what we say. Let me remind you that some pretty substantial changes have gone on here, and from what I can tell, this is a done deal unless God intervenes.

So let me ask you the same questions they asked me. Would you approve of their marriage in light of what I've said? They don't want a large wedding, but would like to get married sometime in the very near future.

Here's the way I figure it. They are both very young, yet very much in love. I've spoken with Carrie about the spiritual issues that Minnie and I must confront, and so would not approve of their marriage at this point. I counseled her to wait and see what God was going to do in Darren's life. But I also understand that waiting might force them to take matters into their own hands. It's a tight-rope walk.

Ultimately, this will be a test of Carrie's personal walk with the Lord and her willingness to submit to biblical counsel. Frankly, this will be your decision and not mine. Carrie said she would call you on the phone in a couple of days following my email because Darren wants to talk with you as well. I'll be praying for you both as you consider this complicated decision. Be sure to weigh the alternatives and don't be hasty in your decision. If you say "no," then be prepared to explain why. If you say it's okay, then share your concerns at the same time. If you advise them to wait, that's fine as well—but be prepared to go to a wedding anyway.

Remember your relationship with Carrie is everything now. You want to support her and guide her, but in doing so you must understand her independence, the pregnancy, some key biblical principles as I mentioned *and* that she's in love. Either way, you can really get behind her and Darren and make a huge difference in the future if you keep your relationship with them intact.

Minnie and I will be praying for your phone conversation.

Carter

TO: CARTER
FROM: AJ and JENNY
SUBJECT: "The fish that got away" is our daughter

Over the weekend, the boys (Troy and Tyler) and I went fishing out in the gulf. We had a great day together. Tyler spent a lot of time driving the boat, which was a lot of fun for him. He's not quite the fisherman that Troy is, and doesn't have near the patience necessary to keep his mind on what he's doing. I know it sounds strange, but he does better driving the boat. Actually, out in all that water it's pretty hard to get in a lot of trouble unless you fail to see an oncoming cruise ship or land which, even for Tyler, would be difficult.

Overall, fishing was just OK. We caught a few smaller fish ranging from 20 to 30 pounds each, but nothing over that until about 1:30 in the afternoon. We were trolling with about 150 yards of line when all of a sudden everything went nuts. My reel started spinning like crazy as the fish took more and more line. I could barely hold onto my pole! The harness holding me into the seat was almost cutting me in half.

When the fish finally broke water we couldn't believe our eyes. A magnificent sailfish shot out from the depths of the gulf's beautiful blue water. The tug on the line was almost unbearable, but I held on with all my might. Tyler did a great job trying to move the boat in reverse toward the fish to minimize the strain on the fishing line. The boys and I made a great fish-fighting team.

I know that where you live a big fish is around five pounds, but not down here—not today—not this sailfish. He appeared to be over six feet long and blue as blue could be. I don't know what happened. I might have gotten too impatient, too tired or too care-less, but all of a sudden the battle ended with the snap of the line. This huge fish made one final leap into the air, danced on his beau-tiful tail, winked at us as if to say "Nice try!" and in a second was free again.

There I sat strapped to my chair, perspiring and reeling in the remains of my broken line with both boys asking, "What happened, Dad?" Instantly excitement, joy and anticipation turned into uncer-tainty, frustration and regret as one sailfish was free again.

Once again, I learned a hard lesson. You can't rush the process of landing a big fish. If you pull too hard too quickly, or if you fail to give the fish extra line when necessary—SNAP goes your line! Troy did manage to get one picture of the fish jumping out of the water while it danced on its tail. It will be evidence. Evidence that proves I hooked a really big fish that got away. Now I won't have to put up with your sarcastic comments about telling fish stories.

Both Jenny and I learned something from my fishing debacle. We don't want to lose Carrie again. So we're committed to not pull too hard, give her some line and be patient in the process. But both of us are novices when it comes to this parenting style based upon relationship and biblical principles. Remember, for years we relied on muscle, power, nagging and anger as the means for getting the children to do things our way. In the process, we lost all three of them. So this time around, we want to be more careful with our children. Remember, this is new territory for us.

As we look back on our phone conversation with Carrie yester-day, we feel that once again we probably pulled too hard, didn't give her enough line and weren't very patient with her or Darren. We're afraid we just lost the fish again. Carter, our daughter is very young, pregnant and immature. She wants to marry a guy who is very young, sexually frisky and immature. What are we to do? We're afraid for them! They have their whole lives ahead of them, and it can all be changed in one hasty decision.

We're not perfect in any sense, but we don't want to feed her to the lions either—not that Darren is a lion. *Life* is the lion, and it will tear them to shreds if they're not careful. Initially, our conversation went well but when Jenny and I started disagreeing with them, it all hit the fan. Carrie felt we didn't understand, didn't love her and wouldn't support their decision to get married.

I'll tell you one thing. This time Darren wasn't the problem. He actually was a real gentleman, and said very little. He told us how sorry he was about the way he'd treated our daughter, and promised to never do that again. At one point, he said the arguing wasn't solving anything and that there was no need to continue the conversation. He hung up his extension of the phone at that time. Shortly thereafter our conversation with Carrie ended, and not on very good terms. Both of us are just sick about it, but hesitate to call her back for fear of making matters worse.

Carter, what is it with kids? Whenever you try to talk some sense to them, they go the opposite direction. When you think they should turn left, they automatically want to turn right. If you want them to run, they want to walk. What in the heck is the deal with kids anyway? Can't Carrie see what's going to happen to her life? She gets so defensive, she can't see the start from the finish. After listening to Darren, maybe he's the one we should be warning to not marry our daughter.

Looking back, maybe we should have told her to go get married tomorrow. Then maybe, just maybe, she would've decided to wait until later just to disagree with our advice. Isn't that called "reverse psychology" or something like that?

Anyway, she's living at your house so maybe you can untangle the mess. Most importantly, please assure her that we're learning and we love her. Together, we'll sort it all out. Encourage her to give us a little time.

Carter, thanks for being there for us. We'll try to follow your lead. In the meantime, would you please tell us why kids are so defiant and disagreeable?

Love you,
AJ and Jenny

> P.S. We felt it was appropriate to send Carrie an email apologizing for our impatience over the phone and to ask her to just consider *what* we said in spite of *how* we said it. We also wanted Darren to know that we accepted his apology, and respected him for wanting to be a part of the conversation. I hope he'll be just as understanding of us.

TO: AJ and JENNY
FROM: CARTER
SUBJECT: One step forward – two steps backward

Well, we're putting up our last cutting of hay. Fall is fast approaching, so the last bit of hay needs to be in the barn pronto. Before you know it, our cattle will be back from their summer range and the snow will be flying. That means feeding, and that means we'd better have all our hay ready for winter.

Whenever you mix cowboys, farm machinery and speed, invariably you encounter something you didn't plan on. Of course, I've learned that if you add to that dangerous combination alcohol, cowgirls, dogs, swarms of bees or music, your problems are multiplied ten times. If a swarm of angry bees attacks you because you drove your tractor through their beehive, then you can plan on digging your machinery out of a creek bed somewhere on your neighbor's front 40. Secondly, it's also hard to drive the tractor with a cowgirl on your lap—especially when you're trying to clean out the corral with the front-end loader while rubbing her back. Just ask my son how long it took him to fix the side of the barn after he created a new door into the milk stall during the back rub.

Well this year, I hired on a cowboy to run the swather. A swather is a self-propelled machine that cuts the hay and puts it in a windrow (not a window, a *windrow*). I thought the hire would save me some time. The cowboy said he'd done it before, and that was good enough for me.

As I said before, combining a cowboy with a piece of farm machinery and speed is concern enough in and of itself. But just add some alcohol and—you got it—sure enough, your nice little swather will end up stuck in your irrigation ditch headfirst.

Talk about one step forward and two steps back! This guy kept trying to get out of the ditch by moving the swather a little forward, only to slide sideways about twice as far into the mud. By the time I got there, the swather was stuck clean up to its axle and the poor thing couldn't turn a wheel. I happened to notice the empty beer cans in the cab, and immediately terminated his employment. I can't tell you what I said to the cowboy because this is an email on parenting and self-control, but he was rubbing his temples as he walked out of the pasture.

Well, with the help of a couple tractors, we got the machine back on dry ground and we were off to the races. This time, I drove the swather and Minnie sat on my lap. Now *there's* an interesting combination! We ended up parked at the creek necking and didn't get the hay cut until later in the day. I knew it was safer that way.

AJ and Jenny, some things seem right in the first place (hiring a cowboy) but then it can turn sour (getting stuck) making your initial decision seem wrong in the first place. However, not all things end up disastrously (Minnie cutting hay with me). What I'm trying to say is that "one step forward and two steps backward" isn't always a bad thing.

I know how disappointed you must be about your visit with Carrie and Darren. It does sound like things didn't go the way you planned. I'm sorry! Subsequent to your phone call with Carrie and Darren, I've talked with Carrie and I think she would agree that the conversation was disastrous. I reminded her that if you didn't love her so much you wouldn't even care what happened. I quoted a verse from Proverbs 3:11,12: "My son, despise not the chastening of the Lord; neither be weary of His correction: For whom the Lord loveth He corrects; even as a father the son in whom he delights." (KJV) Then I helped her understand the value of being wise. We looked together at the first seven chapters of Proverbs that teach us to pursue wisdom. I also warned her about the consequences of not listening to the counsel of her father and mother, comparing that to the fools of Proverbs 1:7 who "despise wisdom and instruction."

I also want to point out an important passage for both of you as parents. It's found in 1 Thessalonians 2:11 and 12 where Paul compares himself to a parent. He highlights some of their valuable characteristics: "You know how I **exhorted** and **comforted** and **charged** every one of you, as a father doth his children, that you would walk worthy of God, Who hath called you unto His kingdom and glory." (KJV)

I guess what's important for us to understand is that it's all right to exhort our children, but we must also comfort them. Carrie is in a real predicament. She needs you to comfort her, not just correct her thinking. If we're not careful, she'll simply rebel again. We can give her direction, but we need to comfort her along the way or discouragement will set in. You'll lose the battle unless you can mix your correction and exhortation with comfort and encouragement. A word to the wise is sufficient, so the old saying goes. I'll leave it at that for the time being.

Presently (as I understand it) Darren is frustrated, Carrie is anxious to do something, Darren's parents want something done right away, you folks don't want anything to happen at this point, and Minnie and I are sitting here wondering what God's opinion might be about this whole mess.

Frankly, I don't know exactly what to do but making everyone happy seems rather impossible. I'm having a meeting with Carrie and Darren tomorrow before he starts work to talk through some of the different ideas. So I guess we'll wait and see what comes of it. I don't want to take one step forward and two steps backward again because I think we just did that. I guess we'll wait for our meeting. Maybe Carrie and Darren have the solution for all of us.

In the meantime, think of it this way: God is putting together His perfect plan for Carrie. I don't know if Darren's in those plans or not, but either way God is in control. Now is the time to trust in Him, and enjoy the assurance of His love for each and every one of us. Don't you think? Hasn't God been leading the way toward total family reconciliation? Remember, you planned a reunion when all your family will be back home. All of us (Gerry and Sue, Stu and Stacy, all their children and Minnie and I) have made preparations to join the party in just a few short weeks. Jenny, you'll be back home and so will Troy and Tyler. Let's just pray that Carrie will join us one way or another as well.

I'll email you tomorrow night just as soon as we finish our discussion with Carrie and Darren. Love you all and God bless…

Carter

P.S. I just had a thought. Maybe this time it'll be one step backward and *five* steps forward. Now that's the encouragement I needed. How about you guys?

TO: CARTER
FROM: GERRY and SUE
SUBJECT: Are children "good" or "bad" at birth?

Carter, we noticed AJ and Jenny's question about kids who do just the opposite of what their parents want. We have the same question about our kids. In fact, it was encouraging to us that AJ and Jenny have the same dilemma.

Gerry's mother says he was a perfect child and seldom needed any correction. Apparently, he was very easy to raise because he always wanted to do what was right. Is it possible he's *regressed* into a less-than-perfect husband? Or is it possible that his mother's in a state of denial that comes with senior dementia? Ha!

It seems to us that our children are always pulling against us. We try to correct bad behavior, and they get angry and fight us. On the other hand, when we praise their good behavior it lasts until lunch. Then they're back fighting with each other.

We had a discussion with our neighbors last week about this very subject. They told us that children are basically good, and given time they learn the value of doing what's in their best interest. In other words, children will automatically learn to do what's right if parents will just be patient.

"Let them grow up and they'll naturally do what's right," one neighbor said. "Where parents make mistakes is in forcing good behavior on a child before they're ready."

"Look at the polar bears, seals, chimpanzees, alligators and other animals," the lady from across the street offered. "Their mothers allow them to grow and learn. Eventually, they all grow into adults and are just fine. How many elephants do you see rebelling and leaving the herd?"

When she finished talking, I just shook my head like the Aflac Duck and didn't know how to respond. Carter, does that make biblical sense? Are children basically going to be just fine if we minimize discipline and just overlook things for a while? Maybe Sue and I are just too discipline-oriented and should back off for a while.

What do you think?

Gerry and Sue

TO: THE PARENTING CO-OP
FROM: CARTER
SUBJECT: Going from bad to worse

There have been many very interesting studies lately on the subject of evolution. New research and scientific evidence has provoked many thoughtful students to rethink the whole theory. In fact, even some unbelieving scientists have acknowledged that there must have been "intelligent design" in the universe in order for things to operate as they do.

Your neighbors are giving the parenting skills God gave elephants and polar bears the short shrift. Any biologist, zoologist, or TV viewer who watched "Wild Kingdom" will let you know that animal parents don't just let life happen to their offspring. (Ever try to walk up to a baby bear or baby elephant in the wild? If you have, did you get your injuries on film?)

Gerry and Sue, tell your neighbors that your children—and theirs, too—are different from goldfish. When the moment is right, let them know that your children belong to God. He has greater plans for them than for polar bears, or even elephants. Remind them that being a part of the herd isn't your goal, but rather preparing them for heaven is your ultimate goal. Kids will never make heaven unless their sinful nature is dealt with—and that will not happen automatically, given enough time.

History tells us that things don't automatically improve and get more complex, but in fact de-evolve and gradually fall apart over time. From the moment of birth, every living thing begins to die. Yes, animals may get bigger for a time but eventually their systems wear down and death occurs. We can medicate, massage and exercise our bodies, which might prolong the process, but over time the end will come. Even our sun is gradually burning itself up.

Human beings face deterioration and decline. Just look at my stomach. It's making its way over my belt on its way to my knees. Gravity is pulling me closer to the ground. I'm shorter today than I was 40 years ago. But I'm in good shape if you consider "round" a shape.

Now let's consider your question about children, starting here: children *don't* get better with time. Sorry to disappoint your neighbors. In fact, the Bible makes this point very clear in Psalm 58:3: "The wicked are estranged from the womb; these who speak lies go astray from birth." There's something very important to notice at this point. Children begin going the wrong direction the moment they're born—not just physically, but spiritually as well. From birth they're pre-programmed to disobey, rebel and resist authority.

Now get this! Proverbs 29:15 goes on to say, "A child who gets his own way brings shame to his mother." In simple terms this means that unless a parent interferes with their child's determination to go their own way, the result is shame for the parents.

I've mentioned this to you in other emails, but want to be clear on this point. Your children were born with an evil nature. They are bent toward self-centeredness, anarchy and godlessness. Left to themselves, children will do the wrong thing, behave the wrong way and think wrong thoughts. Time won't correct your child's evil nature. You must reshape them on the anvil of biblical instruction and healthy and consistent parenting every day or else.

Maybe I could say it this way. Children are born sinners; they will live like sinners and will die as sinners unless God intervenes through His sovereign means of parenting to alter their sinful nature through discipline and correction.

Well, there you have it. Don't be surprised when your children refuse to agree, resist your authority and seem determined to do what they want regardless of what you say. They're programmed that way!

Now that you know what you're working with, get back to parenting.

Carter

TO: THE PARENTING CO-OP
FROM: CARTER
SUBJECT: If it wasn't for dad, grandpa and
great-grandpa...

Do you remember the email I sent a couple days ago? I talked about the fact that children don't get better with time, and unless parents take corrective action, a child will go the wrong direction. Do you remember? Well, I failed to mention that our ancestors have a great deal to do with our sinfulness as well. Do you know why? It says so in the Bible. Do you want to know where? It's in Exodus. Where in Exodus? You'll find it in chapter 34, verse 7. What does it say? It says God **"will by no means leave the guilty unpunished, visiting the iniquity of fathers on the children and on the grandchildren to the third and fourth generation."**

What does that mean? It means that our ancestors have left us a very undesirable legacy: namely, their sinful patterns. You'll see in Genesis 20 that Abraham had a bit of a problem with lying. In Genesis 26, you'll find that Isaac followed in his father's footsteps and lied as well. Then in Genesis 27 you'll read of Isaac's son, Jacob, who lied to his father about his birthright. This is a pattern of "family sins" that were passed down from one generation to another.

Here's another interesting thought to ponder. In Genesis 5:1 it reviews God's creative work, and says that "He made Adam in the likeness of God." Remember that Adam and Eve were created perfectly. God saw His work and commented, "It was very good." Then Adam and Eve sinned, and the entire human race fell into sin. Now notice Genesis 5:3 where it says that Adam "...became the father of a son **in his own likeness, according to his image,** and named him Seth."

What this amounts to is that our ancestors pass on to their children, grandchildren and great-grandchildren sins that are typical to them, just like Abraham did to Isaac and Jacob. Now let's not overstate this. I'm not looking for a place to hang the responsibility for our sins. I can't do that, because *that* responsibility rests directly on our personal shoulders. What I'm trying to accomplish is *identifying sinful tendencies that come from our lineage.*

You can understand it, can't you? When a father like Abraham lies all the time, his children learn how to lie and they pass it right down to their children. You've heard the old saying "Like father, like son," haven't you?

Life at the Lazy-U says it a little differently ...
> "like mother, like daughter."

So where does it stop? Exodus 34:7 tells us of God's mercy. His loving kindness will stop the landslide of sinful behavior at the third or fourth generation. This prevents the total destruction of the entire human race through specific sinful patterns like lying, adultery or envy. But understand one thing: we are all sinners. That never goes away. The nature of our "sin of choice" is an inheritance from our dad, grandfather, and great-grandfather. Sorry.

It's frightening when we see our nasty disposition in our children, isn't it? Practically speaking, maybe it would be good for you to examine your family tree to see what sinful present you received from dear old dad. Maybe it would help you to understand the behavior of your own children. (Come to think of it, what did I give to my children? YIKES!)

Carter

TO: AJ and JENNY and
THE PARENTING CO-OP
FROM: STU and STACY
SUBJECT: Jumping to conclusions, running other
people down and pushing their luck

You all know Stacy and me pretty well. We love exercise. Ever since we joined the Recreation Center, we both feel so much better. You'll find us there usually twice a week working out on the Stair Master, running on the treadmill, lifting weights or playing a pickup game of basketball. Both of us really believe in it.

But it's not for everyone. Take Carter, for example. He exercises by running to the refrigerator or doing the stairs on the way to bed. He always tells me he exercises at least three times a day. When he first told me that, I was really impressed. He told me he especially enjoyed lifting weights. He said he does about 20 reps with one weight, and then about 20 reps with a heavier weight, and 10 reps with the heaviest weight and then wraps up his workout session by lifting all three weights together and carrying them over to where they belong. Amazing!

"What a man! How many guys do that at his age?" I thought to myself. Then I learned that the weights he was talking about were the knife, fork and spoon. He lifted them three times a day for breakfast, lunch and supper and put them in the sink when he was finished. What a rascal! He's nothing but a sissy!

I got suspicious when I asked him if he did any running. "Not very consistently," he responded, "but I can still run a mile or two without breaking a sweat."

"Now that's pretty impressive," I told him. Then I asked why he didn't run more regularly.

"Well, Stu," he said, "it's too tough on my horse." He runs all right, but on the back of his horse. It's no wonder he doesn't break a sweat. Carter, you know I'm just kidding you. I know you'll be reading this email and probably write me something sarcastic back. Love you brother!

Well, treating your wife and children with respect and honor along with compassion and love is a lot like getting exercise. You need to work at it! Exercise is something you actually *do*, not something you just talk about. Right Carter?

Stacy and I have been reading all the emails being passed around. The one from AJ and Jenny about the fish that got away really got to us. AJ and Jenny, our hearts went out to both of you. It seemed like everything was going to work out fine with Carrie, but then disagreement, anger, hurt feelings and despair brought uncertainty. We're both very sorry, but like Carter emailed you, God is in control.

Folks, there are a couple of statements you'll often hear in the gym that go something like this: ***"If you don't use it, you lose it,"*** and ***"No pain, no gain."*** Both of these statements apply right now to your situation with Carrie and Darren.

You've gained emotional and spiritual strength over these past few months. Disciplining yourselves has been good for both of you. Today you're different people than you were when we first met. AJ, you're a stronger man in character, commitment and understanding. You've really been working hard building up those muscles in your character—no pain, no gain. Jenny, Stacy and I have seen your endurance improve so much. Your flexibility gives you tremendous versatility and adaptability. When we first met, depression ruled in your heart. Now, the muscles of optimism have been conditioned into peak performance. Your spirit was suffering from malnutrition, but look what the exercise of Bible study has done to those spiritual muscles!

You're both becoming strong in spirit and in character. Spending as much time as you have in building your inner man and inner woman has turned both of you into people of discipline and purpose and all of this in just a matter of a few months. However, if you don't use it, you lose it! This is the time to use it, or believe me you'll lose it!

Some people jump to conclusions, run other people down and push their luck. They fail to understand the eternal benefits of real spiritual exercise. Paul the apostle told his spiritual son Timothy to train himself in godliness, knowing that bodily exercise profits a little but godliness is profitable in all things.

AJ and Jenny, recently you've chosen to take the high road of selflessness rather than jumping to conclusions, pushing your luck and running others down. By trusting in God, and thinking of your spouse first and your children next, you have altered the direction of your family. You're no longer running away from each other but working together with growing relationships. Hopefully, all of you will never be the same.

Now, we said all of this in order to say this: *why did you resort to your old habits when dealing with Darren and Carrie?* You both knew better than that. That kind of response was the old AJ and Jenny. Anger, impatience and loss of self-control are the very attitudes that have broken your family to pieces and destroyed your relationships. Why would you want to go back to that sinful behavior?

As two of your spiritual trainers, we were personally disappointed in your performance. We know you can do better than that because you're stronger people than that. You've been trained by consistently disciplining yourselves to be strong when tempted. You've practiced not caving in to fleshly desires and emotional outbursts. You're acting like an Olympic athlete that goes out the night before he competes and gets drunk, stays out late and sleeps in the next morning. His coach will never accept that kind of behavior, and we don't either as your spiritual coaches.

We love and believe in both of you, so get busy and fix this situation with Carrie and Darren. Don't delay! Time is wasting! Show them the real you! Model for them what it means to be committed to relationships both in heaven and on earth. What do you say?

We know you'll love us for writing this because you know how much we care for you both. We are so proud of what God is doing in your lives we could SHOUT TO THE HEAVENS! Remember, no pain, no gain! Use it or lose it! The ball's in your court.

Love you lots,
Stu and Stacy (your spiritual workout buddies)

TO: CARRIE
FROM: DAD and MOM
SUBJECT: If at first you don't succeed—try, try again!

Well, Carrie and Darren, this will be our next effort at Parenting 101. When Mother joined the Parenting Co-op I was very hesitant. Some would say "stubborn," but I say "hesitant."

OK, I *am* stubborn and bullheaded. I didn't want anybody telling me how to be a better parent. Even to this day, I'm not convinced why I felt that way. I suppose it's a man thing in a way, because men never like for anybody to tell us that we're wrong or that we've lost our way.

But I began reading the various emails from Carter and the others anyway. Before you knew it, I was intrigued with the thought of becoming a better parent. It took some time, but I gradually began to gain ground on my poor parental habits. Carrie, I didn't say I *conquered* my poor parental habits but rather was slowly building new and better parenting skills.

That rascal Stu has been a great accountability partner. He has really been a good friend and teacher. Working with Social Services, going through the anger management classes and attending the parenting stuff at Stu's church has actually made a difference in how I think. I seem to be growing in spiritual understanding.

Carrie, you know I've got a long way to go. I merely ask that you'll be forgiving and patient with me when I slip back to my old ways. I feel I did that when we talked over the phone last week. I wasn't understanding, and spoke in a hurtful way to both you and

Darren. We might have differences in our opinions about what to do next, but that should *never* be an excuse for the way I talked to you. I'm sorry, and ask you to forgive me and give old Dad another chance.

Carrie, your father needed a break so I'm going to take over for a minute. Ever since he became interested in the Parenting Co-op, he's become so emotional. Just like now. He typed one paragraph and tears started running down his cheeks. It's like for years he's been expressing his emotions in negative ways through his control, manipulation, fear, anger and impatience. But now, his emotions surface in gentler and more positive ways. He's kinder and more understanding, yet he continues to be strong and confident in so many good ways.

Personally, I'm becoming much more comfortable trusting his leadership in our family because he's putting others before himself. Yes, there are times when he loses it. But I can see that he's really trying to better our home and family relationships.

Carrie, I must confess that my attitude over the phone was also completely unacceptable. As a parent it's so easy to become self-willed and self-righteous (as Carter would say). Often a parent's love for their child is replaced with their own self-centered feelings, personal expectations or selfish embarrassment and shame. I feel I made your pregnancy and marriage to Darren more about how I felt than what you must feel. I'm sorry.

Well, Dad's back and has once again regained his composure. I'll turn the keyboard over to him.

I wasn't crying; I had something in my eye! Maybe my allergies kicked up, or maybe I've got a little sinus cold. Men don't cry unless it's something really important, like acting stupid to their daughter!

Well my dear, I want to attempt once again to give you some fatherly advice in a way that is helpful, not hurtful as before. You must remember—as your mother and I must remember—that we might disagree, but that doesn't mean we don't love each other. So together, let's tackle the problem.

We've thought a lot about your situation. I've personally discussed the matter with Stu and Stacy, and since Mother is still living with them it's convenient for us to talk together. Here's what we've concluded for the time being.

You're a minor legally (age 17), pregnant physically, in love relationally, distressed emotionally and worn out mentally. Nice going! Behind it all is a wonderful, exciting, loving, compassionate and willful young lady that we both love with all our hearts. Sweetheart, you've gotten yourself in an awkward situation. But I've learned lately that God seems to specialize in "against the odds"-type situations.

Stu was telling me about a guy named Gideon in the Old Testament. God's people, the Israelites, were preparing to go into battle against the Midianites. The Israelite army was made up of 32,000-plus warriors but God felt there were still too many soldiers, lest in winning the battle the people would believe that their own power had delivered them. So God instructed Gideon to send away over 32,000 soldiers, leaving a measly 300 to fight the Midianites. Well, those 300 men (with a craftily designed plan) defeated the Midianites through God's power.

Carrie, all we need is a craftily designed plan and with God's power, we too can overcome this situation. What do you say? Here are some ideas. Ultimately we can't, nor will we, force you to make any decision. I'm going to list some options for you and Darren to consider:

A. First and foremost, I'm thankful that both you and Darren have agreed against abortion. Both Mother and I join your belief that abortion is murder in the first degree. Two wrongs will not make it right.

B. If you decide to keep the baby, Mother and I will do all we can to help you. You can move back home for a while until we can arrange permanent housing elsewhere. Eventually, you'll want to be on your own anyway. But until then, we'll help.

C. Both you and Darren will have to agree on adoption. That's something you can't decide on your own, because Darren has rights as the father. I know you've discussed this option as well.

D. This is where it gets sticky! The final option is for you and Darren to raise the child together. The question of marriage surfaces in our thinking, as does the two of you simply living together or living apart while trying to raise the baby. Frankly, neither of them leaves a very good feeling in our thinking. Every father and mother wants to have a great marriage, have their own children and live happily ever after. Carrie, we want that for you as well. At this point, however, we're not sure about Darren even though he seems more stable and in control of himself. To top it all off, you're both still pretty young. Yet we know of couples who were married at your age and are doing very well today. It all is very confusing to everyone.

E. Here's what we would like for you and Darren to consider. We would like for you to continue as you are until after the baby is born. As soon as the baby is born, then let's begin to contemplate marriage. You could both get some pre-marital counseling and in a matter of months we could have a nice wedding in your honor. Mother and I will support you regardless.

I know you'll let Darren read this email, so I want to say something to him as well. Darren, I forgive you for treating my daughter so terribly. You hit her! You hurt her! You had no right to do that! You'll appreciate a father's love only when your child is born. If some angry person intentionally hurts your new baby, only then will you understand my anger against you. However, Darren, I did the same to her and to my family and I'm ashamed of myself for it. Maybe together we can learn how to be good husbands and fathers. Thanks for taking good care of Carrie while I'm not there to protect her. Please don't ever hurt her again. If you really love her, please consider what I've written.

Well, for now Mother and I will sign off. We look forward to seeing you soon!

Love you,
Dad and Mom

TO: AJ and JENNY
FROM: CARTER
SUBJECT: Questions! Lots of questions

There's been a volley of phone calls over the past couple of days. You must be worried sick. There are so many decisions to make, with so little time for contemplation. This must be so stressful for both of you.

I guess I'm writing for my own therapy and to summarize the latest events. You never know when you might need the facts.

I went through my daily planner and couldn't believe how many times we've been together with Carrie and Darren. In fact, just two nights ago we all went out to dinner at Lettuce Alone, which is a soup and salad shop on the edge of nowhere near Littleton. Carrie wasn't feeling the best at the time, so we decided against steak and taters for the moment and became temporary vegetarians surviving on lettuce and pickled beets. I lost seven pounds overnight! On the way home, we actually laughed thinking Carrie's illness might be because of Darren eating so much blue cheese on his veggie-burger. It was so disgusting to Carrie and Minnie, they wanted to move to another table.

Anyway, she didn't go to work the next day thinking that a bit of rest might be just what the doctor ordered. I thought she just caught a flu bug from one of the cats. That was Thursday evening.

But come Saturday, it wasn't the flu that was the problem. It was the blood running down Carrie's right leg. She got up in the morning, had breakfast and almost immediately started bleeding very severely. I mean blood was almost gushing out onto the kitchen floor. Both Minnie and I knew this was not the time for discussion. We had no time to lose. We loaded Carrie into the Explorer and literally shot down the highway to the hospital. It was actually faster for us to leave then and there than to wait for the ambulance. Trust me, folks, I turned every red light into a green one and every speed limit sign into an "unlimited" sign. I was hoping for a police escort, but they couldn't catch me. (Go figure!)

I knew Carrie couldn't lose blood that fast for too long, or she and her baby would both be in jeopardy. We arrived at the emergency room. The doctors immediately assessed the condition of Carrie and the baby. Things weren't going very well for either of them. Carrie's blood pressure had fallen; she was very light-headed and in shock. The baby was in fetal distress.

Carrie had suffered a placental abruption. Her heart rate had dropped to 70, and if something wasn't done quickly, the baby wouldn't survive. In order to save both their lives, the doctors took the baby by a caesarean section around 9 AM. When it was all over, Carrie had lost two units of blood and the smallest baby I think I've ever seen was lying on the table. That little boy topped the scale at 4 pounds, 10 ounces. (What can you expect when the little guy arrived over a month too soon?)

With some extra special attention and care, the little guy will be fine and Carrie should have a normal recovery. Thank God for taking care of both of them!

Minnie and I were so thankful you were able to get a flight to Denver. We were happy to pick you up from the airport and be the first to welcome the new grandparents to Colorado! I could see in Carrie's eyes how thankful she was that you came. She didn't know you were on the way, so it was a huge surprise. Frankly, she needed her parents more than anyone else.

AJ, after you left the hospital Tuesday morning and headed for home, Carrie expressed to Minnie how much better your relationship is with her. She cried when reflecting on your love for her and just loved the little baby outfit that said "Grandpa's Little Fisherman." Jenny, wasn't it nice for Carrie to invite you to stay on for a few more days? Nothing's more important than having Mother by your side when you're not feeling the best.

AJ, you handled the situation with Darren beautifully. I know it must be hard, but recognizing that this was his baby as well was very meaningful to him. I was also impressed with his parents. They were very understanding of how awkward the whole situation was. Jenny, you were magnificent with Darren's mother. Encouraging a picture with both mothers, Carrie and the baby was an outstanding suggestion. I'm sure it made everyone more relaxed.

I thought Darren tried real hard to include everyone. I've watched fathers and mothers get so selfish and controlling that they don't want anyone around. That wasn't Darren. He was just the opposite, and wanted everyone to share in the joy of the moment. I was personally very proud of him. I think it shows a real maturing on his part!

I was glad Darren got hold of Vanessa. It was terrific to see her and meet the Street Ministry gang. When they all arrived Monday afternoon, it was a total surprise for Carrie. It was so exciting! Maybe it was because they were all so young, but each and every one of them was so excited for Darren and Carrie. They saw the baby through the glass at the nursery and just giggled and giggled. It was so wonderful to see! They all gathered around the bed holding hands and, one by one, all ten of them prayed for the quick recovery of Carrie and the growth of the baby. They prayed that Darren and Carrie would be great parents and that together, they would teach the baby about Jesus Christ. One guy actually prayed that Darren would be a loving husband to Carrie after they get married. (I kept my head bowed but nearly choked on my tongue having heard such a prayer. Did this guy know more than I did about their marital intentions?)

I concluded the prayer service with a word of thanksgiving to our great God. Not only for the health of Carrie and the baby but also for what He is accomplishing in the lives of every person in the room. They left! We left! Darren, Carrie and the baby were finally alone.

Weren't you encouraged that Vanessa wanted Carrie to move in with her until the baby is released from the hospital? It would be so convenient. She lives just a few blocks from the hospital. Now Carrie and Darren can easily get to the hospital to be with the baby. Vanessa is a great "care giver" and is spoiling Carrie something awful. Since Carrie is nursing the baby, it wouldn't even be practical for Carrie to commute to the hospital several times a day from the ranch. Doesn't God have great administrative skills?

I'll tell you one thing. That little community of believers is really caring for them. But here's the kicker! Get ready for this! This group of young Christian people doesn't want them living together until they get married. Basically, they're supporting everything you suggested in your email to Carrie. How's that for some reinforcements?

All parents should take notice of this very important parenting principle. It often takes more than just parents to raise children. A loving community of believers is a tremendous add-on, don't you think? We can get so "parent focused" we fail to utilize other parenting resources that come through our friends, extended family and the Christian community. Your children should know that Bill, Jack, Harry, Susan, Alice, Cindy and others in the community will hold them accountable for their actions and attitudes.

Carrie has taken a leave from her job at the Quik Stop until she gets back on her feet. I don't know how long these arrangements will last, but for the time being she's in good hands. I don't know what all this will look like in the future, but God does, so brace yourselves.

Congratulations again,
Carter

> P.S. Minnie read the email and said, "Carter, you forgot the most important fact of all. I knew I should have married a fencepost instead of you!" We laughed! Then we played our famous game of "I know the answer and you don't." I asked for clues to the mystery fact, but she wouldn't help. She's relentless at this game! After reading through the email another two times it dawned on me: I failed to include the baby's name. Oh, well!

TO: CARTER
FROM: DARREN and CARRIE
SUBJECT: Let's talk about a wedding

Greetings to you, Mr. Carter!

Carrie wanted me to tell you how much she misses being at the ranch. I think she misses Minnie's country cooking and your unforgettable popcorn! (Don't forget to remind Minnie of her promise to keep us in cinnamon rolls, because we're just about out.) My friend Vanessa wonders why you aren't 400 pounds overweight after tasting one of them!

The cherry pies you sent down last Friday for our coffee house ministry were a fantastic hit. A couple of our gal leaders and one guy we call "Sally" (we razz him because he loves to cook) asked if Minnie would consider holding a little cooking class as part of the ministry's outreach program. Carter, maybe after the cooking class you could also teach how to rope cattle using some parking meters! We're thinking "evangelism."

Anyway, I just wanted to give you a little update since we haven't been in touch lately. Carrie's more beautiful than ever, in spite of her surgery and a little baby that keeps her occupied night and day. Her countenance just shines every time she looks into his little blue-colored eyes. She's a great mommy. I'm thankful we decided to follow her dad and mom's advice about getting married. They thought it would be better to wait until after the baby was born, get some pre-marital counseling, then plan a wedding. You know something? Carrie and I think the time has come to start counseling and planning. One of our elders at church is willing to handle most of the pre-marital counseling, provided you give him some help along the way. Would this be all right with you? It isn't because we don't want you to do it, but we're pretty stuck in downtown Denver until the baby is roadworthy. He's still so small that the doctors would like for us to protect him a bit from the elements. But don't worry, we can still counsel with you provided Minnie brings down more cherry pies and cinnamon rolls. Ha!

Carrie's parents are supportive of our beginning premarital counseling. We speak with them over the phone two or three times a week. We've just begun thinking about some options for the wedding. Carrie would like to have a small ceremony and Jenny would like the wedding somewhere close to their home if possible. She's checking with some churches about their wedding policies. Is this exciting or what?

Two questions for you. First, what do you think about all this? Secondly, would you be willing to officiate the wedding? While asking those questions, my knees are shaking a bit. Please email us what you think. But I need to bring you up to speed on one other thing before you make a final decision.

We attend a weekly Bible Study with our friends. We were talking about influential people in our lives and I was telling them about you. They wondered how we met you. Now *that* was a very interesting conversation.

For Carrie, the answer was pretty easy. For me, the answer was pretty embarrassing. It was difficult explaining our first encounter on your porch that painful day (literally) a few months ago. They understood by the end of my explanation that you're a no-nonsense type of guy when it comes to caring for those you love. However, I reminded them of how much I've come to respect you as a spiritual leader and the influence you've had on my life. Up to that very moment on your porch, I believed that Christian men were a bit like sissies. I don't want to be offensive, but that's the picture I had in my mind. I know now it's not true at all. Christian men are (or should be) principled, determined and protective. They are men of God's Word.

Anyway, I told our friends that I wanted to protect Carrie from all the shame and disgrace connected with us living together until we were formally married. They agreed and that's been the case since the baby was born. This whole discussion ended with my final announcement. Here's the good news! With Carrie sitting right next to me holding my son, I let them all know that I'd become a Christian.

Silence fell over the entire group and everyone looked as if they'd seen a flying saucer. Then there was clapping, cheering, hugs and tears as one by one they welcomed me into their fellowship as a brother in Christ. I wept, too. I was so thankful as I knelt down in front of Carrie and my son. I gave thanks to God for them, and for sending His beloved Son, Jesus Christ, into the world to save the likes of me. It was just like Luke 15 and the story of the prodigal son. Great joy and celebration followed my decision to receive Christ and repent of my evil ways.

All this happened because God simply chased me down. I was active in the street ministry, but only as a warm body. Everyone knew I wasn't a Christian but loved me anyway. But God set His everlasting love upon me and I was drawn to Him in simple faith. God used an old man who lives in a shelter in downtown Denver to finally knock me off my guard. He's around a lot and we've become a bit like friends if that's possible to understand. His story of personal destruction began when he, too, was a wild and unbelieving young man. God spoke directly to me out of the despair of this man's ruined life. I could see my future written in the wrinkles and scars on his wind-blistered face.

He was once married to his childhood sweetheart but became abusive, arrogant and unfaithful. What was a "marriage made in heaven" soon became a marriage lived in hell. They were divorced. He hasn't seen his two children for over 23 years. As I sat there on a bus bench, I couldn't help but think of "Old Carter" because you, too, have a wind-blistered face, a wife and children. You're pretty wild, too. But unlike my homeless friend, your life is marked with discipline, belief in God and submission to divine authority. I couldn't help but compare your two lives.

Then I remembered a tract I'd stuck in my jacket pocket after church last Sunday. John 1:12 was printed in bold red letters on the front: "But as many as received Him, to them He gave the right to become the children of God, even to those who believe in His name." Those words hit me square between the eyes. No question about it; I was a sinner in need of a Savior and became fearful of my life without the Creator. I recited the verse under my breath several times, then simply received Christ as my personal Savior and asked Him to make me His child and live His life through me.

So there you have the first chapter of my new life's story, Carter. Thanks for being my friend and teacher.

Finally, I want to throw out something for your so-called Parenting Co-op to think about. I've been reading the emails sent back and forth the past several months. My own story gives another angle to parenting.

You see, my parents (you met them at the hospital) are nice people but to a fault. When I was in middle and high school, they gave me just about everything I wanted. They were afraid that I'd explode in a fit of rage if they didn't. No question about it, I was a problem teenager with a lot of determination mixed with anger and frustration. My parents felt that the only way to avoid a conflict was to cave in. Rather than fixing our broken relationships, installing healthy boundaries and sticking with them, they quit parenting and became emotion managers.

Looking back now, I see that you don't build respect in your teenager by taking the path of least resistance or the hands-off approach. Kids need to hear what their parents think. They want the necessary structures to protect them. Sure, young people push for additional freedoms; but when a parent disconnects, it expresses a lack of love and care. My dad was a whole lot more involved when I was nine years old. When I became a teenager and wasn't quite so cooperative, Dad disconnected and got busier at work. Well, what does that say to a 13-year-old facing bodily changes, emotional struggles and girls? It says, "We used to be friends, but now I have other more important things to do."

I talk with a lot of the street kids at our coffee house ministry. I'm shocked at how alike our stories are. In most cases, the dad and mom are either disconnected, or angry and controlling. Teenagers want and need parents that are people of the Word of God—teaching, admonishing, correcting and guiding their children. They long for parents who are principled, involved, understanding, and available and who are willing to go through some tough times without either exploding or defecting.

Parents don't have to wave the white flag and surrender, or pull out bigger threats to demand compliance. Just because a kid becomes a teenager, don't quit parenting. Talk to your teenager. Understand what makes them tick. Be reasonable with your teenager and explain things carefully. Be the one person in their life that *doesn't* overreact to their emotional outbursts. Define loving boundaries, demonstrate respectful attitudes and model Christ-likeness in the midst of disagreements and stay the course. When the winds of disobedience and defiance blow hard, don't tuck tail and run. Again I say, stay the course. Trust me, it'll pay great dividends in the future.

Well, that's all I can say. I hope it makes sense. I'll probably see it differently when my little baby turns 13, and *we* start disagreeing. We'll be anxious to hear from you. Wedding bells are ringing, lights are flashing and I think I just got hit on the head with a falling star. Whoa! Life is good! Let us know what you think.

Your new brother and sister in Christ,
Darren and Carrie

TO: DARREN
FROM: CARTER and MINNIE
SUBJECT: Out of darkness, into light

Not often does it happen to Old Carter, but when I hear of someone who becomes a Christian, I'm speechless.

Darren, I thanked God this morning for the light that has entered your heart, driving the darkness out. I realized afresh that during the past months God has actively been pursuing you. You were running, but He runs faster! You were hiding, but He has a big flashlight! You were resisting, but He is stronger!

You were spiritually blind, but He gave you eyes to see! You were lost, but He has discovered you! You were impatient, but He was patient with you! You were indifferent, but He was deeply concerned! You hated yourself, but He loved you! You were spiritually sick, but He became your Physician! You were filled with anger, but He was full of kindness! You were indifferent, but He became the difference! You were filled with sadness, but He brought you joy! You were seeking life, but He gave you the abundant life! You had lost your way, but He became the way, the truth and the life! You wanted happiness, but He gave you contentment! You wanted to do whatever you wanted, but He gave you true freedom. You wanted to experience life, but He wanted you to experience HIM in your life. To God be all the glory!

Darren, always remember you didn't find Christ, He found you! You didn't pursue Him, He pursued you! You didn't come to Christ, He came to you! As you reflect on these things, thanksgiving will continue to grow in your heart. You'll never, ever conclude you were saved by your good works. Salvation is all about Christ, and nothing about us! Isn't that wonderful? Let's both be careful to never forget it!

Thanks for sharing your experience with us. It means so much to hear of our God's great salvation in your heart. Carrie must be thrilled as well. Just think of it! Your baby will grow up with a Christian father and mother in a home filled with God's love and forgiveness. Peace, gentleness, patience, self-control, kindness and all the other fruits of the Spirit will be the norm. Isn't that great?

Minnie sends her love to you as well. She wanted me to remind you to start *immediately* with regular Bible reading, meditation on the Word and prayer. The Bible reminds all Christians to be like newborn babes, to "long for the pure milk of the Word, so that by it you may grow." (1 Peter 2:2) Darren, you're a newborn baby Christian. You need the Word of God in order to grow in your faith and keep from evil (read Psalm 119:11). Follow Minnie's advice and get started on the right foot.

Give our love to Carrie and the baby.

Carter and Minnie

P.S. Darren and Carrie, I'd love to do your wedding and will participate gladly in your premarital counseling. Let's get on with the PARTY!!!

TO: CARTER
FROM: AJ and JENNY
SUBJECT: The good old "family reunion"

We were watching a movie last night that reminded us about our upcoming "family reunion." The movie was an old western. It's one you've probably watched at some point in time. You might have even ridden your horse in it when you were a young man back in the early 1900's. Just kidding!

The bad guys had burned down the poor helpless farmer's house, barn and blacksmith shop. Then these tough outlaws worked the defenseless father/husband over pretty good before heading to the saloon for a shot of whiskey. Of course, the good guy was "coming 'round the mountain," so help was on the way.

To make a long movie short, many friends and neighbors from all around gathered together one afternoon and had an old-fashioned barn raising and house building. When the good guy got tired of pounding nails, he decided it was time to go to town and pound the bad guys. That's when everything got real exciting. While their women were eating fried chicken and watermelon, the good guy and some of his friends got on their horses and headed to town to take on the bad guys. After 537 rounds of ammunition, the good guys claimed victory.

When it was all said and done, all the bottles of whiskey were destroyed by shotgun fire, every mirror in town was completely ruined and every piece of saloon furniture was either busted to pieces or had bullet holes in it. There wasn't a stock tank that held water and not a horse left in town when the story ended. Whoa!

Now a story like that will cause you to push out your chest and wish you lived 100 years ago. Men were men back then, and their watermelons looked better than ours! They never needed to reload their guns; they shot straighter and could run faster with bullet holes in their legs. Anyway, it's off to our email.

It's time for *our* reunion! The bad guy (namely me) has been dealt with, and our home has been rebuilt from the inside out. There'll be no ammunition at our reunion, no broken mirrors and no whiskey—just a lot of fun. Jenny and I want to personally invite you and Minnie to come join us on the 20th of November, which is the week before Thanksgiving. We'll make all the overnight arrangements at the local hotel for Friday and Saturday night if you'll just get here. We thought that everyone could come and spend the weekend celebrating.

We've written to Gerry and Sue and talked with Stu and Stacy, and they're all set to come. Troy and Tyler are so excited about Jenny coming back home, and so am I. Do you think they're tired of having soup for dinner every night? According to them, they just want to be a family again.

Carrie and Darren would like to come, but a great deal depends on the baby. It would be sad if they couldn't make it, but we'll understand and we'll just plan another party with them later. We've also invited some other people from our church. In addition, some friends I made while taking the anger management classes would like to come as well as some folks from Social Services. I think this whole event will really be helpful to these guys and gals who have marriage problems. I'd especially like for them to meet my spiritual support group. None of them have such a thing as a spiritual support group. Who knows, maybe we could get them to come with us to church sometime or maybe join our next EMAIL GROUP.

Here's a question for you. If you can come, would you be willing to do a ceremony uniting our family together? All of us would like to get off to a good start. We want to repeat our wedding vows and exchange new rings symbolizing our renewed relationship. Would you do this for us? I want the boys to stand with me, and Jenny would like for Carrie to stand with her if she can make it. If she can't, then Stacy said she'd be glad to.

We've discussed this with the boys, and they think it's a terrific idea. Each person could recite their commitment to the family and promise to work together as a family that loves each other. Afterward, we'll have dinner at a very nice restaurant across town. How's all this for a strange idea? Have you ever done a family unity ceremony? Will you? Please just let us know.

For now, we'll sign off. We just both happen to be over at Stu and Stacy's house for Bible study and took a moment to use their computer. We really need to get back to our Bible study friends and the refreshments.

Carter, we both love you and Minnie so much. Thanks for being such a vital part of our family these many months. I don't know where we'd be if it weren't for the folks in the Parenting Co-op.

With thankful hearts,
AJ

P.S. Following the fun and games, we're going on a five-day family vacation to Disneyland in California. It's the kids' fall break so we can have a few days just to ourselves to mess around. After that, it's back to the old grind with new intentions.

TO: CARTER
FROM: CARRIE
SUBJECT: A day late and a dollar short!

Wouldn't you know it? Dad and Mom beat me to the punch. They're going to get married to the same person for the second time before I can even get married to the first person the first time. It seems like I'm always a day late and a dollar short. Oh, well. There are plenty of other dates and times.

I was thinking about getting married shortly after the party in Texas. Darren and I discussed this with Dad and Mom, but they thought it would be a pretty tight schedule because of their trip to Disneyland following their reunion ceremony.

If we decide to have our wedding just after Thanksgiving in Colorado, would you be able to do the ceremony? I'd like to have the wedding in the park with all the fall colors. Doesn't that sound beautiful? I know Mom would like for us to get married down in Texas, but all our friends from the street ministry live here.

I'd like for my Mom to be in the wedding. Are moms ever bridesmaids? Are they ever the maid of honor? I don't know about these things. Maybe you could email us back and tell us. Thanks!

Changing subjects, our counseling has been absolutely wonderful. Who wouldn't want to get pre-marital counseling anyway? The man that's counseling us has great insight into how to be a biblical husband and wife, how to develop a godly marriage, how to communicate better with each other and how to manage finances.

Keeping ourselves sexually pure before marriage didn't happen for us early on. However, since we got back together it's a different story. Our counselor gave us reasons at our very first meeting to practice sexual purity. We've been sexually pure ever since we got back together. You made sure of that, Mr. Carter, right from the get-go. However, our counselor told us to make a covenant of purity to protect ourselves for the balance of our courtship.

After the doctor gave the baby a clean bill of health, Darren took us all out for an ice cream sundae to celebrate. Just going outside together was terrific! Anyway, around the table in the ice cream parlor, we vowed to stay pure until our wedding even if it isn't until next year. We made a chain of ice cream spoons as a reminder, and hung it from the rear view mirror in the "old clunker." The baby was a witness to the proceedings. So was God. (That's really scary!) We get so excited to learn more every time we get together for pre-marital counseling.

Enough for now. The baby's crying, and Darren says he refuses to nurse the baby. Go figure!!

Thanks for everything,
Carrie

TO: AJ and JENNY
FROM: CARTER
SUBJECT: A weekend from Heaven

You can bet Minnie and I are set for whatever you folks plan. We can hardly wait to share in the festivities! All of our hopes and dreams for your family are coming together. It's so exciting even my horse is jumping around in the corral and the pigs are rolling in the mud. God has certainly been busy, and our prayers are being answered. So let's get the party rolling!

Let me get this straight. The first weekend will be for the Family Reconciliation Celebration and renewing your vows in Texas. Then later, Darren and Carrie will get married in Colorado. (Hold on. Let me catch my breath. You know I'm not as young as I used to be.) Do I understand correctly that in between those two week ends you're going to *Disneyland* for a few days of R & R? You certainly know how to fill up a calendar in a hurry!

Whose idea was the Family Reconciliation Celebration, anyway? I really like it. After a family has gone through what you folks have experienced, a special ceremony followed by some heavy fellowship seems very appropriate.

Jenny, you must be very excited to return home. AJ, you've been growing like a weed. Stu has been so impressed with your progress with the boys. Frankly, you've become quite romantic again. Your special surprises for Jenny have demonstrated your selflessness. Loving your wife as Christ loved the church is certainly sacrificial/ servant leadership at it's best.

Jenny, your life just shouts with exciting changes. How your understanding has increased! Stacy says your countenance is brighter, and your skin even looks softer and more beautiful. Stu tells me you appear rested and relaxed. What a change a couple of months of personal reflection and discipleship can make! Right? Being the "helper" of your husband and a woman of spiritual determination pays great dividends.

I know AJ and the children can hardly wait. None of them can afford to lose any more weight! The time you spent living with Stu and Stacy has allowed both of you some extra time to learn about becoming a biblical family and rekindle your love for one another. You were going the wrong direction, but the controlled separation gave time for both of you to evaluate, grow your relationship with God, and forgive each other. Now you're implementing biblical principles for parenting, learning to control your emotions and healing from the many hurts sustained over the years.

It's been so exciting for Minnie and me to watch your transition. You've grown not only as parents, but also as partners!

I've already chosen a passage of Scripture to use at the celebration. Since you'll have many of your friends there, I'd like to suggest that you invite them to share some words of encouragement during the reunion service. What would you think about that? Also, maybe we could have all the people from the Parenting Co-op write a personal email explaining how the Co-op has affected them and what they've learned about parenting as a result. How does that sound for a Friday evening? Whoa! I'm getting a bit emotional. I sure hope Darren, Carrie and the baby can come. That would be so exciting, wouldn't it?

Then comes Saturday evening and the renewal of the wedding vows. Now you're talking! Every family unit is built upon strong marriage vows. You forgot yours many years ago so it wouldn't hurt to recite them again, especially after the controlled separation.

I'm sending a copy of this email to Darren and Carrie because this next paragraph might just apply to them as well. They want to get married a couple of weeks later. But Minnie and I were wondering, why not have their wedding Sunday afternoon on the same weekend down in Texas? Carrie wants Jenny to be in her wedding. You want their wedding down in Texas so your family and friends can attend. Since we're all down there anyway, why not "kill three birds with one stone?" Sunday would be Darren and Carrie's day, Saturday would be AJ and Jenny's day, and Friday afternoon and evening would be the whole family's day. What do you think?

I'd be honored to do all three ceremonies no matter where they're held, so count us in. Please understand this is only a suggestion. Maybe the four of you could discuss this and get back to us.

You know what's impressive to Minnie and me? Your resolve to be a loving family is lived out in the way you're cooperating with each other over the reunion and wedding plans. So often families argue and fight over the most happy events because they're thinking only of themselves. The new pattern for your family is to "regard one another as more important than yourselves; do not merely look out for your own personal interests, but also for the interests of others" (Philippians 2:3,4).

It really does work better when the Spirit of Christ is present, doesn't it?

Warmly in Christ,
Carter

cc: Darren and Carrie

TO: CARTER, MINNIE and EVERYONE
IN THE PARENTING CO-OP
FROM: JENNY and CARRIE
SUBJECT: "Two are better than one"

Like a handprint in fresh cement, so our plans have been set in place. We've decided to combine everything into one gigantic week-end blowout. We're both very excited, and look forward to the festivities coming up on the weekend of November 21, 22 and 23 just prior to Thanksgiving week. How does that date strike you? Rather than imposing on everyone's Thanksgiving celebration with their own families, we thought that the weekend before would work nicely.

Carter's suggestion of doing all three ceremonies the same weekend made a lot of sense. Finally, he had a sensible idea! So here's a "Carterised" itinerary:

- Friday the 21st around 6 PM, we'll meet at AJ and Jenny's house for a catered meal from the Road Kill Barbecue House. Afterward, we'll have the Reconciliation Celebration in the backyard. Carter will lead the service opening with prayer and share something from the Bible. Then AJ would like to say something to everyone. Following that, we'd like to open it up to personal comments and expressions of love from everyone. This is when we'd like to read the emails from everyone in the Parenting Co-op.

- Saturday the 22nd, AJ and Jenny will renew their vows. We'll start around 5 PM with some pre-dinner hors d'oeuvres and beverages at Stu and Stacy's home, followed by dinner at the restaurant where AJ proposed to me on the outskirts of town. We'd like for all the Parenting Co-op people to join with us for this intimate evening. Carter will do the service. We'll renew our vows at about 8 PM down at the beach, with beach lanterns brightly burning.

- Sunday the 23rd, Darren and Carrie will have their wedding at 6 PM sharp. Carter will perform the service. I would suspect about 75 people to be in attendance.

So there you have it. We'll see you all then. Travel safely and pray that everything will go smooth as silk (or as Carter says, "smoooooooth as a baby's back side"). It seems like we're stuffing a lot into a weekend, but it'll be the time of our lives. Talk about making a memory; this is making a big one!

Thanks for what you've all done for our family. We want to celebrate each of you over this weekend, as well. God bless!

Jenny and Carrie

P.S. Carter, do you have a suit or anything other than jeans and boots? Well then, wear it!

DARREN: Carter, thanks for meeting me online tonight. When I left the message on your voice mail, I was really stressed out. I was hopeful you'd be available because I could sure use some guidance.

CARTER: I can't imagine why. You're 18 years old, impulsive, a new Christian, father of a new baby and soon to be married. Why would you need guidance? Darren, you know I'm only teasing you. In fact, your request is very biblical. Did you know that? In the book of Proverbs we're told that there is wisdom in many counselors. So it's always healthy to get other opinions before making critical decisions. Let's get started.

DARREN: These past several months have been a real ride! Looking back, I can't believe what's gone on. I went from simply dating Carrie to running away with her in about three months. When we found out she was pregnant, I went from total excitement to incredible fear in about 20 minutes. Then I went from caring a great deal about her to abusing her physically and emotionally. It wasn't very long before I began feeling pretty guilty about the whole thing.

Then, I went from deep sadness and loss to the excitement of getting her back. Life seemed as if it was turning around. We were back dating once again, only this time in Colorado. Joy came back into our relationship and before you knew it, BINGO, the baby was born. To top it all off, I'm a new Christian. Now a wedding is right around the corner, and I'm scared to death. It seems as if everything is moving so fast, I can't catch my breath. I've gone along with the wedding plans because I don't want to hurt Carrie again. Yet I'm overwhelmed with the responsibility of it all. Carter, I can't believe I'm even writing this to you.

CARTER: Whoa, big fella! You're going so fast I need some heart medicine. Give me just a few minutes to digest what you're writing. I'll be right back!

Now I've got my heart medicine in hand: ice cold Pepsi and some chips on the side to help me think more clearly. So carry on, my friend.

DARREN: As I was saying, I'm overwhelmed with all of this. The baby, medical bills, the wedding, a place to live, a rather bumpy beginning and no consistent income give me a very insecure feeling. I feel like I have a grapefruit right in the middle of my stomach. I'm a father, and I don't even have the foggiest idea how I'm going to provide for my family. I bring in a little income but by the time I pay rent and pick up a few groceries, there's not a lot left. There's no way I can afford health insurance and all the other expenses related to family life. I don't mind helping with the street ministry, but I sure as heck don't want Carrie and the baby to end up on the street literally.

CARTER: What is it you're trying to tell me? Do you want to change jobs, or are you looking for a cheaper apartment? Maybe you're asking me for guidance about a family budget. Why don't you just tell me what this is all about?

DARREN: Actually Carter, I'm second guessing my decision to marry Carrie. I just don't know if I'm ready. Carter, please don't misunderstand what I'm writing. It's not that I don't love Carrie and the baby, but the timing seems to be all wrong. I feel too much pressure to move forward. Can you understand what I'm thinking?

CARTER: I understand perfectly. Young man, you're a new Christian and I'm curious about what you think God would want you to do. Have you been praying and seeking direction from Him? Have you been reading your Bible searching for divine guidance?

DARREN: You know something, I've actually been doing all three. Part of my answer from the Lord was to call you. How do you like that?

CARTER: I'm not sure! Anyway, God will give you the guidance you need even if it comes from an old rancher like me. Tell me one other thing. Have you mentioned anything to Carrie about this?

DARREN: No, I haven't. I'm so afraid of what it will do to her. It would be so easily misunderstood and it will break her heart. I promised AJ and Jenny that I would never hurt her again and I meant it, but something isn't right about what we're doing. Frankly, I don't think either one of us is ready for marriage. We've known each other less than a year.

CARTER: Darren, I think God is working in your heart and causing you to think more responsibly than ever before. When we pray, sometimes God answers "yes," other times "no," and still other times "wait." Which answer do you think God is giving you?

DARREN: I think He's telling us to wait. As I told you, I still love Carrie and I want us to be a family. But getting married now is too dangerous for our relationship. Maybe if we waited until next summer things would feel very different. I could find a better career-type job and lay aside some money for a better place to live. There's not much future in staining furniture. Maybe I could even get some benefits that would include medical insurance for my family.

CARTER: Now you've got me thinking about a very important biblical principal. The great apostle Paul tells us in 1 Timothy 5:8, "If anyone does not provide for his own, and especially for those of his household, he has denied the faith and is worse than an unbeliever." Darren, you must be able to provide for your family. If that's not possible now, then to wait is a wise move on your part. If your relationship with Carrie is of the Lord, then waiting won't end it but rather protect it. What would be wrong with staying in your separate living situations, growing your relationship with Carrie, loving the baby, growing spiritually together, locating a better job, gaining some financial independence and waiting until next year to get married? What do you think?

DARREN: That's what I'm asking you.

CARTER: Then my answer to my question is there's nothing wrong with waiting. Darren, you're a young man. In 1 Timothy 4:12, Paul gives you some healthy advice: "Let no one look down on your youthfulness, but rather in speech, conduct, love, faith and purity, show yourself an example of those who believe." Waiting and trusting God with your family is a sign of maturity. I believe God will honor that in the future.

Carrie will also need to trust God, and suffer through the disappointment. She may question whether you love her at all, but like the passage says—through your speech, conduct, love, purity and faith you'll be an example she can follow. Don't you think it's about time you told Carrie and her dad and mom?

DARREN: I suppose so. I just hate doing it. Do you have any ideas about how I should go about it? Maybe I should write a letter. What do you think?

CARTER: Well my friend, I need to get Minnie's input on that question. Hold on a second and I'll be right back. Hang on.

Minnie thinks that a letter is too cold and distant. She thinks you should take Carrie and the baby out for a special dinner and begin your evening by giving her a gift that will speak of your love for her and your sincerity. Something like a necklace or an engagement ring, if you haven't done that yet, assuring her that you want to do things right this time. She should feel your decision is protecting something you love, not "jumping ship" politely. Darren, you need to communicate to her that your decision is about *timing* and not about her and the baby. She needs to understand that this is what true spiritual leadership is all about for her husband-to-be. While there might be shock and even despair, waiting is safer for everyone.

DARREN: Would you be willing to support my decision with Carrie? I don't want to lose her and my baby. Could I tell her that we discussed this before I talked to her? Would Minnie be available as well to talk with her? What should I do about AJ and Jenny?

CARTER: Darren, you have our complete support and we're happy to help. We'd even be glad to visit with AJ and Jenny after you break the news to them. After you tell Carrie, maybe both of you could call them. I really believe that they'll agree with your decision. In fact, I think they'll appreciate your love for their daughter as expressed in your tough decision.

DARREN: All right, Carter. I'm moving forward with Carrie. Please pray for both of us as we go through this mess. Thanks for helping me, and we'll see what happens.

CARTER: Well my young friend, we serve a great God and He will be your strength. I'll be praying for you. Minnie wants me to remind you to be gentle, understanding and loving. Carrie might let off some steam. That might be hard for you to accept, but just keep pressing forward to next summer. We'll talk soon. Bye for now.

TO: CARRIE
FROM: CARTER and MINNIE
and THE PARENTING CO-OP
SUBJECT: When God shuts the door,
He opens the window

Carrie, we all love you and know that Darren's decision must be very disappointing to you. I was thinking of a beautiful verse of scripture that has often given me a different perspective when I've faced disappointing events in my own life. 1 Thessalonians 5:18 says, "In everything give thanks; for this is God's will for you in Christ Jesus."

Carrie, you need to see that changing the wedding date is according to God's will for your life. Then you can look at this in the spirit of thanksgiving, and your disappointment will vanish. Rejoice in the fact that God has a plan for you life that is bigger than your momentary disappointments!

Each of us in the Parenting Co-op wanted to express our love to you in this email so I'm forwarding it to each of them for their loving encouragement.

From Stu and Stacy:
Hi Carrie, it's Stu and Stacy. We received this "love email" from Carter and Minnie and we'll forward it to other members of the Co-op. We heard about Darren's decision to wait on the wedding. That must have been difficult to hear. By accident, I met your mom at the grocery store. She told me about your phone call to her and AJ explaining what happened. We wanted to contact you because we understand so well the sad and disappointing side of life. You

remember that my husband died and left me alone. But now God has worked in my life to bring new joy, excitement and renewal.

When a door shuts, God often opens a window. God gave me a wonderful husband and a loving father to my children. Carrie, it's so easy to focus on the disappointment that you lose track of the anticipation and the excitement of the future. Maybe God wants you to take a deep breath, slow down and enjoy a meaningful engagement with Darren instead of going full speed into matrimony. Stu wants to remind you that marriage is something you prepare for, not something you hastily jump into. So what if you have a baby? You can still take some time to prepare your heart and character for marriage. Hang in there. We love you.

Stu and Stacy

From Gerry and Sue:
Carrie, it's Uncle Gerry and Auntie Sue. We're so proud of you. You are a beautiful young lady with the cutest little baby. Carrie, the baby isn't going to know the difference between a November wedding and a summer wedding. Don't let your concern for the little baby push you into a premature wedding date. You and Darren owe it to yourselves to go slow and be confident in your decisions. To hurry into marriage is foolish. What has happened has happened, and an early wedding won't change that. You and Darren need time to love each other as single people before you love each other as a married couple.

Darren needs to demonstrate his love for you through sexual purity, patience, kindness and self-control. His acceptance of Christ needs a time of testing, and your faith in Christ needs a time of trusting. Why not sit back and enjoy the ride until summer? We love you a bunch!

Uncle Gerry and Auntie Sue

From AJ and Jenny:

Carrie, our weekend celebration will be different than we had planned but, together, we can work toward a new wedding celebration *whenever*. Sweetheart, Mom and I don't want you to make some of the same mistakes we have. Our life is a testimony of impatience, self-will and marital failure. Yes, we are doing much better. But we made so many mistakes in the beginning of our relationship. We rushed into marriage without considering the serious consequences and the unbelievable commitment necessary to sustain it and make it work. You don't want to hurt the prospects of a healthy marriage by acting prematurely. Remember, an unhealthy marriage will produce unhealthy parenting practices.

Darren was wonderful over the phone with us. He specifically wanted us to know that this was about timing, not about whether he did or didn't love you. We actually agree with his decision. A little more time will allow both you and Darren to drive the roots of your life together deeper into the soil of your love. Then when the winds of marriage blow and the rain and snow seek to destroy your family, it will stand firm and tall. Don't forget that we love you. We're sorry we haven't been a very good model for you to follow. With God's help, we're certainly going to give building healthy relationships a try.

Remember one thing, Carrie. The controlled separation between Mother and I actually saved our marriage, not destroyed it. A little separation between you and Darren for a while won't hurt you either. Use this time for growth and discipleship.

Love always,
Dad and Mom

Carrie, your dad and mom sent the email back to us by mistake so we'll add just a footnote to it and send it on to you.

Dearest Carrie, Minnie and I love both you and Darren a great deal. We're so thankful for his loving leadership. Something tells me this young man is going to be a great husband and father in the future. But for now he needs time to digest all that's been happening. Don't focus all your attention on yourself and the disappointment you feel. Remember, it's not very easy for Darren to protect his family either. The decision he made came with a great deal of concern for you and the baby. Don't lose sight of that as you get control of your emotions. He does love you a lot.

Darren realizes that he has taken advantage of you and deprived you of a meaningful courtship and proper love. A shotgun wedding isn't the answer to anything. He wants to make it up to you by doing the right thing this time around.

Before we sign off, Minnie wants to say a couple of things so I'm turning the keyboard over to her.

What's wrong with you, girl? Any time you can put off marriage, take advantage of it! Darren needs more time to learn how to do the laundry, iron his shirts, do the dishes and cook. You're still recovering from having a baby. Think "rest and relaxation" while Darren catches up on the household chores. Now you're talking, girl! Trust me. You don't want a Carter on your hands. We both love you!

Carter and Minnie

TO: PARENTING CO-OP
FROM: GERRY
SUBJECT: "Hot time in the old town"

Sue and I are back in Wyoming and we just can't get the weekend off our minds.

I can tell you one thing; this was truly a weekend to remember. Will we ever forget AJ and Jenny's day for the Reconciliation Celebration? From the limo AJ hired to bring Jenny home to their reunion with all their children (and grandchild) in the driveway, to AJ's public announcement before us, his friends, his anger management group and—best of all—his family that he had become a Christian, it was a powerful day. Hearing the commitments of Troy, Carrie, Tyler, Jenny and AJ to be a strong family in the power of Christ was a perfect ending.

Then the renewal of AJ and Jenny's vows on the beach the next evening. What a beautiful time after a great dinner—warm sand between our toes and a service by torchlight. Words of promise and hope out of AJ and Jenny that we'd have never expected just a few months ago. What a demonstration of God's power to renew and restore shattered relationships! And what a surprise to see Darren and the gang from the Street Ministry show up at the end of the service! When all those young people made a human circle around Darren, Carrie and the baby, AJ and Jenny, Troy and Tyler, I couldn't hold back the tears, but I wasn't alone either. It was one of the most touching moments I've ever witnessed. One by one they started praying for each of them. Some of the guys and gals wept tears of joy while asking God to bless Darren and Carrie.

Others thanked God for holding AJ and Jenny's marriage together. Still others praised God for protecting Tyler and Troy during the separation time.

What went through your mind when Carrie, Darren and the baby walked down the beach into the darkness? Personally, I'm so glad they decided to postpone their wedding. A more glorious day awaits them.

Carter, just when I think you can barely pull your boots on the proper feet, you orchestrate something amazing. Things look good for Carrie and Darren, too, don't they?

So we're home, and "the kids" are in Disneyland. Who would have guessed it? A weekend to remember, but there's one thing that remains to be shared. I have eight emails in my possession that were read at the Reconciliation Ceremony. These were a real hit to all the visitors from Social Services, AJ's anger management team and other friends. I want you to have a copy of them so you can all benefit from what the others have learned about parenting and family life over the past several months. They were written by our friends in the Parenting Co-op. I hope you enjoy reading them. I'll send them in one final email tomorrow.

With love,
Gerry

TO: THE PARENTING CO-OP
FROM: GERRY
SUBJECT: Eight emails from the Parenting Co-op
participants

Rather than sending eight separate emails, I am including all of them in this email for your personal review. They provide a summary of some of the lessons we've learned over the past months. I know all of us have benefited from this experience with AJ and Jenny. Now some of those insights are in print through this email. Here we go!

TO: THE PARENTING CO-OP
FROM: DARREN
SUBJECT: When the going gets tough,
the tough get going

As one of the youngest participants in the Parenting Co-op, I want to offer this little piece of insight. Proverbs 29:15 says, "The rod and reproof give wisdom, but a child who gets his own way brings shame to his mother."

I've learned that parenting can be a very, very difficult proposition. It must become wearisome over time, especially if your kids are like me. Many parents like my own quit fighting. They just give in to a complaining, angry child. They desert the child. They give in to anything and everything he or she wants.

My parents probably didn't know what to do with me, so they just caved in and let me do as I pleased. I felt they didn't care about me. Is it any wonder that I disconnected from them?

My recommendation is for parents to stay involved (Proverbs 13:24). Even when your children get older, grow your parenting skills. Be intentional. Give direction. Offer counsel. Demonstrate your love by setting limits if necessary, but don't let them figure out life on their own. It's a shame, but Carter was the first one who set things straight for me on his porch some months ago (Proverbs 15:5). He was the only person who said "NO!" and meant it. In doing so, he let me know he cared about Minnie, Carrie and eventually me.

Actually, I want to speak on behalf of those in our street ministry. They make a very good observation about parenting. It's simply this. Parents need to train their child's freedom. In other words, teach them to make wise decisions by allowing them to make some personal choices along the way. Start the process when they're young and grow their independence as their thinking matures. These street kids complain that their parents never let them make decisions. They were constantly under the thumb of their parents and everything needed to be done accordingly. It drove them to rebellion because their choices were never validated and independent thinking was never encouraged. It's something to consider.

Thanks, Carter! And thanks to all of you for loving me.

Darren

TO: THE PARENTING CO-OP
FROM: CARRIE
SUBJECT: Proverbs 15:1: "A gentle answer
turns away wrath…"

The Bible verse I quoted above goes on to say, "…but a harsh word stirs up anger." A little later in the same chapter, verse 4, it says, "A soothing tongue is a tree of life, but perversion in it crushes the spirit."

I'm a new mother and so my advice hasn't been tested with time. However, I've learned how *bad* parents talk to their children. It's summarized in the verses above. My dad and mom (AJ and Jenny) have encouraged me to be honest with you and share their failings in order to make my point.

My point is this. Good parents watch their tongues. They don't let abusive language slip out of their mouths. The Bible reminds parents in Colossians 4:6 to "Let your speech always be with grace, as though seasoned with salt." I've learned that in order to teach, guide, discipline or give advice, a parent must control their tongue and their anger. Screaming and yelling (or barking and biting) don't work very well with children. Our friends at the Street Ministry see their parents not as loving, kind parents but instead as raving maniacs who can't control their mouths.

I want to guide our little baby following the advice of Proverbs 15:1-4. There should be a plaque made with these verses inscribed on it and given to every parent the moment their first child is born. Thanks, Dad and Mom, for being willing to change the way you talk to your children. I forgive you. Let's learn together from these emails.

Love you all, and thanks for accepting Darren and me into your Parenting Co-op.

Carrie

TO: THE PARENTING CO-OP
FROM: GERRY
SUBJECT: The parent as teacher

Since we started the Parenting Co-op, I've been more aware of the need for fathers to be teachers in the home. Early on, I noticed how I let Sue do almost all of the teaching while I massaged the TV remote or the keyboard on my computer. She was the one to read the children stories. She handled the potty training. She showed them how to make peanut butter and jelly sandwiches. She taught them Bible stories.

Carter emailed us about a passage in Deuteronomy 6:1-9 that deals specifically with the subject of being a teacher of your children. The great Shema (verse 4: "Hear, O Israel! The Lord is our God, the Lord is one!"), which became Judaism's basic confession of faith, was to be recited morning and night. Parents were charged to ingest the Shema into their lives, and then to consistently and persistently teach it to their children. The parent was to be the primary teacher, not the Rabbi or any other substitute.

Recently, this reality has been indelibly impressed upon my mind. Fathers are especially weak in this area. I was no exception. I was willing for Sue to do all the teaching. However, I see the urgency of my taking up a teaching role with my children.

It's unacceptable for me to find or allow a surrogate teacher to teach my children in my absence. Yes, there will be school teachers, Sunday school teachers and others, but they should enhance my primary teaching responsibility, never be a substitute for it.

This has been a life-changing lesson I've learned over the past months. It's exciting to see how it's already impacting my children.

Carter, thanks for calling this to my attention. I love you all very much. Let's keep in touch!

Gerry

TO: THE PARENTING CO-OP
FROM: SUE
SUBJECT: Discipline "to the child" or "for the child"?

When we were asked to provide an email for the Reconciliation Celebration, my decision regarding what I would say was a very simple matter. Why? It's because my discipline skills have been almost non-existent.

Disciplining the children was something I did "to the child" with the hope of getting them under control and out of my hair. While I've been reading the emails from Carter, something has constantly stood out. Discipline is something I should be doing "for my child," and that's a whole lot different than what I've been doing "to my child." Discipline is something that parents do *for* a child so they might learn to live life skillfully with discernment and an understanding of God. To merely lash out at a child in careless anger is unacceptable.

Proper discipline requires careful strategy and initiative. First, parents must accept the responsibility to discipline their children, and then strategically initiate **effective** and **healthy** forms of correction for their child's best interest. We must also determine what type of discipline effectively reaches our parenting goals, rather than using any form of discipline that accomplishes nothing except irritating the child (and giving everyone else a headache).

Furthermore, discipline must fit the child, not the event. A good parent knows and understands what discipline will work for each of their children. Discipline isn't a one-size-fits-all procedure. Effective discipline is specifically tailored to fit one child. Therefore, "KNOW YOUR CHILD" and discipline correctly.

I've begun to see discipline as something very exciting and challenging, and not something I just have to do because I have to do it. Discipline has become the means of building character and spiritual strength in my children, not just the means whereby my children fear me and reluctantly obey me. For the first time, I see the connection between discipline and our training objectives.

I hope my insights will be helpful to everyone in the Parenting Co-op. Minnie, thanks for sharing your personal struggles with me. Now I don't feel so alone.

Love you all,
Sue

———————————————————————————————

TO: THE PARENTING CO-OP
FROM: STACY
SUBJECT: The friendship factor

Last year on our volleyball team, our team captain said that we played together "like a hand in glove." That meant we encouraged each other, sacrificed for each other and helped each other. We worked together as a team. This email is a hand in glove message.

First and foremost, I want to thank all of you for your friendship. Sharing the load of parenting together has been a real help to me. You have encouraged me, sacrificed your time and effort for me and have helped me understand how to be a better parent.

I feel so sorry for all the parents out there going it alone. While they try to do their very best, they often lack support and creativity from their friends. When I've had concerns about my children, you were just an email away. Besides that, I felt your loving pressure and accountability upon me to improve my parenting skills. You've all held me accountable for my impatience and irritability. One of the most important things I've learned over the past several months is the need for friends while parenting.

Secondly, I've learned that there are three A's to successful parenting: ATTENTION, APPROVAL and AFFECTION. My children need all three desperately. They want me to pay **attention** to them and not be distracted with a thousand other things. They want me to look them in the eye and not ignore what they're saying. Eye contact, I've found, is very important to my children. They don't like it when I talk to them while I'm preoccupied with something else.

They also need me to say, "Well done!" more often. **Approval** seems to be the backbone of a successful parenting style. Showing my approval creatively, too, is so much more effective than just saying "Nice job." If I do something unusual (write a note, buy a small gift at the store, or pass out on the grass) it drives the message of approval home because I've gone out of my way to make the point.

Finally, what child doesn't need **affection**? A hug is always nice, but why not develop some new ways to express your affection? Special privileges, special drinks, special cereal for breakfast, or a special outing with Mom have certainly worked well for my children. My mom expressed her affection by using a special plate at the supper table. It came out of the cupboard only when one of the kids needed some special affection. Get this! Sometimes Mom would put the special plate in front of the child that had been the most disobedient. She felt that was the time a child needed the greatest demonstration of affection.

Now Stu and I work together with our children like a hand in glove. I've learned so much from all of you. Thanks again for your friendship.

Stacy

TO: THE PARENTING CO-OP
FROM: STU
SUBJECT: Time-release parenting

I guess the lesson I've learned revolves around this idea of "time-release parenting." The thought came to me after reading once again Proverbs 22:6: "Train up a child in the way he should go: and when he is old, he will not depart from it."

Parenting takes time. It doesn't happen overnight, nor do children shape up after one week of parental consistency. The Parenting Co-op has been emailing back and forth for many months. While the emails have been very helpful in our parenting, I would love to see better and faster results from my parenting.

When it comes right down to it, I prefer parenting to be like a 50-yard dash instead of a 26-mile marathon. What I've learned is that day after day, I must continue to teach, train, love and discipline my children knowing full well that many of the results of parenting are yet to come. Yes, the parenting process is a slow process but consistency will pay great dividends in the future.

Let me illustrate a bit. There are medications that are time-release. The doctors will use those medications to treat you now but there is a time-release factor that allows the medicine to release its ingredients at intervals over a longer period of time, not all at once. So it is with parenting. Much of our parenting will show up later in the lives of our children. We parent today, but there is a time-release factor that shows up later in the lives of our kids. There's a scary side to this as well. If I don't parent properly today, then very negative attitudes and actions as well will show up later in my children.

My point is this: don't become discouraged if you don't see results immediately. Your parenting will kick in sometime out in the distant future. Just stay the course! Keep parenting!

Being involved with other families at my work has made me so appreciative of your involvement with me. Thanks for taking Stacy and me under your wings!

Stu

P.S. Don't you feel sorry for those parents who aren't a part of a PARENTING CO-OP?

TO: THE PARENTING CO-OP
FROM: AJ
SUBJECT: Relationship or Technique?

By now you surely know the answer to my question. Relationship is everything!

Among parents, so much emphasis is directed toward technique (aka behavior modification). "Do this or that, this way or that way, and this will be the result!" Hogwash! "When you do this, be sure *not* to do that or this could happen to whomever, whenever." Hogwash again! All of this technique business has a place in the subject of parenting, but not to the exclusion of RELATIONSHIP.

You know my past history. I was an abusive husband and father. Both my wife and children grew to hate me. My indifference and lack of affection for my family eventually blew up right in my face, and I found myself emotionally destitute. My self-centered ways finally caught up with me, and my family was gone.

You're also aware of how we got back on track. Was it because of the controlled separation, or playing more basketball with the boys? Was it because Jenny and I went out for dinner more often? Was it because I didn't say hurtful things to my family anymore, and didn't pound my fist and demand my own way? Yes, it was those things—but not entirely.

Always remember, you can do the right things but still not have right relationships. Did you get that? You can be a family administrator or taskmaster, but not have meaningful relationships with family members. My family is different today because I understood what I had lost in the first place. I was alone and was without relationships with my family.

I remember crying early on that my daughter didn't even care if I existed, and my sons wanted nothing to do with me. Jenny just wanted out period! I coveted the relationships you had with your families. Carter, I read about your hunting experiences with your boys in *OOPS! I Forgot My Wife*. It was more that just hunting together. You actually loved being together. I also wanted what you enjoy with Minnie and your daughters. You laugh together, tease each other, and go to church together. I wanted that with my family. It all seemed so far away.

Thank God for helping me see this biblical principle of relationship, first with Jesus Christ and then with my family! Yes, we did do basketball but there was a hidden agenda. I wanted a relationship with my boys. The same has been true of Jenny and Carrie. I want them to love and respect me not just because I do the right things, but because they *enjoy* a loving relationship with me.

Well, that's the lesson I learned over the past several months. Hope it helps keep us all on the track of building relationships! Thanks to all of you for being patient in the process.

AJ

TO: THE PARENTING CO-OP
FROM: JENNY
SUBJECT: Loving my children's father

I don't have a lot to say because the lesson I've learned is very simple: parenting should be in addition to your marital responsibility.

I made my children substitute recipients of my affection for AJ. I built my life around them. The children were always there, and if AJ didn't pay attention to me then the children would. I could care for them. Even when AJ was uninvolved and distant, my emotional needs could be met other ways—namely, through the children.

Don't allow your children to stand between you and your husband, or you're likely to have problems in your marriage. Don't attempt to fix those problems by directing all your time and energy toward the children. It won't work! You must face your marriage problems and get help ASAP.

When a wife focuses only on her children, the marriage erodes away like a sandcastle on the beach. Just look at where AJ and I were. But you say, "My husband doesn't think there's a problem!" Well then, it's time for you to read *OOPS, I Forgot My Wife!* and then give it to your husband. Be prepared to act on your marriage problems, not just talk about them.

Remember, when I returned home, I returned to AJ first and my children second. Pray for me that I keep it that way.

Thanks for being there for us. I love you all very much.

Jenny

TO: THE PARENTING CO-OP
FROM: MINNIE
SUBJECT: Psalm 127:1

Did you read Psalm 127:1? I'll do it for you. "Except the Lord build the house, they labor in vain that build it: except the Lord keep the city, the watchman waketh but in vain." (KJV)

This is the lesson I've learned while sharing in the Parenting Co-op. From the very beginning you could see God going to work on each of our families. How futile it is for us to believe that we can parent successfully in and of ourselves! How outrageous is that kind of thinking? Left to myself, I can't even take care of me, let alone Old Carter! I can't manage my own life, let alone my children. Yes, all my children are grown and out of the house except Carter. (Ha!) However, even when they were in the house, I couldn't possibly protect them, guide them, and teach them without God running the interference.

Behind our feeble parenting there will always be God who makes the difference in our children. His Word instructs us, His Holy Spirit holds us accountable, His Son died to remove our failures as parents and God Himself has the ultimate say in how it all turns out. This is true, my friends! Unless the Lord builds His life into your children, your parental labors are in vain. Hence, your personal spiritual condition is extremely important. God hears the prayers of parents. God wants to bless our families, if we'll only ask Him to. See 1 Peter 3:7 about how to avoid a hindered prayer life.

I've learned over many more years than I care to admit that parenting isn't something you do on your own. God is your eternal partner in parenting your children. He will give you the creativity, patience, wisdom and direction necessary if you'll only ask Him. Don't go it alone!

One final comment! I've learned once again how important it is for older women like me to teach younger women like you. The Bible tells women like me in Titus 2:4, 5 to teach the younger women "to be sober, **to love their husbands, to love their children,** to be discreet, chaste, **keepers at home,** good, obedient to their own husbands, that the word of God be not blasphemed." (KJV) I've been trying to do that the last several months. So now I have a personal investment in each of you.

The time has come. Carter and I are passing the baton and getting out of the way so you can take over the Parenting Co-op and minister to others. But I'll always be available as your loving mentor. On with it, ladies! I love you all very much.

Minnie

TO: THE PARENTING CO-OP
FROM: CARTER
SUBJECT: What's for dinner?

Not chicken, I can tell you that!

Last night I walked down to the barn around 10:30 PM to say good night to my barn kitties, and my chickens were having a tizzy. I thought it strange at that time of night because they should have been roosting and sound asleep. I went into the hen house to see what the heck was going on with my egg-laying girlfriends. To my surprise, up from behind my feeding trough stood a big raccoon on his back legs with feathers hanging out of his mouth as if to say, "You're late for dinner, old man!"

I took off on a dead run for the house to retrieve my 12-gauge shotgun so I could defend the rights of my poor sleeping chickens to have an uninterrupted night's rest without getting their heads chewed off. I grabbed my gun, a handful of shells and a heavy-duty spotlight so I could give one raccoon a lesson on eating etiquette.

Using my spotlight on the way down to the barn, I spotted the rascal coon just outside the chicken yard. He must have heard my threats as I ran up to the house and decided he better cut bait and run. I stopped to chamber a shell while the raccoon continued to make faces at me. He was so cute! In the process of all the excitement the gun jammed, and I think I heard the rascal coon laugh as he walked out into the night and over the hill.

"What an idiot!" I thought to myself. "I should have been more prepared for action."

Well, my young friends, this is the lesson I've learned. Parents had better be prepared for action. If you want to be an "honored parent" (Proverbs 31:8) and want your children to rise up and call you blessed, then you need to be prepared for action as a parent. Personally, you must be a growing parent (not only around the waist, but in your heart and character). You should be striving every day to be more biblical, more patient, more informed, more talkative, more interesting, more humorous, more self-controlled, more spiritual, more involved, more, more, more everything. Your relationship with God should be growing at an outrageous pace. You should be excelling in creative parenting ideas because you're reading books and listening to tapes. You can learn a lot from others can't you? We've proved that with the Parenting Co-op. Right?

When your child is in distress and is crying out for help, it's a horrible thing that you don't even know there's trouble in the chicken house because you're not tuned in to the needs of your children. When you must guide or rescue your children, it's an awful feeling when your gun jams because you weren't prepared for action. When your children are being "eaten alive" by the villains and you have no shells to fire in your gun because you're unprepared, that's a major problem. To make matters worse, if you don't even have a spotlight bright enough to shine into the darkness, then you ought to be ashamed of yourself.

My counsel? Get prepared for action, you sorry bunch of slackers. Your kids are counting on you to be prepared. So don't forget it!

Love you all, and stay in touch with Minnie and me because you never know what's just around the corner.

Carter

— —

Well, there you have it my friends. This is the conclusion of a journey that's brought Sue and me much joy. I hope you enjoyed the "thrill of victory" and learned how to avoid the "agony of defeat" in your parenting.

Gerry

TO: THE PARENTING CO-OP
and OTHER READERS
FROM: CARTER
SUBJECT: Hallmark cards vs. "Hallmarky" endings

After reading the summary email Gerry sent, I had my friend Blake read it. He's experiencing a boatload of marriage problems himself, and is getting some help at our guys' midweek study group.

I thought the exciting details surrounding AJ and Jenny's reconciliation might just be an encouragement to him. He'd been following their story through my weekly prayer updates. "What could it hurt?" I thought to myself.

Well, I don't think it *hurt* because Blake was excited for them, but he said the ending felt very "Hallmarky" to him. "It seemed almost too good to be true, like many of the Hallmark movies," was his conclusion.

I understood why, because our email story wasn't consistent with what he was experiencing in his own family. You see, his divorce is still pending after a pretty ugly eight-year marriage. Both he and the children are really struggling with no real solution or reconciliation even in sight.

I know what you're thinking. "With God all things are possible!" Of course that's true, and I believe it from the very core of my being. As we helped AJ and Jenny, we could see God's hand arrange and rearrange the details. Was it miraculous? Of course it was! The months were stuffed full of unbelievable surprises as AJ,

Jenny and the children made their way down the path to reconciliation.

At the same time, I can see Blake's point of view. Not every situation has a Hallmarky ending. There are sincere, loving and committed people of prayer and faith whose marriages don't work out and whose children go astray. (Trust me, I've been counseling for years. I know the drill.)

Have you ever wondered what it would take to give your personal story a Hallmarky ending? Well, there were several important factors that led up to that kind of ending for AJ and Jenny. Maybe we could learn something about Hallmarky endings by looking back over the participants in their story.

1ˢᵗ, GOD: Never minimize the supreme importance of God's divine intervention in your family. Unless God builds your home and family, your ending will be less than Hallmarky.

2ⁿᵈ, GOD'S WORD: Never trivialize God's Word in developing and growing your family, either. "All Scripture is given by inspiration of God, and is profitable for doctrine, for reproof, for correction, for instruction in righteousness." (2 Timothy 3:16, KJV) And as you'll see in Psalm 1, keeping God's Word on the front burners of your hearts and minds will bring great blessing to you and your home!

3ʳᵈ, AJ: His life was a complete mess at the beginning of our story. Yet take careful note that he was willing to listen to the advice and counsel of others. His male ego didn't hinder him from taking a humble position, confessing his failures and saying "I'm sorry." While he was a bit resistant at the beginning, his heart was open to hear what God was saying to him. He even acknowledged his own children's anger and fears and set out to be a better father. Finally, he adjusted his priorities to accommodate his hurting family and gave them time to heal.

4th, JENNY: Jenny was fed up with her husband and all the stress related to family life and the children. And yet she was willing to take some time to heal and wait upon God to work in her life and in AJ's. We watched her gradually lay aside her bitter feelings and pursue reconciliation with her family. Her respect and love for AJ was gone, and yet she demonstrated faithfulness to her marital commitment. As a hurting mother, she was unwilling to walk away from her family.

5th, TROY AND TYLER: These two boys were willing to re-enter a relationship with their father, even though it was scary. You see, family reconciliation is impossible without the children making adjustments as well. These two boys saw the importance of family life and were willing to sacrifice time with their friends in order to save their family. Is your family a priority to your children?

6th, DARREN and CARRIE: As in almost all stories where sexual purity is compromised, their relationship fell on extremely hard times. His abuse, her pregnancy and their mutual self-centeredness set the stage for problems. What was so Hallmarky about this young couple was his determination to love her and her deep love for him. How many young men would ever take responsibility for their actions, and say they're sorry? Not many, I'll bet. Hallmarky endings include commitment to Jesus Christ. Both Darren and Carrie became people with spiritual commitment.

7th, GERRY AND SUE, STU AND STACY: I can't say enough about the necessity of loving friends who come alongside of a hurting family and help them alter the ending of their family story. Good friends tell it like it is, and these friends were true friends to AJ and Jenny. They were right alongside of them supporting, listening, confronting, caring and counseling right down to the reconciliation ceremony. Now let me ask you a question. Do your friends push your family forward to excellence, or do you just get together with them to talk about the weather and watch a Hallmark movie? If you want to live a great Hallmarky ending, then you'll need more than a good movie! Think friends!

8th, CARTER AND MINNIE: It doesn't hurt to throw a little age and wisdom into the mix. In reality, everyone needs a senior mentor. Husbands need one, and so do their wives. These older folks have experience-tested wisdom that you just can't get from the sports page of the local newspaper. They generally don't worry about bluntness because they've got only a short time to live anyway. So they just tell it like it is. I guess it's important to ask, "Do you have someone like Carter and Minnie that's mentoring your family?" Look around. You'll always find them reaching out to you. It might be because they can't find their glasses or they're about to fall down the stairs, but most likely they just want to help you have your own personal Hallmarky ending in your family.

Well for now we'll say Goodbye! Our best wishes to each of your families.

Til the next email, love you all!
Carter and Minnie

TO: OUR READER
FROM: CARTER
SUBJECT: Being an observer and learning
by "default"

Now that you've finished the book, I'd be curious to find out what you've learned about parenting.

When you first cracked the cover on *OOPS! We Forgot the Kids*, you did so with certain questions and expectations. You wanted to learn more about parenting, didn't you? Did you see yourself through the lives of my friends? Where? How?

No matter what age your children are, the principles of parenting always outweigh the everyday techniques. Many parents relentlessly search for some new tricks of the trade, all the while ignoring foundational principles that are just as plain as the nose on your face. So let's take a moment to review.

The basic principle of discipline is what you do **for** your child, not what you do **to** your child. Right? It's also important to understand that no formula for tweaking a child's behavior can replace **trusting in the Sovereign God** as you parent. Yet many parents continue down the path of outcome-based parenting with fear and trembling. They actually think that the future of their child rests 100% on the dos and don'ts of parenting.

Or maybe you're one of those parents who forgot about the importance of **knowing your child before correcting your child**. Or could it be that you assume your **relationship** with your child is less important than Little Albert's being perfect all the time? And what about biblically training your child? Do you use **creativity** and **strategy** to bring about true heart change, or do you simply put out fires in order to survive? And finally, is your parenting marked by **biblical love** (1 Corinthians 13) and **consistency**?

As you reflect on your parenting style, there might be some areas where change would be a good thing. Maybe you're stuck in the proverbial parenting rut. (We've all been there!) You know there's a need for more consistency and less anger, but you're short on energy. You also want to be more proactive in training, and less reactive in discipline but....but.... *but what*?

Offering up excuses never changed anything. It's time to re-think, rebuild and revitalize your parenting. Remember, God specializes in new beginnings. He wants us to turn from ineffective parenting habits and commit to selfless, God-centered parenting.

Regardless of where you find yourself as a parent, good parenting starts with good decisions: a decision to trust the Sovereign God, a decision to live Christ at home, a decision to follow biblical parenting principles—and remember, *all* decisions made today must be lived out tomorrow. So *start right now* and make *good* parenting decisions! You'll see the difference in your family so fast it'll make your head swim.

There you have it. May God bless your family and cause it to thrive!

Warmly in Christ,
Carter and Minnie

> P.S. My egg-laying girlfriends will sleep good tonight.
> See? Persistence pays! Turn the page and see one final
> *Life at the Lazy-U* !

How do you think my coonskin hat looks?